ALL THINGS
DRACULA!

ALL THINGS
DRACULA!

An A–Z
Of The Count Who Refuses To Die

MAGGIE HALL

© Maggie Hall, 2020

Published by Maggie Hall

All rights reserved. No part of this book may be reproduced, adapted, stored in a retrieval system or transmitted by any means, electronic, mechanical, photocopying, or otherwise without the prior written permission of the author.

The rights of Maggie Hall to be identified as the author of this work have been asserted in accordance with the Copyright, Designs and Patents Act 1988.

A CIP catalogue record for this book is available from the British Library.

ISBN 978-1-9989917-0-9

Book layout and design by Clare Brayshaw

Cover design by Rachel Oldroyd & Clare Brayshaw

Small Count Dracula on back cover © Bertos | Dreamstime.com

Prepared and printed by:

York Publishing Services Ltd
64 Hallfield Road
Layerthorpe
York YO31 7ZQ

Tel: 01904 431213

Website: www.yps-publishing.co.uk

DEDICATED TO

Whitby ... without which there would be no *Dracula*.

And to my lovely Gary, whose last words to me were:

"Get *the* bloody book finished!"

MAGGIE HALL

FOREWORD

As an 18-year-old, sitting on the top of a double-decker bus, on my own, late at night – I wished I was a good Christian churchgoer with a crucifix round my neck. I had just seen a *Dracula* film (I can't recall exactly which one, but assume it was the first Hammer offering in 1958) and I desperately needed protection from my over-zealous imagination! Once off the bus I scurried home – which as it was opposite the town cemetery did nothing to help calm me down. Safely indoors, I laughed off my stupid fears with my family and never gave Dracula another thought. Until, that is, in the mid-70s when I was travelling in Cyprus and a Turkish-Cypriot musician I met went into raptures when I told him, that while I lived in London, I had a "bolt hole" in Whitby. "Dracula!" he screeched.

I had no clue as to the reason for his boundless excitement, which is why his delight at meeting someone with a home in Whitby quickly gave way to incredulity. He was totally shocked that someone who loved Whitby knew nothing of the historic fishing town's link with the Prince of Darkness. I felt foolish. But then I had not read the novel. Indeed, I had no idea there was one, believing, like so many, that Dracula was a character created for the silver screen. And in those days the good folk of Whitby, diehard, superstition-fueled families going back generations and the town councillors, conspired to deny the connection. They wanted none of this vampire nonsense tainting the town and its burgeoning tourism.

All that has, of course, changed – but only since the early 1980s. Quite dramatically. For those who don't know, the connection is that Bram Stoker, the author of *Dracula,* got the idea and was inspired to write his legendary story during several holidays in Whitby. In the book, published 1897, Dracula arrives in a gale-lashed Britain from Transylvania, on a Russian cargo boat. The boat is heading for London but the storm-ravaged vessel seeks refuge in Whitby and goes aground on the harbour beach. All aboard are dead, with the skipper's body lashed to the mast. The only survivor is the ship's black dog. It leaps ashore onto the stone fishing pier, shakes itself and bounds through the narrow, cobbled streets, racing up the famous 199 steps leading to the Abbey, high on the cliff – and turns into Dracula. Nothing it seems will ever dull or diminish the power, lure, and penetrating influence of *Dracula* ... be it the novel, the character or some pop-culture force.

The following pages gather together "all things" *Dracula* and show how a literary "undead" character is alive and well. Displaying no signs of ever dying!

* * *

The book is a compilation of a myriad of *Dracula*-related subjects and topics, but not always in minute detail. For instance whole books/theses/academic tomes, etc, have been produced, analyzing societal mores and sexual attitudes, as reflected in the novel and the multitude of films and plays it has spawned. Where possible, entries that do have extensive material about them – out there in the big wide world – have been marked with: **FYFI** (For Your Further Information) followed by either a website, an internet link or how to buy the book, etc.

* * *

Now (with thanks and apologies to the most famous quote from the novel): *Welcome* to my book. Read *freely*. Enjoy *safely*. Gain something of the *happiness* that – despite his evil – Dracula has spread throughout the world.

ABBEY: one of Britain's most famous abbeys is inextricably associated with *Dracula*. It is, of course, Whitby Abbey. Dating back to a Christian community founded in 657 AD, a Benedictine monastery was founded on the site in around 1078 and the current church was built in the 13th century. The edifice – which was badly damaged by German bombs during the early days of World War I – is a massive character in the novel *Dracula*. Its presence lingers on every page from Chapter 6 through Chapter 8. It is within its imposing, and invariably eerie shadow that Lucy has her fatal meeting with The Count. So it is little wonder that English Heritage (in whose care the Abbey is) advertises it with the luring slogan: "Sink your teeth into a great day out. Uncover centuries of stories and explore the Gothic ruins that inspired Dracula."

ABBEY-2: floods of visitors roam the grounds looking for signs of Dracula, in the misguided belief that, not only was Dracula a real person but that he is buried in the graveyard of the nearby Norman church of St Mary's (also mentioned in the book). But there are just as many who visit for another – and very real – reason. Whitby Abbey is famed as "the home of Easter". It was here, at the Synod of Whitby in 664, that it was decided how to calculate when Easter would fall. As a result it is on the first Sunday after the first full moon after the spring equinox. This means it's always between March 22nd and April 25th. So, if Easter falls too early or too late for your liking you know who to blame!

FYFI: The Abbey's gift shop is stocked with a splendid array of books about Dracula, along with the novel and a range of trinkets and food, all vampire inspired. And to see a short film on the Abbey and *Dracula*, https://www.youtube.com/watch?v=XqFyWtw14O8

ABEBOOKS: this is the global online marketplace – with sellers in 50-plus countries – to (apart from your local bookshop) go to find any book, along with comics, posters or photographs with "Dracula" in the title. While it has new and out-of-print books, it specialises in rare copies and first editions. At the time of going to press it listed 37,553 items with "Dracula" attached to them – among them a first edition of Bram Stoker's book (see FIRST) for $75,000.

FYFI: https://www.abebooks.com

ADVERTISING: it is astonishing how creative minds have used Dracula, the character, to flog the most unlikely products. Be it cars, toothpaste, mosquito repellents, highlighters, painkillers, pizza, cream cakes, soda pop, locksmiths, banks, ice cream, bottled water, gin, biscuits (cookies in the US), insurance, and heck (thanks to Switzerland) even tampons, ingenious copywriters have found ways to persuade customers to sink their teeth into everyday items, products and services.

FYFI: for a sample of TV ads see BANK, CAKES, COCA-COLA, GEICO, OREO and SCHLAGE; For the link to the tampon ad, https://www.adsoftheworld.com/media/print/ob_vampire

ALL: to see, read online, borrow or buy all the books written by the author of *Dracula*, Bram Stoker (12 novels, three collections of short stories), or books about him or *Dracula*, go to: openlibrary.org and search his name or *Dracula*.

ALUCARD: doesn't take much working out. It's "Dracula" backwards. It's turning up in all sorts of places – in book titles, comics, TV shows and other forms of media. The name is particular prominent in the top-rated video game *Castlevania* (see CASTLEVANIA). Alucard has been a main character in *Castlevania* since 1989 and as his father is Dracula and his mother is human, he is half vampire, half human. However there is nothing new about the backwards name. It was first used in 1943 in the film *Son of Dracula* (see SON–2) where Count Alucard was played by Lon Chaney Jnr.

FYFI: to watch the movie, for free, https://archive.org/details/UniversalStudiosMonsters1943SonOfDracula

ANALOGY: several have invoked – surprise, surprise – Donald Trump. Towards the end of July, 2020, when his bid to win re-election as President of the United States hit the doldrums, columnist Patrick Cockburn of The Independent issued a warning. "Donald Trump has fallen far enough behind in the polls as to raise the hopes of the world that it will soon see the back of him as US president come the election in 100 days' time. Given his calamitous handling of the coronavirus pandemic, the decline in his popularity is scarcely surprising. Yet Trump has always shown a Dracula-like ability to rise from the political grave...."

FYFI: https://www.independent.co.uk/voices/trump-biden-coronavirus-election-chances-media-strategy-a9635936.html

ANALOGY-2: there's a great one connected to football (soccer, for the American reader). It was coined by humourist author – sometimes sports' writer – Neil Humphreys. Reporting on an utterly pathetic performance by Manchester United, when they failed to capitalise on an English Premier League record of 81 across-goal shots (when there's two chances to score) in one game, he wrote: "Dracula was more effective around crosses". The game was in February 2014, when United drew with Fulham – bottom of the Premier League at the time – 2–2. Humphreys' report appeared in the Singapore publication, *The New Paper*.

ANALOGY-3: the media have been likened to Dracula – most famously by legendary US defence lawyer Robert Bennett who, in 1998, represented President Bill Clinton in the Monica Lewinsky affair. In 2012, when asked what should be the top priority for those involved in high-profile cases he answered: "The primary rule is to get it out and get it all out." He likened the media frenzy that often surrounds scandals to Count Dracula. "He needs blood every day," said Bennett.

ANALOGY-4: when Jean-Claude Juncker, who was President of the European Commission from 1 November

2014 to 30 November 2019, was running for the office, a fierce critic attacked him by invoking Dracula. Tim Costello, a member of the Civil Society 20 (C20) that liaises with G20 leaders, said putting Junker in charge of European efforts to combat tax avoidance was akin to placing Dracula in charge of a blood bank.

ANALOGY-5: in April 2016, Cher copied Costello's comments. Only she replaced Juncker's name with Donald Trump, who at the time was in the middle of his first battle to win the White House.

ANALOGY-6: and a similar charge was made when the 2020 corona-virus ravaged the world. As millions were plunged out of work, an anti-lottery group in America tried to get all states with lotteries to close them for a month – to stop addicted gamblers spending their Federally issued $1,200 relief cheques on scratch cards and numbers. Les Bernal, spokesman for Stop Predatory Gambling, a group that believes gambling – from lotteries to casinos – places a disproportionate burden on the poor, said: "Federal tax dollars are being sent to American families in order to put food on the table, make rent or mortgage payments, or provide for other daily necessities – not to subsidize state lotteries." The group sent letters to governors and attorney generals calling for the moratorium. When the bid failed Bernal said: "For lotteries to continue running when so many citizens are financially desperate is like putting Dracula in charge of the emergency room blood bank."

ANITA: a fictional vampire-hunter/executioner, called Anita Blake, works as a supernatural consultant to the police in the US city of St Louis, Missouri. The creation of American author Laurell K Hamilton, the series is 29 books long. The first one, *Guilty Pleasures*, was published in 1993; the latest, *Sucker Punch*, was published in August, 2020. The series has sold six million copies and counting. Paying tribute to her inspiration for her massive success, Hamilton has said: "Without Dracula I might never have created my own vampire stories – perhaps no one would have. Yes, Dracula really is that important to the genre."

FYFI: www.laurellkhamilton.com

ANTS: Madagascar is home to a species of ant that survives by feeding on the blood of its larvae, ie, its young. Predictably the ants – proper name *Adetomyrma venatrix* – are popularly referred to as "Dracula ants". The manner in which they suck the blood of their babies is called "nondestructive cannibalism". They were first discovered in a rotting log in Madagascar more than a decade ago. Then in April 2014, after years of painstaking research by entomologists at the California Academy of Science, six new species of Dracula ants were identified in the genus *Mystrium*. While some of the ants appear to be black, the majority are mainly a pale orange in colour, so are not all Dracula-like in appearance. They form small colonies, usually not more than 200 strong. Their main habitat is in one of the last remaining high plateau forests left in Madagascar – very close to the capital, Antananarivo. Despite its name, this was not named after the ants!

FYFI: www.livescience.com/44479-new-dracula-ant-species.html

ANTS-2: in December 2018 the cheetah lost its title as the fastest animal in the world. As hard as it is to believe, the Dracula ant (Mystrium camillae) moves faster. Not in running but in the snapping of its jaws. In late 2018, scientific research made headlines when it showed the ant clamps onto its prey at a startling 200 mph – 5,000 times swifter than the blink of an eye, making it the fastest moving animal known.

FYFI: if you are really, really serious about knowing the anatomy of this ant in excruciating detail,

https://royalsocietypublishing.org/doi/10.1098/rsos.181447

APPS: of course there are *Dracula* "applications". Search "Dracula apps" and a slew of them will come up – from games to music. But the number one is Draculapp – a very serious, top notch company (with offices in London, Turin and Dubai). Its website welcome says: "Are you ready to be bitten and boost your Brand Identity to the next level with the Digital Integration? If you feel comfortable, then you are ready to enter in the House of Digital".

Explaining why the company, established in 2008, chose Dracula as its front-man, the website says: "Who is Dracula? A romantic fictional character, strong and highly controversial. Thinking about it, when he bites, he forces you to change." Italian Claudia Marino is the Marketing Director of Draculapp and one of her favourite films is *Bram Stoker's Dracula*, Francis Ford Coppola's 1992 take on the most famous of vampires. Fellow Italian Edoardo Valente is the Creative Director of the company and he came up with the logo of a smartphone with bat wings. "I certainly cannot deny Dracula's ferocity," Edoardo explains, "but I also wanted him to be the symbol of this company, because he is a nonconformist, non-conventional character, a man with his own passions who stokes the imagination and fantasies through entire generations; nobody can deny his huge magnetic and communication powers."

FYFI: www.draculapp.com

ARCHETYPAL: the novel *Dracula* fits the definition – relating to or denoting an original which has been imitated – perfectly. Since its publication in 1897, it has spawned a massive, wide-ranging genre revolving around other written materials, movies, stage productions, philosophies, art, comics, fashion, accessories and all manner of other products. All of them share a common link: that of the character central to the book – a vampire. And this book (the one you're reading) is a tribute to Dracula's archetypal power.

ARCHIVE: the novel *Dracula* is a veritable archive of the age in which it was written. It's jammed with Victorian attitudes, geographical facts, customs and lore in varying countries; a social history and a tourist guide to various parts of Britain and Eastern Europe.

ASHES: on his death on 20 April, 1912, aged 65, Bram Stoker, the author of *Dracula*, was cremated at the historic Golder's Green Crematorium, London. His ashes lie at rest there, in a grey marble urn that also contains the ashes of his only child, Irving Noel Thornley Stoker, who died, aged 81, in 1961. The plan had been for the ashes of his wife, Florence Balcombe Stoker – who died at age 78 in 1937 – to be added to the urn, mixed with first those of her husband, then with those of their only child. However, she opted out of the agreement. Instead, her ashes were scattered in the crematorium's Garden of Rest. For fear of vandalism and out-of-control-fan-obsession, visitors to the crematorium wanting to view the urn of father and son have to be vetted before being escorted to where it's housed.

ASWANG: is the Dracula of the Philippines. Cemented in folklore since the 16th century, the mythical creature is, like vampires, repelled or killed by using garlic and religious artifacts. And yes, there are four *Aswang* movies – dating from 1992 until 2019 – made on location in the Philippines.

FYFI: https://www.imdb.com/find?q=ASWANG

AUCTIONS: all manner of high-end Dracula memorabilia constantly comes onto the market. First editions of the book, movie posters, film props and artwork are the mainstay items which go under the "going, going, gone" gavel in auction rooms around the world. New York-based Live Auctioneers has a comprehensive online database covering auctioneers from the leading houses of Sotheby's, Christie's and Bonhams to those that just have a very local, high-street presence. It lists forthcoming items and those that have already been and gone. The latter works as a guide to what you might have to pay, or might get, if you have something Dracula-related to sell, or fancy buying.

FYFI: www.liveauctioneers.com

AUDIO: there are 27 unabridged versions of the novel as audio-books. Some are read by a single narrator, others have multiple actors. The star names include Alan Cumming, Greg Wise, Saskia Reeves, Susan Duerden, Gildart Jackson, John Challis, Timothy Ackroyd and Amanda Friday.

FYFI: find them all at www.audible.com or, https://www.audiobooks.com/search/book/Dracula?resetFilters=1 and for free recordings (by volunteer readers), https://librivox.org

AUSTRALIA: the only dining-cabaret spot in the world highlighting *Dracula* is Down Under. In 1980, the famed Australian Newman family – known for its singing/dancing/acting talent – opened the unique Dracula's Cabaret in Melbourne, followed five years later with its Queensland, venue. Sadly the Melbourne restaurant closed in 2017. But the nightly Gothic show in Broadbeach, near Brisbane, still terrifies with its underworld setting, and is constantly claimed as a "howling" success. Ticket prices start at A-$59 for the show only; an A-$95 ticket includes a three-course dinner; for A-$115 you get dinner plus complimentary canapes, sparkling wine, premium seating and a VIP Dracula pendant. There's nothing particularly Dracula-like about the food, apart from the "death by chocolate" desert which is served in a chocolate coffin. In addition, among others, there's a special-order A-$48 cake, which should be called Renfield's Pleasure after the insane, insect-eater in the book, but for some inexplicable reason it is not. It's a chocolate ganache, decorated with a spider's web and a redback spider.

FYFI: https://www.draculas.com.au

AUSTRALIA-2: when the 2020 corona-virus took its global toll, Dracula's suspended its operation. Until it opened again, it promoted the closure with telling humour. It made the world's biggest face mask and wrapped it round the huge, colourful skull that marks the entrance to the restaurant. The bright turquoise mask certainly sent the "we're protecting you" message to its legion of customers.

FYFI: to see the mask, https://cdn.newsapi.com.au/image/v1/a81ccaaefed212b872701b0a2c125b37?width=650

AUSTRALIA-3: is going to be the setting for the upcoming movie *Outback Dracula*. Full of maniac madness the horror-comedy plot is set in 1880s Australia, where a psychic, lesbian schoolteacher sets out to find her missing girlfriend but ends up having to try and defeat Dracula and his Golden Army of the Undead. The low-budget movie – being made by Hollywood writer/director Brendan Steere – will be shot on location Down Under, either towards the end of 2020 or early 2021. It's planned as a sequel to Steere's award-winning 2019 cult-status offering of *VelociPastor*, which had nothing to do with Dracula or vampires but revolved around a priest going to China and turning into a dinosaur.

FYFI: http://brendansteere.com/film

AUTOGRAPH: to find Bram Stoker's autograph is a true find. In February, 2020, there were two on eBay. One was in a 1911 edition of *Dracula* – in which Stoker made an inscription to a "Mr Knight". It sold for $22,750. The other was a rebound 1908 copy of the book, sold along with a business-sized card bearing Stoker's signature. Its price was $3,500.

In 2019, Stoker's autograph sold for a mere £608. But then it came on a slip of paper, not in an early copy of the book. The signature was contained in an antique Irish autograph album, in which it had been glued after being cut off the end of a letter. It was sold on the global website Etsy. This can be deemed a giveaway price because on specialised autograph sites, letters handwritten by Stoker on behalf of his boss Sir Henry Irving (see IRVING) and signed by Irving, not Stoker, go for £1,000 and more.

AUTOGRAPH–2: never mind the man who made him famous, the signature of Bela Lugosi is worth a fortune. See entries LUGOSI–3 and –4.

B

BABIES: there is a Dracula-themed book for the very young. For toddlers learning to count there is *Dracula: A BabyLit Counting Primer*. It's part of the American *BabyLit* series that introduces toddlers to the world of classic literature. It goes from 1 to 10 – counting castles, coffins, tombstones, vampire-hunting heroes, friends (Mina and Lucy), rats and garlic flowers.

FYFI: https://www.babylit.com/catalog/product/viewid/2329/s/dracula

BABY: there is a musical comedy called *Dracula, Baby*. It was first produced in 1970 – and is still a popular production, particularly for amateur dramatic societies and high schools.

The synopsis reads: "When the chorus opens the show singing, 'Transylvania after dark. Rather grim and rather ghoulish! Walking by ourself is foolish …' we know that we're in for an entertaining if not fiendish evening. When Count Dracula sets out for England, intending to make the beautiful young Lucy his 93rd bride, Lucy's future looks pretty anaemic. Her principal defenders are Arthur, her milksop fiancé – who is so proper that Lucy sometimes worries about him – and Van Helsing, the clumsy professor who is out to thwart the evil vampire. An unexpected ally is the nurse who works in the sanatorium run by Dr Seward, Lucy's guardian. The nurse, a tough and very good-looking chick, kind of digs that crazy Count Dracula. Count Dracula is a great exponent of the wisdom of evil, advising that, 'The man who is pure is generally poor and frightfully sad, that's why it's good to be bad'. If you're looking for a fun musical that is easy to do, has lovely, singable music, clever lyrics and lots of modern box-office appeal, this should be just your thing."

FYFI: to buy the script/licence to produce, etc, https://www.dramaticpublishing.com/dracula-baby

BABY-2: if you have a compulsion to dress your baby, or infant, as Dracula there are plenty of costumes out there. Most come with all the expected bits and pieces, ie, black pants, white shirt with a bow tie, and a black-collared cape with red lining.

FYFI: search "Dracula infant costume" (followed by your country) for offers.

BAGS: you can clutch your favourite book – ie, *Dracula* – wherever you go with a purpose other than reading it. Used, hard-back copies of *Dracula* are constantly sought by highly talented women – on both sides of the Atlantic – to be turned into bags. With enormous skill they produce totally eye-catching handbags, clutches and purses.

BAGS-2: Jo Tittershill – who trades under the name Bookarelli – turns book covers into exquisite bags and purses. The way she will convert a vintage copy of *Dracula*

– all black and red leather cover, complete with a skull clasp, a tiny silver bat adorning the silk-rope closure and satin-lined interior – is a show-stopper. Jo, from Calverton, Nottinghamshire, who sells on Facebook and the worldwide craft online store Etsy, said: "This is one of my absolute favourite clutches in my collection. It is not for everyone but seems to be favoured by my Gothic fans, young and old. It's a definite conversation starter. Dracula is certainly a to-be-noticed choice. Everyone knows of The Count and his story … while not being my biggest seller, this creation has a following all of its own."

FYFI: www.etsy.com/uk/shop/Bookarelli?ref=shop_sugg

BAGS-3: Kate Lowe, of Tingewick, Buckinghamshire, also leads the field with her BagsyMeFirst company. Like Jo (see previous entry) she has a worldwide following. Kate will, for around £100, fashion a handsome black, gold and red leather edition of *Dracula* into a satin-lined clutch bag that doubles as a jewellery or keepsake box. At the other end of the price scale she will, for just a few pounds, back a small hand mirror with a page from the book, showing a famed passage.

FYFI: https://www.bagsymefirst.com/store/c1/Featured_Products.html; also search Etsy and Facebook.

BAGS-4: in the States the book-to-purse craft is executed by Karen Higham, of Euless, Texas, who trades as Novel Creations.

Specialising in horror books, she started out converting *Twilight* titles and was honoured to turn an Ann Rice (see

RICE) novel into a purse – for the author herself! As for *Dracula* bags she searches for leather-bound editions, embossed in silver and scarlet. Expect to pay around £50.

FYFI: like the others she trades on Etsy, www.etsy.com/listing/158316588/bram-stoker-dracula-book

BAGS-5: also in America, Caitlin Phillips, of Washington, DC, performs the same book-to-bag magic. Apart from bags and purses, she specialises in producing wallets, bracelets and bookmarks out of the remnants of unwanted books. And if she doesn't have *Dracula* in her collection she will seek one out for you or use the copy you give her. Her Rebound Design studio is in the Arts Walk section of Brookland, close to downtown DC, and she is often at the arts and crafts weekend market at the famed Eastern Market, on Capitol Hill.

FYFI: www.rebound-designs.com

BALLET: *Dracula* was first turned into a ballet in 1899, just two years after its publication. Titled *Prince des Tenebres* (Prince of Darkness) it was the work of Hungarian Laszlo Szilagyi and it was performed at the Budapest Opera House in 1899. Since then there have been over 20 ballets based on *Dracula* – all, with the exception of a couple, called *Dracula* – and these days one or another is in constant production by dozens of ballet companies around the world.

BALLET-2: probably the most famous and critically acclaimed *Dracula* ballet is choreographed by Michael Pink and directed by the late Christopher Gable. It premiered in 1996 as a production of Northern Ballet at the Alhambra Theatre, Bradford, West Yorkshire. Since then the ballet has been staged in America and New Zealand. The internationally renowned Pink is currently Artistic Director of the Milwaukee Ballet. Born in York, he won a scholarship to train at the Royal Ballet School in London and went on to join the London Festival Ballet (now the English National Ballet) where he worked closely with such luminaries as Natalia Makarova, Rudolf Nureyev and Lynn Seymour. Gable, who was awarded a CBE (Commander of the Order of the British Empire) for services to dance in 1996, sadly didn't live long enough to see the ballet go from strength to strength. He died in 1998, aged 58.

BALLET-3: in 1999 along came another version, from award-winning Canadian choreographer, David Nixon. He came up with it when he was Artistic Director for BalletMet, Columbus, Ohio. Since 2001 he's been Artistic Director for Britain's Northern Ballet (the position once held by Michael Pink – see previous entry) based in Leeds, West Yorkshire. In 2005, he revised his version of his *Dracula* ballet and it was staged in Leeds at what was then known as the West Yorkshire Playhouse, but is now the Leeds Playhouse. Northern Ballet has since staged Nixon's *Dracula* twice, in Leeds – in 2009 and 2014. In October 2019 they staged it at The Marlowe in Canterbury and then, a few weeks later, back home in Leeds. And over Halloween it was live-screened into cinemas throughout the UK. The latest production was shown on BBC 4 on May 31st, 2020, then streamed throughout June on BBC iPlayer.

The music, not original to the ballet, is drawn from various sources, including Rachmaninov's *Symphonic Dances* and

Schnittke's *Faust Cantata*. In 2010, David Nixon was made an OBE (Order of the British Empire). The blurb for the 2019 production reads: "With darkly Gothic sets and costumes, Northern Ballet is resurrecting Bram Stoker's classic horror story for special LIVE screenings in cinemas this Halloween. The haunting tale of passion and immortality is played out through a unique blend of sensuous dancing and gripping theatre – this is ballet with a dramatic bite, a thrilling adaptation that will leave you thirsty for more."

BALLS: there are Dracula Balls – not the bouncing variety (though I'm sure they're out there, somewhere) but the dancing sort. The longest established is staged in Philadelphia, USA. It celebrated its 22nd anniversary in May 2020. Or, it should have done. But the grim corona-virus pandemic put a stop to that. The balls are usually twice a year – in Spring and, for obvious reasons, in October – and are the work of Patrick Rodgers who sports a splendid (if you're into that sort of thing) pair of "implant" fangs.

The other one is, in relative terms, newly minted and is held to raise funds for the Conservatory of Flowers, a prime attraction in San Francisco's Golden Gate Park, which has a wonderful display of *Dracula* orchids (see ORCHIDS–1). Balls were held in 2017 and 2018. The one planned for 2020 was, because of the corona-virus pandemic, postponed until 2921.

FYFI: http://draculasball.com and https://conservatoryofflowers.org

BANDS: there are several rock 'n' roll, punk, hard-metal bands out there which have turned to Dracula for their name. See: BOND, DRACULA, MUSIC and PLAID.

BANK: it's hard for even the "oldies" to remember – never mind today's "generation-z" to imagine – there once was a world where banks did not have a "hole-in-the-wall". In 1985 Abbey National (now Santander) used Dracula to introduce customers to its ATM system. The TV ad starts with Dracula leaving his castle, at night, and going into town. The voice-over script goes: "If you can't get out much during the day depositing cash can be a pain in the neck. So Abbey National is introducing Abbey-Link. Now you can pay in money day and night, seven days a week … and with a limit of £250 a day you can take money out. Which could be very handy if you're nipping out for a bite to eat …" With the last sentence the camera zooms in through a window. Dracula is outside and his eyes – with fangs at the ready – land lustily on the exposed neck and cleavage of a beautiful woman.

FYFI: this ad used to be listed on www.horrorpedia.com and could be seen on YouTube, but, bizarrely, it's disappeared.

BANNED: during the Communist era, "all-things" Dracula were banned in his country of origin, Romania. The book, the films, any mention of Bram Stoker were all "illegal". But that didn't stop the Romanian Ministry of Tourism creating a tour of Transylvania that was injected throughout with images, thoughts and deeds of Dracula, without actually mentioning his name or the vampire legend. And as the Soviets could not put a stake through Vlad Tepes, aka Vlad the Impaler – upon whom Stoker based Dracula – they turned him into a good guy. A portrait of him, in the house in Sighisoara where he was born in 1431, had a plaque underneath which was inscribed: "Patriot, Defender of Freedom". As the late Associated Press journalist Hugh A Mulligan wrote after taking the everything-but-in-name Dracula tour in 1979: "Vlad the Impaler, with his incisors removed, has gone to government rectification school and emerged as a Marxist folk-hero."

BARDOT: bringing Brigitte Bardot, the famed sex-kitten of the 1950s, into the mix is a convoluted way of telling the inter-linked stories of a speedboat and a model boat, both called Dracula. They deserves a mention here because, in 2012, the model was sold by Sotheby's for an astonishing £9,375.00. But then it was a prized possession of Gunter Sachs – renowned German playboy, heir to the Opel car industry – who was Bardot's third husband. Fearing the onset of Alzheimer's he committed suicide in 2011.

Sachs had commissioned the model because he so loved the real thing ... which he, of course, owned. For years he, Bardot and his jet-setting, high-flying pals raced around the Mediterranean in Dracula, his Riva Aquarama Speedboat. It sold at the same auction for £385,250.00. But his boat was not his only link to our man, see CLUB.

BATS: although the novel made vampire bats famous there is nothing fictional about their existence – although they do not (despite their presence in the book) exist in Romania. Bats are the only mammals that fly and vampire bats the only mammals that exist entirely on blood. There are three species, the most common – and therefore known, in layman's terms, as the common vampire bat

– is *Desmodus rotundus*. Then there is the hairy-legged vampire bat, officially *Diphylla ecaudata* and the white-winged vampire bat, whose proper name is *Diaemus youngi*. All three are native to South America and are alive and well, particularly in Mexico, Brazil, Chile, Uruguay and Argentina. Their prey is usually sleeping livestock but occasionally they will feed on humans. Known to man for aeons they were labelled "vampire bats" by the Spanish explorers who conquered the Americas.

BATS-2: there is a likeable, loving side to vampire bats. Simon Barnes, the British journalist and wildlife writer, pinpointed this little known fact in his October 2014 book: *Ten Million Aliens: A Journey Through the Entire Animal Kingdom*. In it he says: "As so often, the truth and beauty of the creatures we live with are obscured by human traditions and untrue assumptions. We are not encouraged to look closely or think afresh about non-human animals because, after all, we know everything. Or do we?"

As an example of how we don't, he wrote: "Vampires are social creatures, coming back to the same day-roost at the end of every night. There are some big colonies, up to 2,000, but most are much smaller, and centre on a core population of females who, even if not related, tend to know each other well. A bat which has failed to find blood in a night's flying will beg a meal from a neighbour. From a friend, we would say, if we weren't so terrified of sounding anthropomorphic. The friend will then regurgitate blood, thus sharing a meal. Under this system, females have been known to live for up to 15 years. Reciprocal altruism is still altruism; obviously this is a system that works on a mutual back-scratching basis. Human society depends on the small kindnesses that you perform as a matter of course and that you expect to be performed for you in turn. But it is not just humans who are humane."

FYFI: https://www.goodreads.com/book/show/22609418

BATS-3: as though what goes on in that great capital of the good old US of A – Washington, DC – is not batty enough, there is a proposal to make the bat a city symbol. Councillor Charles Allen, who represents the Capitol Hill neighbourhood, proposed that the big brown bat – official name *Eptesicus fuscus* – be declared the city's "mammal". He ran with the idea after the Girl Scouts (Girl Guides in the UK) in his constituency – who did a survey on the critters indigenous to their community – urged him on. It turns out that all 50 states have a mammal symbol, some have several, but DC (which is not officially a state, for reasons too complicated to explain here) does not. But there's nothing original about claiming a bat to represent the mammal population of a jurisdiction. Texas, Hawaii, Oklahoma and next-door-to-DC, Virginia, have adopted bats as their non-human mammal symbols. Needless to say, having a bat as a symbol of an elected authority leads to tons of daft jokes about human "bloodsuckers" that drain public coffers of taxpayers' money. But that has not deterred the Girl Scouts of Capitol Hill and, in January, 2020, they argued their case in front of the Council. A decision was expected late 2020.

BATS-4: make great eating. Well, the ones from Bridgewater, Somerset, do. No, you don't have to go night-hunting. They're made of sugar – by Nice Buns. Every Halloween party should have cupcakes, puddings and ice cream sprinkled with them. They're also great to give out, by the handful, to the trick-or-treaters.

FYFI: https://www.nice-buns.co.uk/black-bat-sugar-sprinkles-333-p.asp

BEER: the Americans are nothing if not inventive when it comes to craft beers. The Black Bottle Brewery of Fort Collins, Colorado, produces a milk stout made with Count Chocula cereal (see CHOCULA). And, like the Dracula-linked cereal it uses, it's only available around Halloween. The brew relies on the cereal with its added milk, sugars and chocolate to round out aggressive tendencies with an aftertaste of bittersweet chocolate and sweet cream. For obvious reasons the brewery labels its seasonal stout "Cerealiously Count Chocula".

FYFI: www.blackbottlebrewery.com

BEFORE: long before *Dracula* there was a slew of novels about bloodsucking "humans". While it's rarely acknowledged, these earlier publications had an enormous influence on Bram Stoker as he created his fictional masterpiece. See: CARMILLA, VAMPIRE, VAMPYRE and VARNEY.

BENCH: in the early 1970s, the Dracula Society applied to Whitby Town Council for permission to erect a bench in Bram Stoker's memory. It was to be placed high on a cliff top overlooking the town and the Abbey – the view that inspired him so much in the writing of *Dracula*. The application was refused. The town, it was argued, did not need or want to be associated with such fictional nonsense.

But finally, in 1980, when Whitby had been taken over by Scarborough Borough Council, a bench was allowed and it was erected to mark the 68th anniversary of Stoker's death. Sadly, the bench – which sits high on Whitby's Spion Kop, on the West Cliff overlooking the harbour, the old town and the Abbey – is fraying round the edges a bit but it's still very much a pilgrimage spot for Stoker and *Dracula* fans to visit. They can sit awhile to soak up the largely unchanged scene that is so wonderfully echoed in the novel, with observations like: "The houses of the old town ... are all red-roofed, and seemed piled up one over the other ..."

FYFI: to see photos, https://www.atlasobscura.com/places/bram-stoker-memorial-seat

BERGIN: in 2002, Irish actor Patrick Bergin played the lead role in the Italian-produced TV movie series *Dracula*, aka *Dracula's Curse*. A modern day interpretation of the novel – it featured a Porsche instead of a horse and carriage – set in Budapest, it made little impact, basically going straight to DVD. However, Bergin – one of those wonderful, never-out-of-work journeymen thespians – was acclaimed as a "crusty and malicious" Dracula. And *Dracula* movie expert Charles E Butler (see FILMS–2) proclaimed his performance as "very underrated" and the film generally as "a very well thought out version of the tale".

FYFI: to buy or rent, www.swapadvd.com/Draculas-Curse/dvd/48102

BIOGRAPHIES: there are five Bram Stoker biographies. The first out of the gate was by Harry Ludlam in 1962. It was titled

A Biography of Dracula: The Life Story of Bram Stoker but it was re-issued in 1977, with what was deemed the catchier title of *A Biography of Bram Stoker: Creator of Dracula*. Ludlam first got his hands on a copy of *Dracula* as a young teen. He read it at night in bed under the sheets, by torchlight. It so terrified him he didn't finish it. Years later he bought a copy for a few pence at a church garden fete. He devoured it. As a reporter on a local newspaper, he was amazed not to be able to find anything out about the author. So he set out to make Bram Stoker known. After years of research and digging through library archives, he finally made contact with Stoker's son, Noel, who gave him access to family documents and letters. The result was the public's first proper look at the creator of *Dracula*. Ludlam, who died in 2011, aged 87, went onto write dozens more books, fiction and non-fiction, many involving "true" ghost stories and accounts of military action in World War II.

The next biography was in 1975, with the latest in October 2017. Bram Stoker's great-nephew Daniel Farson (see FARSON) – the late famed British writer and broadcaster of the 1960s and 1970s – published *The Man who wrote Dracula: A Biography of Bram Stoker*. Then in 1996 came *Bram Stoker: a Biography of the Author of Dracula*, by the late American author Barbara Belford. She followed that in 2002 with *Bram Stoker and the Man Who Was Dracula*. The latest, in October 2017, was *Something in the Blood: The Untold Story of Bram Stoker*, by David J Skal.

BLACULA: say it slowly and deliberately and you'll get it! There are two movies portraying a black Dracula. In the 1972 movie *Blacula*, an ancient African prince, turned into a vampire by Dracula hundreds of years earlier, ends up in modern day Los Angeles. Although it received mixed reviews it ended up as one of the top grossing films of the year. In 1973 there was a sequel, *Scream Blacula Scream*. Both starred the late William Marshall, famed for his rich operatic voice and Shakespearian training.

FYFI: to rent or buy, in the UK, https://uk.chili.com/country-selector and in the US, https://www.vudu.com ; the sequel can be seen for free, https://www.youtube.com/watch?v=99SS1PnW7Jk

BLOOD: is the common theme that runs, pervades and dominates *Dracula*. Suffice to say the fluid that holds the story together is common to all vertebrates – ie, all "animals" with a spinal cord. So that includes humans, snakes, dogs ... well, you get the picture. We all happily bang on about "blood" but probably few of us, put to the test, could come up with the exact definition. According to most dictionaries it is: "The fluid that circulates in the heart, arteries, capillaries, and veins of a vertebrate animal carrying nourishment and oxygen to and bringing away waste products from all parts of the body". Consult the *Oxford English Dictionary* and it tells you: "Blood consists of a mildly alkaline aqueous fluid (plasma) containing red cells (erythrocytes), white cells (leukocytes), and platelets; it is red when oxygenated and purple when deoxygenated. Red blood cells carry the protein haemoglobin, which gives blood its colour and can combine with oxygen, thus enabling the blood to carry oxygen from the lungs to the tissues. White blood cells protect the body against the invasion of foreign agents (eg, bacteria). Platelets and other factors present in plasma are concerned in the clotting of blood, preventing haemorrhage". And that's as much, even more, that anyone – unless you're a doctor – really needs to know!

BLOOD–2: on a more prosaic note than above, there is a product called Dracula's Blood. Despite its grisly name it's a sweet treat. The "blood" is sugar crystals – black ones that are a must for decorating cakes and buns for Halloween. Also a wonderful way to add a Goth touch to ice cream, cereal, yoghurt and puddings.

FYFI: www.nice-buns.co.uk/sparkling-sugar-crystals---halloween- draculas-blood-50g-409-p.asp

BOLLYWOOD: and now India has got into the act. *Dracula Sir*, released in the summer of 2020, is a Bengali horror-thriller movie, layered with poignancy. A handsome primary school teacher, with a beautiful girlfriend, has one big problem in life. He has protruding canine teeth. Consequently he is plagued by the nickname, and known to all his pupils as "Dracula Sir". He is driven, by the dual powers of love and revenge, to becoming a vampire. Starring two of the leading lights of Indian movies – Anirban Bhattacharya and Mimi Chakraborty (who is also a member of the Indian parliament) – it is (at the time of going to press) only available in Bengali. But it has the makings of a *Dracula* offering that would do really well if translated into English or was given subtitles.

FYFI: to see the trailer, https://in.bookmyshow.com/movies/dracula-sir/ET00126095

BOMB: no, nothing explosive here – except for the way it explodes in your bath. The Jet Black Soap Bomb will turn your bathwater into exactly what the name implies. So if you want to soak and dream of Dracula, this is for you. American-made, the "bomb" lists activated charcoal and bentonite clay in its ingredients – all aimed at helping you detox as you submerge in black suds.

FYFI: in UK, https://www.amazon.com/MIDNIGHT-Bath-Bomb-Soapie-Shoppe/dp/B01DSTHOZ8; in the USA, https://soapieshoppe.com/products/midnight-jet-black-ring-bath-bomb-by-soapie-shoppe

BOND: so many bands have incorporated "Dracula" into their name. But one of the most intriguing is *James Bond Dracula* – a punk-rock trio that hails from El Reno, Oklahoma. They came up with the name, not because they're fanatical about either Bond or Dracula in equal measure, but thanks to a dog called CJ. Now what sense does that make? None. But ask the band and the backstory goes like this: "When asked what CJ stood for, the owner of the dog would reply in a smart-arsed tone, 'it stands for James Bond Dracula', which clearly it didn't. Over time it turned into a personal joke as people always asked and he always replied with the same answer. With no reasoning. Years later, when in need of a band name, one of our trio just spat it out. James Bond Dracula. Sounds good. Has the horror touch. Both were suave, badass, undying, chivalrous (disregard motive), edge-of-your-seat thrilling kind of characters ... and so, it was."

FYFI: to get an earful of what Trevor, Mike and Justin (such ordinary names for crazy punkers) have to offer, https://www.youtube.com/watch?v=VUwNsHNMfS8

BOOKS: apart from the novel *Dracula*, there are scores of books about the book; about its author Bram Stoker; the origins of the character Dracula; the films based on the novel. Plus there are many that are spin-offs or use the basic story or the name Dracula to tell a tale. These books run the gamut from desperately serious academic tomes to children's comic strips.

Many have separate entries here but the most expansive and expensive is *Dracula and the Gothic in Literature, Pop Culture and the Arts*. Published in 2015, it a compilation of academic articles examining the influence Dracula still holds over all media today. The blurb for the book reads: "This volume brings together fourteen articles that reappraise the productivity of Stoker's *Dracula* and the strong influence it still exerts on today's generations. The volume explores various multimodal and multimedia adaptations of the book, by critically examining its literary, cinematic, theatrical, televised and artistic versions. In so doing, it reassesses the origins, evolution, imagery, mythology, theory and criticism of Gothic fiction and of the Gothic (sub)culture. The volume is innovative in that it congregates various angles to the Gothic phenomenon, providing an overview of the interdisciplinary relationships between different cultural, artistic and creative reworkings of the Gothic in general and of Stoker's legacy in particular."

FYFI: https://brill.com/view/title/32469

BOXING: Sugar Ray Leonard, the legendary boxing champion, once told *Boxing News*: "When I hurt you, it was intuitive and it was instinctive, and especially if I saw a little blood, I went at you like Dracula."

BRADSHAW'S: is the legendary train guide that Bram Stoker used to add authenticity to Jonathan Harker's travels from London to Transylvania. Founded in 1839 by George Bradshaw, there were many titles in the series. Stoker undoubtedly consulted the *Continental Railway Guide* that was published annually. Bradshaw's continued being published long after George Bradshaw's death in 1853. It finally ceased publication in 1961. In 2012, Michael Portillo, the former Conservative MP, used the 1913 edition of the *Guide* to plot his travels around Europe for his BBC programme *Great Continental Journeys*.

FYFI: to buy an original, consult an antiquarian bookshop or go to eBay (expect to pay £200 plus); for reproductions of the earliest editions, along with the one Portillo used, go to your local bookstore or AbeBooks.

BREASTS: come into play in the novel. All to do with being close to the location where the fangs finally sink and do their evil. But now we have "Vampire Breasts". They are created by plastic surgeons (well, some) who inject blood into the droopy breasts of a sad patient – to perk them up. That's both the treated breasts and the patient.

FYFI: to read more about this somewhat pathetic zeal for alleged perfection see FACELIFT–1.

BRETT: in 1978 the sadly lamented British actor Jeremy Brett – best remembered for his title role in the TV series *The Adventures of Sherlock Holmes*, 1984–1994 – toured America in a stage production of *Dracula*. It ended up for a limited season on Broadway. Whichever city he was in he garnered huge publicity for his thoughts about playing The Count.

He told the *Milwaukee Sentinel*: "... all of us have our Draculas inside us. We all have somebody we like to scare ... our little brother, our mother, someone. Each of us knows the most scary thing about us – whether it's short-sheeting someone's bed, jumping out from behind a door or rigging a bucket of blood above it." About his nightly, on-stage seduction of Lucy, he told the *Chicago Tribune*: "That scene amazes me. Here a man in a black cape comes in the window with a blast of mist and he seduces a girl on the bed and there isn't a laugh or a titter in the place. I think it affects women terribly. To be swept off their feet, to be possessed, is their wildest dream. Men get an enormous fizz from it, too."

During the tour he developed what he called "Dracula elbow" in his left arm. He blamed it on the way he had to constantly fling around the cape he wore. It weighed 30 lb. And another great bit of trivia from his time as Dracula in the US was the way – in a bid to add authenticity to the production – a load of Romanian soil was imported. The plan was to put the soil in the stage coffin, in which Dracula slept, as per the mythical custom that vampires need to sleep on soil from their native land. Nice idea. But sadly the soil was confiscated by customs – for fear it would contaminate wherever it was disposed of after the tour ended.

FYFI: for complete Brett quotes and other fun trivia about his *Dracula* tour, www.brettish.com/later-stages.html

BRIDES: as in *The Brides of Dracula,* the 1960 Hammer film. The verdict of movie critic George E Butler (see FILM–2) is that it is "still the best treatment of the story".

BRIDES–2: in early 2020 *Dracula* fans were beyond excited. The American TV network ABC announced it was making a *Dracula* drama series, *The Brides*. Set in the present day, it would center on what happened to the trio of empowered, immortal women – the brides of Dracula – and the things they did to maintain wealth, prestige, legacy and their non-traditional family. Croatian-born actor Goran Višnjić – who rose to fame, playing Luke Kovac in TV's hospital soap *ER* – was all set to play Dracula. Then the dreaded corona-virus struck. And, along with so many other theatrical and film productions about to enter the pipeline, *The Brides* was axed. But the Hollywood buzz is that when the "new normal" gets back to being just "normal" *The Brides* will – like Dracula himself – rise from the dead.

BRIGHT'S: as in Bright's Disease – which Bram Stoker suffered from. A condition that reflects the poor state of the kidneys, it was that – along with a couple of strokes – that was the cause of his death. Having said that, there is a popular conception that in fact he died of syphilis. See DEATH.

BROWNING: John Edgar Browning is one of the most high-profile and lauded academics when it comes to analyzing the hidden and erudite meanings lurking in the pages of *Dracula*. Previously a visiting lecturer at the esteemed Georgia Institute of Technology, he is now Professor of Liberal Arts at the Savanah College of Art and Design in Atlanta, Georgia. Vampires are his subject; *Dracula* his speciality. He has eight books under his vampire-zombies-monsters-belt. In 2010 he penned the award-winning *Dracula in Visual Media* – in which he examined more than 700 *Dracula* movies, TV programmes, documentaries and video games, plus 1,000 comic books and pinpoint adaptations. In 2011 it won him the prestigious Lord Ruthen Award (see RUTHEN) and high praise from another leading Dracula expert, Dr Elizabeth Miller (see MILLER). She said: "A superb book ... a magnificent piece of scholarship".

FYFI: https://www.goodreads.com/book/show/8703107-dracula-in-visual-media

BUFFALO: as in Buffalo Bill. Bram Stoker met William F "Buffalo Bill" Cody on at least three occasions. The first time was in America in 1886, when the author was on tour with thespian Sir Henry Irving (see IRVING). They met again, a year later, in London and Glasgow when Buffalo Bill staged his famed Wild West show in both cities.

Louis S Warren – who teaches US western history at the University of California, Davis – paid special attention to their friendship in his 2005 biography *Buffalo Bill's America: William Cody and the Wild West Show*. In it he made an amazing, bizarre claim. He wrote: "Weird as it may seem Buffalo Bill and his Wild West show were important inspirations for Bram Stoker's *Dracula*. In Cody's drama, as in *Dracula*, the frontiers of racial encounter were infested with the possibility of degeneration and the necessity of race war."

FYFI: to explore Warren's theory in depth,

https://historycooperative.org/buffalo-bill-meets-dracula-william-f-cody-bram-stoker-and-the-frontiers-of-racial-decay

BURTON: another notable influence on Bram Stoker was undoubtedly Sir Richard Burton. No, not that one (he, the late, legendary actor – when it came to British honors – only got a CBE) but the British explorer, diplomat, linguist and author, who died in 1890. Among his many and varied works – including translating the *Kama Sutra* and *1001 Arabian Nights* into English – was *Vikram and the Vampire*. It helped sow the very early seeds of *Dracula*. Burton freely adapted the legendary Indian collection of tales about how a king called Vikram tries to capture a "baital" (equal to a vampire in Western literature). Published in 1870, the content intrigued Stoker. The two finally met in 1879. Later Stoker said: "The man riveted my attention. He was dark and forceful, and masterful, and ruthless. I have never seen so iron a countenance."

BUTLER: horror movie buff Charles E Butler (see FILMS–2) is no longer just a well-versed fan of *Dracula* and other vampire movies. He is now a *Dracula* comic-book writer. In March 2018 he produced *Dracula Reborn No. 1*, the first in an e-book series titled *Dracula: the Unearthed Chronicles*. The introduction to the series says: "Count Dracula is restored to life in the present day and begins his long centuries revenge on Van Helsing and his followers. Caught in the crossfire are Miriam and Jessica, sisters and the great, great, great-granddaughters of Jonathan and Mina Harker. A great evil descends on the United Kingdom as Dracula is finally reborn!" As one reviewer said: "Charles is a very talented illustrator and writer. The storyline follows the original Dracula story and reads well. His drawings offer a fresh interpretation of Dracula in all his gore and all his glory."Before his venture into the comic genre, Butler laboured long and hard to bring his *Dracula* passion to fruition, via film, in 2010 in his first book *The Romance of Dracula: A Personal Journey of the Count on Celluloid*. He followed that up two years later with a review of all vampire movies, *Vampires Everywhere: the Rise of the Movie Undead* and a year after that, *Vampires: Under the Hammer,* covering movies made by the iconic Hammer studio. In 2015 he published the very comprehensive and updated view of the genre with *Vampires: the Final Hunt*. Then in September 2018 he updated his first book with *Dracula: The Ultimate Romance*.

As to the never-ending draw of Dracula, Yorkshire man Butler says: "... he is the greatest fantasy figure ever created and even though undead he will never die as long as there are creative talents to keep him alive ..." And paying tribute to Bram Stoker he says: "I doff my hat to Bram, the father of Dracula, and thank him for my many years of entertainment."

FYFI: https://www.goodreads.com/author/show/1160722

C

CAKE: even Dracula enjoys a luscious cream cake now and then. Well, he did when he was portrayed by the late, legendary character actor Kenneth Williams. In a 1985 TV advert for cream cakes (to promote the consumption of fresh cream by the, then, Milk Marketing Board), Williams, in full Dracula regalia, rose from an ornate, scarlet satin-lined coffin, clutching a large cream cake. As he sinks his teeth into the cake he says, in his celebrated mincing way: " 'ere, the trouble with these midnight snacks is that you get crumbs all over the place." Before uttering the famed phrase of those days, "Fresh cream cakes. Naughty – but ever so nice."

FYFI: to see it, https://www.youtube.com/watch?v=ERFzL7yLxNY

CAMBRIDGE: as in University Press. In November 2017 it published *The Cambridge Companion to Dracula*. Basically it gives voice to 16 *Dracula* experts to reflect on the multitude of complex layers that unite in the novel to make it one of the most celebrated pieces of literature ever produced. The preface reads: "Bram Stoker's Dracula is the most famous vampire in literature and film. This new collection of sixteen essays brings together a range of internationally renowned scholars to provide a series of pathways through this celebrated Gothic novel and its innumerable adaptations and translations. The volume illuminates the novel's various pre-histories, critical contexts and subsequent cultural transformations.

"Chapters explore literary history, Gothic revival scholarship, folklore, anthropology, psychology, sexology, philosophy, occultism, cultural history, critical race theory, theatre and film history, and the place of the vampire in Europe and beyond. These studies provide an accessible guide of cutting-edge scholarship to one of the most celebrated modern Gothic horror stories. This *Companion* will serve as a key resource for scholars, teachers and students interested in the enduring force of *Dracula* and the seemingly inexhaustible range of the contexts it requires and readings it might generate."

FYFI: www.cambridge.org/core/books/cambridge-companion-to- dracula/1B638EB1F3A8F93571B3905DAFC48BD1

CANADA: just say the name Anthony DP Mann in Canada and you might as well have said Dracula. This actor/writer/film-maker has carved his name deep into Canadian thespian life – with movies based on our hero a speciality. In 2008 he wrote, directed and starred in *Canucula!* (aka *Dracula in Canada*) in which Dracula turns up in Canada and sets about his bloodsucking ways. It's become something of a cult movie – particularly because it was made using a scratchy black and white filter giving the scenes a look of the old time horror movies. It also lapses into silent cinema mode. In 2012, Mann repeated all three roles (writer, director and star) in *Terror of Dracula*, which he claimed was a faithful adaptation of Bram Stoker's novel. Both films, which were made in Kingston, Ontario – Mann's hometown – were, when released, available as DVDs. Now they're very hard to track down.

CARDS: if you're after a greeting's card that shows off your love for *Dracula* and or anything associated with the novel or him, there is a global website that caters to all *Dracula* card needs. Whether it's an artist's impression of him, a copy of a movie poster, stills from one of the many movies, a photo of Bran Castle, cartoons or pictures of Whitby. Fine Art America – which displays the work of thousands of artists from around the world – has an amazing 2,410 items with a *Dracula* link. And if you find an image which you love (and you will) it can be transferred not only to a card, but to a mug, a cushion cover, a yoga mat, a T-shirt, a towel, etc, etc.

FYFI: https://fineartamerica.com/shop/greeting+cards/dracula

CARMILLA: before Dracula there was the lesbian vampire called Carmilla. She was the anti-heroine in the 1872 Gothic novella of the same name by Joseph Sheridan Le Fanu. Published 25 years before *Dracula*, its influence on Bram Stoker is well recognised. On top of that, like Stoker, Le Fanu was Irish and spent most of his life in Dublin, and the two got to know each other when Stoker became theatre critic for the Dublin paper Le Fanu owned. *Carmilla* has penetrated the artistic genre of vampires since the Danish film *Vampyr* in 1932. It was followed by many more, all based on or featuring Carmilla. The latest movie take on her, *The Curse of Styria*, was released in August 2014. A few months later its Irish premiere was a highlight of the Bram Stoker Festival (see FESTIVAL) in Dublin. Styria (see STYRIA) is the region of Austria in which *Carmilla* was set, when it was part of the Austro-Hungarian Empire.

FYFI: for the book, https://www.goodreads.com/book/show/48037; for the trailer of the movie, https://www.youtube.com/watch?v=-5nCn0H13yM

CARRADINE: over his 65 years as a celluloid star, Hollywood legend John Carradine chalked up four appearances as Dracula. He played the role in: *House of Frankenstein* (1944); *House of Dracula* (1945); *Billy the Kid Versus Dracula* (1966) and *Nocturna: Granddaughter of Dracula* (1979). In the last film he sported the same cape and tuxedo costume he wore in the 1945 movie.

CAR: want to zoom around in a vehicle that has a distinctive look of Dracula? Then the Lexus hybrid RX range is for you. In April 2020, the *Irish Times* reviewing the upgraded model said: "... it has a dramatically pointy snout, with a grille that appears to have chromed fangs invading, Dracula-like, from the corners of its mouth ... while we accept that Lexus's sharp-nosed styling won't find favour everywhere, it looks ruddy good to us." But to whizz around, showing off your new Dracula-like motor, will set you back a cool £70,000.

FYFI: to see the look, https://www.lexus.com/models/RX/gallery

CASTLE: approximately 120 miles from Bucharest, Romania's capital, you will find the majestic Bran Castle

– nestled in the Piatra Craiului Mountains. While it has no official connection with *Dracula*, of all the castles in Transylvania, it is the one most closely resembling the description in the book. Bram Stoker, surprisingly, never visited the region and is believed to have based Dracula's abode on the castle described so graphically, alongside an illustration, in Charles Boner's book, *Transylvania: Its Product and Its People*, published in 1865. The Castle's only (albeit tenuous) link with Dracula is that Vlad the Impaler (on whom Dracula is, again tenuously, based) was imprisoned in Bran Castle for two months, in 1482.

Built in 1211 by the Teutonic Knights, the castle has a long and rich history. In 1920 it became the summer residence for the Romanian royal family and in 1944 it was converted into a Red Cross hospital for the war wounded. But in 1948 the Communists kicked out the royal family and the State turned it into a museum. In 2009, possession was handed back to the royal family and exiled members returned to Romania to run the castle as a major attraction in the burgeoning tourist industry of the, once again, independent country. The latest plan is for a glass lift to be built in an adjoining, abandoned, mine shaft. It will lead visitors through the escape tunnel – used by Vlad when he fled his fortress prison – into a multimedia show highlighting the history and mystery of the Castle and its environs.

FYFI: www.bran-castle.com

CASTLE-2: in October 2014 word got out that, for the right price offered by the right person, Bran Castle could be sold. While it's never officially gone on the market, a

New York lawyer has been appointed to handle the sale – should it ever come to that. As of going to print, no suitable new owner, with the suitable amount of cash (probably $80 million), has come forward. The current owners – Archduke Dominic and his two sisters, descendants of Queen Victoria's granddaughter who was Queen Marie of Romania – assume any eventual buyers will turn the restored edifice into a tourist attraction. Not that it isn't one already! The sale – if there ever is one – will be handled by lawyer Mark Meyer, of the New York law firm Herzfeld & Rubin, who founded and is president of the Romanian-American Chamber of Commerce.

CASTLE-3: in the run-up to Halloween 2016, an enormous amount of publicity was garnered for Bran Castle. Airbnb, along with Bram Stoker's great-grand-nephew, Dacre Stoker (see DACRE), held a competition in which the winner – accompanied by a friend – would get to sleep in the Castle, in scarlet satin-lined coffins. Contestants had to use their "vampire wit" to come up with what, given a chance to meet him, they would say to Dracula. It was claimed over 88,000 contestants battled it out. Though it wasn't much of a battle because there was no "wit" involved. The winners were sister and brother Tami and Robin Varma from Ottawa, Canada, and they won because of their special connection to Dracula. All they had to do was mention their grandfather!

Those deeply involved and fascinated by the Gothic genre will recognise the name. Tami and Robin's grandfather was the late Devendra Varma, one of the world's leading experts in Gothic novels and vampire lore. He was the author of *Gothic Flame: Being a History of the Gothic Novel in England* which, although published in 1957, still holds a prestigious place in the vast library of Gothic literature. So their answer to the competition question didn't take much time to work out. They simply said: "… our late grandfather was the world's leading expert in Gothic literature, and was considered to be an expert in Dracula … we would do just about anything to stay as a guest with the original vampire who inspired him." So, on the bewitching night of the 31st, the siblings did what their esteemed grandfather would have salivated to do – had a Dracula sleepover in his fictional castle.

FYFI: https://www.goodreads.com/author/show/2847808

CASTLE-4: there's yet another one – in Dublin. Not a real "castle" but a place of entertainment, It's billed as: "Dublin's most exciting, fun & unique Irish adult attraction". The blurb continues: "Millions of Euros have been spent creating this incredible Irish Dracula attraction. Travel back in time and enjoy a heart-thumping visit to Castle Dracula, meeting the weird and wonderful characters from the story of Dracula and learn about Irish writer Bram Stoker. Brave guests journey through the dark castle's tunnels, over spinning bridges to Lucy's courtyard, up to Dracula's lair and down to the world's only graveyard theatre for a show where they promise not to bite, unless …" Castle Dracula also boasts a museum (see MUSEUM-2) which visitors are encouraged to tour before going to the show, which lasts over two hours. The "castle" is in Clontarf, the Dublin neighbourhood where Bram Stoker grew up. It was closed for a while in early 2020 for a total refurbishment. Then, just as it was about to reopen, the corona-virus crisis hit and kept it closed. It hoped to be up and running again – in all its new scary splendor – by the end of 2020 or early 2021.

FYFI: www.castledracula.ie

CASTLE-5: in 2008 another sort of castle became home to Dracula and the usual cast of characters. *Dracula* was performed entirely on a bouncy castle at the Edinburgh Fringe Festival. Produced and performed by The Strolling Theatricals – who made headlines earlier that year with their "X" appearance on *Britain's Got Talent* – it was panned by the critics, but loved by the fans!

CASTLEVANIA: the legendary video game series – which stars Dracula – never seems to lose its prized place in the top ten of such pastimes. In 2017, *Netflix* stepped up to the production plate and brought the ever-popular video game to a device, with a screen, near you. In 2018, the second season aired. Basically the plot revolves around a vampire hunter who fights to save a besieged Eastern European country from an army of otherworldly beasts, controlled by Dracula. Inspired by the classic video game (see entry X), a British trio of well-known actors – Richard Armitage (*The Hobbit*), James Callis (also *The Hobbit* and *Battlestar Galactia*) and Graham McTavish (*The Outlander*) – provide the voices for the lead roles in the animated series, which went into its third season in March 2020.

FYFI: https://www.netflix.com/title/80095241

CAT: no, not the four-legged type. This "cat" is short for "catalogue" – as in WorldCat. It's the global website that finds the location of libraries – from local to university –

that have a copy of the book, the audio-book, video, CD or movie you are searching for. It also tells you where, if available, the item can be bought. WorldCat has two billion items listed in 10,000 libraries. As of August 2019, it had 19,338 listings for items with "Dracula" in the name.

FYFI: https://www.worldcat.org/search?qt=worldcat_org_all&q=Dracula

CELOSIA: and what is that, when it's at home? Of course, as keen gardeners know, it's a plant – with its origins in Africa but now widely grown in Central America, the Caribbean, Indonesia and Asia. There are about a dozen types, all with different-looking blooms. Some are considered weeds, others highly cultivated plants. But, whatever the form, the leaves are edible.

However, that's not got anything to do with why the most stunning of the species is called *Celosia Dracula*. It got its name not because it's out to kill or pollute everything around it but because, like Dracula, it is light-sensitive. Though in the opposite way. Unlike its namesake, without sun and warmth it will not flourish. Not die, but just stay a green plant. Once exposed to strong daylight it jumps into life – with a show-stopping, extravagant blood-red bloom that darkens to midnight-purple in the sun. Which is why it's rapidly becoming a must-have for landscapers everywhere. As for the leaves: they are used in all the aforementioned countries as a nutritious, leafy green vegetable, similar to spinach.

CHAIR: an office chair that's found in the gaming or racing-seat category has been dubbed "The Dracula Office Chair".

Hard to know why it's not marketed under that name. For sure, there's nothing bland or ordinary about it. The black upholstery is slashed with scarlet blazes and the wheels sport red highlights. But the image of Dracula is conjured up via the high back with slanting cut-outs. A truly eerie – but comfortable – look.

FYFI: chairs with the Dracula look can be found everywhere. Search for "gaming racing recliner".

CHATEAU: no, not a proper one – where they make blood-red vino – but a restaurant. "Le Chateau de Dracula" is in the Schaerbeek district of Brussels. Despite the name, the Romanian owners, who are from Transylvania, have gone out of their way to decorate only with artefacts inspired by the folklore of their country. There are no bundles of garlic or images of Dracula's castle on the walls. No posters from *Dracula* movies. Neither do they have anything on the menu that invokes vampires, like a blood sausage pie or a garlic-heavy appetizer. And there are no coffin-shaped deserts or black-iced cakes decorated with blood-red bats or fangs. Julia, one of the owners, says: "We don't have scary things because we are inspired by reality not by the legend of Dracula."

CHINA: a musical version of *Dracula* – especially adapted for Chinese audiences – premiered in Shanghai, in November 2014. It emphasised the gentle and warm side of vampires with a sad, romantic approach. Director Shen Xufei said: "We made some adaptations to the show based on cultural differences and Chinese habits when it comes to enjoying the theatre." He added that scenes and plot points relating to eroticism were toned down, including "fangs, stakes and some other props that represent sexuality and desire". In this Chinese version, such elements are "euphemistically and implicitly staged". But when it came to the music, the Western world won out – with pop, rock and heavy metal being used to add to the atmosphere of horror and to help the actors in depicting their characters.

CHRISTMAS: the sight of Dracula dressed as Father Christmas welcoming guests to a festive party is indeed a sight to behold and one that quite warms the heart ... but not for long. In the indie movie *Christmas at Dracula's,* the cheery mood changes swiftly. It had a limited release in March, 2015, before hitting the worldwide film-festival circuit. The first major production from El Diablo Productions of Cork, Ireland, it was the work – writing and production – of Cork native Simon McKeon. It was greeted with enthusiasm by Film Ireland, which wrote on its website: "Shot at various locations in and around Cork City and County, *Christmas at Dracula's* is a modern, darkly comic take on the vampire myth, interweaving aspects of Bram Stoker's legendary novel and expanding on the Hollywood B movies of the 1930s and Hammer horror creature genres."

The storyline unfolds thus: the once formidable Count Dracula decides to throw a Christmas party to rejuvenate his failing reputation as the Prince of Darkness. The guest list includes an array of famous movie monsters including Frankenstein, The Invisible Man, The Wicked Witch, Dr Jekyll, The Wolfman and many more. This unwittingly sets off a series of events that quickly spirals out of control and threatens to become the party to end all parties, heralding a zombie apocalypse and bringing Dracula to the very gates of hell.

FYFI: www.youtube.com/watch?v=nAHc6tUb7Zs

CHRISTMAS-2: spook your kids at Yuletide with a copy of *Little Dracula's Christmas* by Martin Waddell. First published in 1986, it was re-issued as *Little Dracula's First Christmas* in 2001. For more about the author and his other *Little Dracula* books see LITTLE and WADDELL.

CHRONICLES: very confusing, but there are two sets of novels based on Dracula, with almost identical titles but by two different authors. It's surprising copyright laws have allowed it. However, there is a subtle difference between the titles of the series – namely, one carries the definite article. So we have *The Dracula Chronicles* by Shane KP O'Neill and *Dracula Chronicles* by Victor T Foia.

CHRONICLES-2: Irish writer O'Neill has published ten of his planned 12-book series. *The Dracula Chronicles* stories are a combo of the real man and the fictional character. As the forewords to the books state: "This is a fresh dimension to the Dracula legend, which combines the real historical Vlad Dracula with a new and different version of Dracula the vampire." O'Neill – whose stylised middle initials stand for Kevin Patrick – is not too happy when he is linked to Bram Stoker and the fictional Dracula. For this book he explained: "My character bears no resemblance to Bram Stoker's in any way, but through name. My series is based on the real man, and his life, and is part of a very expansive concept." In a fuller explanation in October 2013, he told an interviewer: "*The Dracula Chronicles* are a concept based on the real historical Vlad Dracula and my own idea of Dracula the vampire. I hate associations made with my work and Bram Stoker's because my character resembles his in name only. My books are historical novels of dark Gothic horror set in a brutal age and often in a brutal context. They are stories of religious corruption; political intrigue; violence; deep romance and erotica set against the vast historical backdrops of 15th and 16th century Europe."

FYFI: https://www.goodreads.com/author/show/6580373

CHRONICLES-3: Victor T Foia was born in Klausenburg, Transylvania, just 90 miles from Sighisoara, the birthplace of Vlad the Impaler, the inspiration for Stoker's *Dracula*. His interest in the novel dates back to visiting the historic city when he was six. At the age of 22, Victor escaped from behind the Iron Curtain and defected to Italy, finally migrating to the United States and setting up home in Bailey's Harbour, Wisconsin. But he never lost his passion for Dracula and spent four decades researching Vlad's life in all the places he lived, loved, fought and was imprisoned. Now retired from a corporate career, Foia is devoting all his time to his *Dracula Chronicles*.

He's published four of the seven planned books. The next one is due in late 2020. As the blurb to *Dracula Chronicles* claims: "Foia has gone beyond the iconic Dracula literature to ferret out the essence of the man behind the Legend." And as the foreword to the series says: "Dracula is certainly among the best-known men in the world, yet arguably the least understood. While many stories have been told about both the real and the fictional Dracula, Foia's account benefits from four decades of research and the unique perspective of a Transylvanian native. Under Foia's pen, *Dracula Chronicles* finally pierces the veil of mystery that has shrouded the Wallachian king for over 500 years. In vivid details, the multi-volume historical novel unfolds Dracula's epic metamorphosis from a naive and trusting prince to the ruthless law-and-order king whose deeds have spawned the most enduring vampire legend. Taking place on the backdrop of the dying Middle Ages and the blossoming of the Renaissance, *Dracula Chronicles* is replete with towering passions, unbridled ambitions, vile betrayals, and righteous revenge. And, as one would expect, blood."

FYFI: https://www.goodreads.com/author/show/6906661

CHOCULA: since 1971, "Count Chocula" – a sugary tribute to Dracula – has been adorning cereal boxes in America, luring youngsters to munch him up with the legendary phrase: "I vant to eat your cereal". The cereal, produced by food giant General Mills, has an almost cult-like following. Since 2010, the chocolate frosted flakes mixed with tiny chocolate marshmallows have only been sold during September and October – Halloween season. Also in 2010, "Count Chocula Energy Bars" were introduced, again as a seasonal product. Until recently the cereal was not available in the UK. But now, thanks to Amazon, it is – along with "Count Chocula" spin-offs, like kids' duvets, backpacks and lunch bags.

FYFI: https://www.amazon.co.uk/Count-Chocula-Cereal-17-8-504g/dp/B00NO3NM14

CHURCHILL: as a young, successful parliamentarian, Winston Churchill – who went on to become the most lauded British leader of all time – always, despite repeated approaches, declined to be interviewed. In 1907 aged 33, while an Under-Secretary of State for the Colonies, he relented and agreed to be profiled by Bram Stoker (who had turned to journalism in a bid to make money after the death of his mentor and boss, Sir Henry Irving). He was writing a series on prominent public figures for the long-gone *New York World*. The series was later published in the *Daily Chronicle*, one of the leading UK newspapers of the day.

And the reason Stoker was able to win him over? In Churchill's own words: "... because you are the author of *Dracula*." Stoker modestly reacted to Churchill's reasoning, pointing out later: "... it was a vampire novel I wrote some years ago, which had appealed to his young imagination ..." The interview can be read in the Penguin Classic's 2003 edition of *Dracula*.

FYFI: to read the article as it appeared in Britain, www.bramstoker.org/pdf/nonfic/churchilluk.pdf; in the US, www.bramstoker.org/pdf/nonfic/churchillus2.pdf; for background notes, www.bramstoker.org/nonfic/churchill.html

CLOTHES: in the book there's a distinct lack of description of any clothing, or references to fashion or style. The only specific mention of any item is when Mina, walking through Piccadilly with Jonathan, observes "... a very beautiful girl in a big cartwheel hat ..." It appears in Chapter 13. Stoker probably restrained from any sartorial mentions for the same reason he left out reference to the year (see DATES) – so the story would not become dated.

CLOTHING: in contrast to the above, there's no shortage of clothing inspired by Dracula and his entourage. One of the most specialised places to find unique and innovative Drac-fashion is "Dracula Clothing". It has a vast array of highly stylised garments for men and women, along with jewellery and accessories. It has no bricks-and-mortar outlet, online retail only, but it ships free, worldwide, from its warehouse in Prague, Czech Republic. While the biggest sales are notched up to customers from the US, followed by most of Europe, there is growing interest from China, Japan and Africa.

Dracula Clothing is owned and operated by Norwegian Truls Stokka. An economist by profession, Stokka started the business in 2007 as a hobby. Two years later he quit his job to concentrate on it full time. His rationale for his, now booming, global business is quite simple: "I have always loved vampire legends, books, and movies. As a kid I admired Bram Stoker's *Dracula* and Anne Rice's *Interview with the Vampire*. I've always been in awe of the outfits worn during the Victorian, Baroque and Rococo eras. This inspired me to make and design 'vampire outfits'." Dracula Clothing has been featured in the Italian edition of *Vogue* and taken part in a special Steampunk edition of the American TV reality show *Project Runway*, hosted by supermodel Heidi Klum and avant-garde fashionista, Tim Gunn.

FYFI: www.draculaclothing.com

CLUB: the ski-Mecca of Switzerland, St Moritz, has a host of "exclusive" night spots. But one of the best known – and hardest to gain admission to – is "Dracula's Ghost Riders

Club". Founded in 1974 by the late playboy-millionaire Gunter Sachs (see BARDOT), to cater to the "vampires of the jet set", it's on (for obvious reasons) Plazza Gunter Sachs. The club, which demands its guests "dress elegantly" and charges £224 for 30 grams of caviar, rocks away from midnight to 5:00 am. The name comes not just from his love of Dracula – his speedboat carried the name – but his obsession with bobsleighing. His team was called the "ghost riders" and he was European champion in 1958.

FYFI: http://www.dracs.ch

COCA-COLA: has used Dracula over the years in several TV commercials, with one of the best airing in 1992. With wind howling, Dracula crashes through the window into the boudoir of a beautiful blonde who is in bed. As he lunges for her, she screams – while grabbing the familiar red can and holding it up to his face. He starts, reeling away, but takes the can and sinks his teeth into its side. His face turns from nasty monster to handsome, smiling, matinee idol type – and as the two of them disappear, arm in arm, into the night, the voice-over says the immortal *Coca-Cola* words: "Can't beat the real thing".

FYFI: www.youtube.com/watch?v=zQ0DFX9qvgQ

COCKTAIL: for that special Halloween or Goth party tipple, try "Dracula's Kiss". There are a slew of recipes for it on the internet – all slightly different, but all using various combinations of vodka (plain or black cherry), cranberry schnapps, grenadine and Coke. Which ever combo you use it packs a colourful punch. But the trick to making it Dracula-like is to use red cake-decorating gel and a clip-on plastic spider. Trim the rim of the glass, preferably a martini glass, with dribbles of the gel to represent blood, along with the spider.

COCKTAIL-2: *The Endeavour* pub is a top hang-out for Goths when they descend on Whitby – the historic Yorkshire fishing town that is "home" to Dracula – for the twice-a-year Goth Festival. Its "Goth Tipple" is a mix of Chambord (the French raspberry liqueur), cherry-flavoured gin, blackberry cordial, fizzy lemonade and ice, topped with fresh raspberries and blackberries.

COFFIN: hard to fathom why, but some people want to own an ornate coffin fit for Dracula. And there is one, designed specifically to fulfil that dream. It's sold by Halloween Express, a US chain of shops, and it will set you back over a thousand bucks. And a lot more than that if you want it shipped overseas. The coffin, which will take a six-foot body, is described thus: "In the tradition of Vlad the Impaler, this coffin comes with the most old-world look possible. From the sculpted wooden angular construction to the ornate sculpted-on brass handles and skull doorknobs, this coffin truly has the Transylvanian feel."

FYFI: www.halloweenexpress.com/dracula-coffin

COFFIN-2: at the other end of the price range, from the coffin above, is the one with Dracula lying in it. It's the creation of Design-Toscano, the US-based global mail-order company that manufactures and sells statuary, historical reproductions, furniture and home decor. The coffin – 8" x 3" x 2" – which can be shipped overseas, sells in the US for around $25. Customers are lured by a description that reads: "Our suave, charismatic vampire statue can be lifted from his faux woodgrain and bat-emblazoned coffin in this chilling collectible, sure to add an eerie measure of vampire panache to your desktop or display shelf. Cast in quality designer resin, our Design-Toscano-exclusive vampire sculpture is hand-painted in bone-chilling tones straight from the grave. Our eerie vampire figurine deftly captures the macabre spirit of Hungarian vampire legend."

FYFI: to buy, https://www.designtoscano.com/product/ the+vampire+coffin+of+dracula+statue+-+wu73309. do?from=Search&cx=0

COFFIN-3: and for something in between – which will be the hit of any Halloween party – get the 6' long, self-inflatable, red and black, illuminated coffin with the pop-up Dracula. And as it's made of waterproof polyester it's great for outside so you can "frighten" passers-by.

FYFI: in the UK it sells for around £100, http://www.karnival-house.co.uk/inflatable-up-and-down-dracula-in-coffin-18mtr-p-3526.html; in the US for $100, from Amazon.

COFFIN-4: in the end, the most palatable Dracula-linked coffin is a chocolate one. And to get it you have to visit Whitby (but then, as a Drac-fan, that's hardly an ordeal). Justin's – the town's famed chocolaterie – does a drop-dead massive trade with its "choc-coffs". The basic version, for £2.50, is milk or dark chocolate, shaped like a coffin, four-inches long by an inch wide, filled with a strawberry-champagne truffle and decorated with a scarlet crucifix. But Justin's will make any size you want and orders for foot-long versions – which give "death by chocolate" a new meaning – are not uncommon.

FYFI: https://www.facebook.com/Justinchocolatefudgetoffee

COIN: in October 2018 the Central Bank of Ireland issued a commemorative silver €15 coin to honour Bram Stoker. It depicted a glowering Dracula behind his moonlit castle. At the unveiling ceremony Dacre Stoker, his great-grand-nephew (see DACRE) said: "On behalf of the Stoker family, it is wonderful to see Bram commemorated in the city of his birth in such a magnificent way." A limited-edition of 3,000 collector coins were minted – for a selling price of €60 each.

FYFI: amazingly there are still some coins left. To see it and buy go to, https://www.collectorcoins.ie

COMEDY: a bid to turn the classic tale into a comedy film was far from being a huge success, though it did star a huge name – David Niven. He played Dracula in the 1974 *Old Dracula* – also known as *Vampira* – in which he romps with a castle full of Playboy Bunnies. In this spoof of the Transylvanian legend, Niven sinks his fangs into a bevy of centre-fold playmates in order to find the right blood type to resurrect his dear-departed wife. With other top names of the day involved – Jeremy Lloyd of *Are You Being Served* scriptwriter fame and *What's New Pussycat* director Clive Donner – it should have been a sure-fire hit. But no. The late and legendary US film reviewer Roger Ebert gave it one star, describing it as "a mess" with only Niven – with "his weary charm and seedy elegance" – being a "highlight". But these days, because of how awful it was, it has something of a cult following.

FYFI: For the trailer, https://www.youtube.com/watch?v=kTTrytHGuJc

COMICS: *Tomb of Dracula – Lord of Vampires*, put out by Marvel Comics from 1972 to 1979, broke the 1950s US imposed "ban" on vampire stories in comics. Over its seven-year life, the immensely popular series earned legendary comic status. The 70-issue run featured a group of vampire hunters who fought Count Dracula and other supernatural menaces. It is now available in a series of books, which are collections of the original comics.

FYFI: to buy, search eBay and Amazon; expect to pay £15 and upwards.

CONCERTINA: no, no one in *Dracula* played one. but writer/illustrator Lyndon White has done a concertina book about the novel. The story – per Bram Stoker's original – is told in highly stylised, graphic illustrative form that looks like a book – until it is opened. The pages unfold like a concertina. Manchester-based Lydon picked 10 key points from the novel on which to work his artistic magic. His introduction goes: "A young lawyer on an assignment finds himself imprisoned in a Transylvanian castle by his mysterious host. Back home, his fiancée and friends are menaced by a malevolent force which seems intent on imposing suffering and destruction. Can the devil really have arrived on England's shores? And what is it that he hungers for so desperately? The clock strikes midnight and all the evil things in the world come full sway, lost souls are falling under the Count's horrifying spell and one thing remains certain – Dracula must be destroyed."

FYFI: https://lyndonwhite.bigcartel.com

COOKERY BOOKS: the most entertaining, among a clutch of them, is *The Dracula Cookbook of Blood* by Ardin C Price and Trishna Leszczyc, published in 1993. Every recipe has blood in it! The dishes range from variations of black pudding and blood sausage, to a tasty liver pate from Italy and stews and soups from all over the world. In the introduction, the authors write: "Mention blood as a food and most of the modern world would consider it the private reserve of vampires and the odd werewolf. But in reality, blood has a long history as a food source for humans."

FYFI: the book is easy to find – put the title into any search engine.

COOKERY BOOKS-2: published in 1978, *The Dracula Cookbook*, by Marina Polvay, has the secondary title: *Authentic Recipes from the Homeland of Count Dracula*. Born a Russian Princess, Marina – who died in 2002, aged 74 – was brought up in Budapest, studied cuisine throughout Europe and finally moved to America, where she carved out a name as a gourmet cook and food writer. She travelled throughout Romania and Hungary to collect the best Slavic recipes that fitted the Dracula mould. As she wrote in her foreword: "These flavourful and lavish recipes are sure to make every meal a bloody success!"

FYFI: to buy, same as above.

COOKIES: in 2013, Oreo, the legendary American cookie – or biscuit for Brit readers – used a cartoon Dracula in a worldwide TV advertising campaign. An impish looking Count is given an Oreo (two dark chocolate cookies sandwiched with a white cream filling) and a lilting singing voice asks if, with the taste, he would "act less undead and thirst for milk instead?"

FYFI: to see the ad, www.youtube.com/watch?v=43YAc20tAog

COOKIES-2: conjure up some grisly "Dracula Denture Cookies" for Halloween. It's a very simple procedure. Cut a large chocolate chip cookie in half; spread red icing (aka frosting in the US) on the two halves; place mini white marshmallows on the edge of one side, interspersing every two or three with slivered almonds; sandwich together and voilà – a tasty Dracula grin!

FYFI: To see how it's done, https://www.the-girl-who-ate-everything.com/draculas-dentures-for-halloween

COOKIES-3: and for that special place to store them, search for a hard-to-find vintage Dracula Cookie Jar. With a limited edition of only 1,000, it is so very collectable. Issued in 1997, as part of the Universal Monsters' Collection, it was made by the now defunct Treasure Craft. If you can find one, expect to pay $300 or more.

FYFI: in the hope of finding one, go to eBay, or, in the US, https://sundryshop.com/catalogsearch/result/?q=Dracula+Cookie+Jar

COOPER-1: Alice Cooper (real name Vincent Darmon Furnier) penned a song in tribute to Hollywood star Dwight Frye (1899–1943) who, in 1931, famously played the demented Renfield in the first *Dracula* movie. *The Ballad of Dwight Fry* (it is not known if Cooper dropped the "e" to avoid a lawsuit or just plain forgot it) – which was on his 1971 album, *Love it to Death* – was also featured in the 2012 Tim Burton movie *Dark Shadows*. In part the lyrics go:

See my lonely life unfold
I see it everyday
See my lonely mind explode
When I've gone insane.

I wanna get outta here ...

FYFI: www.last.fm/music/Alice+Cooper//
Ballad+of+Dwight+Fry

COOPER-2: in a guest appearance on the 1978 *Muppet Show Halloween Special*, Alice Cooper adopted the Dracula persona, rising from a coffin, and singing *Welcome To My Nightmare*. It goes:

Welcome to my nightmare,
I think you're gonna like it,
I think you're gonna feel you belong.
A nocturnal vacation,
unnecessary sedation,
you want to feel at home
'cause you belong.
Welcome to my nightmare,

whoa, ho, ho, ho.
Welcome to my breakdown.
I hope I didn't scare you.
That's just the way we are
when we come down.
We sweat and laugh
and scream here.
'cause life is just a dream here.
You know inside you
feel right at home, here.
Yeah, welcome to my nightmare,
yeah, hey, hey, hey ...

FYFI: www.youtube.com/watch?v=TQK5TbgopKw

CORONA-VIRUS: yes, yes, in the year of the worldwide lockdown, Dracula was invoked many times over. In a feature headlined "The Lighter Side to Covid-19", the *Malaysia Chronicle* wrote: "Yes, Covid is more horrifying than even Dracula the Vampire, as Dracula kills only an average of 365 people a year ..."

A face mask (mandated apparel in so many places) with Dracula-like fang teeth was a huge seller. In Florida, a lawyer sued the Tampa region of Hillsborough County for imposing a night-time curfew saying: "It's not like the virus is Count Dracula. The virus isn't just going to come out at night; the virus is 24/7."

COUNT: is a title used only in mainland Europe. In Britain the equivalent is an Earl, but, because the Brits failed to come up with a title for the wife of an Earl, they resorted to the European Countess. The word Count comes from the Latin "comitem", which translates to "companion".

COPPOLA: in 1992, the famed film director Francis Ford Coppola made *Bram Stoker's Dracula*. Coppola adopted an effective publicity ploy by claiming that, unlike many filmmakers before him, he'd actually read the book ... hence the title of the movie, which was greeted with mixed reviews. Also, in a fascinating look behind the camera – in a short documentary *The Blood is the Life: The Making of 'Bram Stoker's Dracula'* – Coppola reveals that he was taken with the *Dracula* story from an early age. And Gary Oldman, who play Dracula, reveals: "I tried to play him like a fallen angel."

FYFI: to watch the documentary in UK, https://www.youtube.com/watch?v=b9EgIzTWF2M; in US, http://www.youtube.com/watch?v=PvSqFcGr5LU

CRAB: part of the folklore surrounding Bram Stoker is that he came up with the idea of *Dracula* – well, at least a mythical character who terrified people – after a restless sleep punctuated with a nightmare featuring a "horror monster". The night before, while on holiday in Whitby, he'd eaten crab. The book was seven years in the making and later, so it's claimed, he explained: "Dracula was born of a nightmare following a supper of dressed crab." In those long ago days, a Whitby-caught crab was a treat. It still is.

CRITICS: when *Dracula* was published in 1897, it garnered nothing but barbs from the critics. *The Athenaeum* – the literary magazine that reigned from 1828 to 1921 – dismissed it thus: "Dracula is highly sensational ... it reads like a mere series of grotesquely incredible events ..." *The Spectator* – still going after 192 years – was not impressed by how up-to-date it was. "The phonograph, diaries, typewriters, and so on, hardly fit in with the mediaeval methods which ultimately secure the victory for Count Dracula's foes."

As for the *Daily Mail,* it slammed the book with the warning: "Persons of small courage and weak nerves should confine their reading of these gruesome pages strictly to the hours between dawn and sunset. The recollection of his weird and ghostly tale will doubtless haunt us for some time to come ... a horrible story ..."

Even Stoker's mentor and friend, the great thespian Sir Henry Irving (see IRVING), had nothing good to say about it. In a one-word scathing verdict he pronounced it "dreadful".

CRITICS-2: however, there were a couple of voices laden with enthusiastic praise. Stoker's mother had no doubt he'd penned a winner. She wrote to him saying: "No book has come near yours in originality or terror. In its terrible excitement it should make a widespread reputation and much money for you."

And more high praise came from one of the most powerful literary personalities of the day. Conan Doyle, creator of Sherlock Holmes – who burst on the reading world a decade before *Dracula* – wrote the following, handwritten, letter:

> *My dear Bram Stoker, I am sure that you will not think it an impertinence if I write to tell you how very much I have enjoyed reading Dracula. I think it is the very best story of diablerie which I have read for many years. It is really wonderful how with so much exciting interest*

over so long a book there is never an anticlimax. It holds you from the very start and grows more and more engrossing until it is quite painfully vivid. The old Professor is most excellent and so are the two girls. I congratulate you with all my heart for having written so fine a book.

With all kindest remembrances to Mrs Bram Stoker & yourself.

Yours very truly,

A Conan Doyle.

FYFI: to see a copy of the original letter from Doyle, https://www.arthur-conan-doyle.com/index.php?title=Letter_to_Bram_Stoker_(20_august_1897)

CROSSWORDS: Dracula clues keep cropping up. They are not the hardest in the world to work out. They are, with the answers:

Dracula's delight? Delicious blood.
Dracula's mother-in-law? Old bat.
Dracula's breaking point? Fang.
Dracula's least favourite time of the year? Daylight savings.
Daybreak or Dracula's bedtime? Dawn.
Dracula repellant? Cross.
Name on cover of Dracula? Bram.
Dracula's bed? Casket.
Garment for Dracula? Cloak.
Dracula's laundry problem? Bloodstains.

CRUDEN BAY: Bram Stoker spent many holidays – from 1893 to 1910 – in this remote coastal village 26 miles north of Aberdeen. With its beautifully desolate beaches and cliff-ringed coves – and Slains Castle (see entry by that name) dominating the landscape – it was the perfect spot to inspire Stoker to conjure up Dracula. Early chapters of the book were penned there – along with some of his later books. At first he stayed in The Kilmarnock Arms (see entry by that name) then later rented Crooked Lum Cottage in the nearby hamlet of Whinnyfold. From both places he looked onto the castle, which – with its gaunt turrets and towering walls – inspired him to describe Dracula's lair. This image was then reinforced by a book about Transylvania.

FYFI: *When Brave Men Shudder: The Scottish Origins of Dracula* by Mike Shepherd provides a powerful insight into the many times Stoker visited Cruden Bay – and was inspired by it. To buy, https://www.goodreads.com/book/show/42203307

CRUDEN BAY-2: a housing estate, built on the edge of the village in 2020, pays homage to the novel. The names of half a dozen roads reference *Dracula*. Cruden Community Council was invited by the developers to come up with names they thought appropriate to the area, They came up with: Westenra Gardens, Renfield Street, Renfield Park, Harker Place, Stoker Road and Stoker Close. So how come Dracula Drive didn't make the cut? That suggestion – barely without discussion – was spiked.

FYFI: https://www.pressandjournal.co.uk/fp/news/aberdeenshire/2201447/councillors-back-dracula-themed-street-names-to-boost-local-tourism

CRUZ: remember Senator Ted Cruz who wanted to be President of the USA? He battled and failed to beat Donald Trump for the 2016 Republican nomination. In a bid to knock him off his campaign perch, the former Democrat Senator for Minnesota, Al Franken, jibed: "Republicans are in kind of a bind since their best hope for stopping Donald Trump is a guy who's the love child of Joe McCarthy and Dracula."

CUMBERBATCH: he's played just about everything going, so why not Dracula? Benedict Cumberbatch – he of TV's Sherlock fame – is tipped to take the star role in the upcoming movie *Renfield* (see RENFIELD).

CUSHING: the renowned British actor Peter Cushing (1913–1994) will be forever associated with Dracula, though he never played the role. He appeared as vampire hunter Dr Van Helsing in five Hammer *Dracula* films. They were: *Dracula*, in 1958 (known in America as *Horror of Dracula*); *Brides of Dracula*, 1960; *Dracula AD 1972*, 1972; *The Satanic Rites of Dracula*, 1973; *The Legend of the Seven Golden Vampires* (known in America as *The Seven Brothers Meet Dracula*), 1974. Interestingly *Brides of Dracula* – despite being billed as "the most evil blood-lusting Dracula of all" – did not feature a Dracula role. In all the *Dracula* movies (bar *Brides of Dracula*) Cushing starred in, Dracula himself was played by Christopher Lee (see LEE). The two iconic British thespians became best friends.

D

DACRE: is the first name of Bram Stoker's great-grand-nephew, who has introduced a new generation to his famed ancestor's creation – revitalising *Dracula* and the astonishing history surrounding the book, and author, along the way. Born in Montreal in 1958, and now living in Aiken, South Carolina, USA, he tours the world giving lectures on his inherited Dracula life.

Dacre Calder Stoker burst onto the Dracula scene in spectacular fashion. In 2009 he co-wrote, along with screenwriter and Dracula expert Ian Holt, *Dracula: The Un-Dead*. A best-selling novel, it picked up on the *Dracula* story, 25 years after it ended.

The preface of the book reads: "The true Stoker sequel. Family secrets, unfinished business and an evil unlike any the world has known. Twenty-five years have passed since the band of heroes destroyed Dracula, in his castle in Transylvania. Since then Jonathan and Mina Harker have raised their son Quincey into a fine, if at times naive, young man, even while their once happy marriage disintegrated. Dr Seward, the brilliant physician, is plagued by drug abuse and mania. Arthur Holmwood, Lucy's brave and dashing fiancé, is now full of anger and regret. And Van Helsing, leader of the brave band, is a sickly old man.

Bram Stoker's Dracula introduced us to these characters and in this fully realised sequel, we see how these lives will forever be entwined with each other and the vampire they so courageously fought to destroy." Dacre dedicated the book to Bram Stoker with the inscription: "For Bram: thank you for your inspiration and your guidance".

Publishers' Weekly greeted it with high praise, saying: "Energetically paced and packed with outrageously entertaining action, this supernatural thriller is a well-needed shot of fresh blood for the Dracula mythos." Then, in 2012, Dacre co-wrote, with leading academic *Dracula* expert Professor Elizabeth Miller (see MILLER), *The Lost Journal of Bram Stoker*. It's based on the sensational discovery of Stoker's journal, found in the attic of his great-grandson Noel Stoker (see JOURNAL–1). Dated 1871 to 1881, the journal contained Bram's private thoughts, how his writing style was developing and, as the preface to the book says: "A veritable treasure trove of oddities, musing and anecdotes".

In October 2018 came *Dracul* – the prequel to *Dracula* – which Dacre co-wrote with novelist J D Barker. The preface to the story goes: "It is 1868, and a twenty-one-year-old Bram Stoker waits in a desolate tower to face an indescribable evil. Armed only with crucifixes, holy water, and a rifle, he prays to survive a single night, the longest of his life. Desperate to record what he has witnessed, Bram scribbles down the events that led him here. A sickly child, Bram spent his early days bedridden in his parents' Dublin home, tended to by his caretaker, a young woman named Ellen Crone. When a string of strange deaths occurs in a nearby town, Bram and his sister Matilda detect a pattern of bizarre behaviour by Ellen – a mystery that deepens chillingly until Ellen vanishes suddenly from their lives. Years later, Matilda returns from studying in Paris to tell Bram the news that she has seen Ellen – and that the nightmare they've thought long ended is only beginning."

Publishers' Weekly welcomed it with: "Bram Stoker fans and scholars will find this a satisfying exploration of his legacy." And The Financial Times raved: "It's a thrilling exploration of the novel's creator. It is also, as with the best literary horror, genuinely creepy. In its crafty structure and unhurried layering of dread, this addition to the canon is a brilliantly entertaining read." In its review the Pittsburgh Post-Gazette – the hometown paper of JD Barker – wrote: "To their immense credit, the authors have created a standalone book. 'Dracul' can be read without any knowledge of 'Dracula', or knowledge of any other vampire tale. However, the more you know, the more apparent are the layers and nuances added by these authors. They have skillfully interwoven characters, themes and settings from the original novel into their book. And because 'Dracul' is a prequel, they have taken pains to end this novel in such a way as to segue naturally and logically into the next book, the original 'Dracula'."

And now (at publication time) Stoker is writing a play based on *Dracula* (see PLAY–5).

FYFI: for all three books, https://www.penguinrandomhouse.com/books/305346/dracula-the-un-dead-by-dacre-stoker; http://dacrestoker.com/books/the-lost-journal-of-bram-stoker-the-dublin-years and http://draculabegins.com

DACULA: no, not a typo! And not an exotic cocktail. Dacula is a town in Georgia, USA. In 1850 it was named Chinquapin Grove. That was changed, in 1891, to Hoke – after a railway executive. But it was quickly changed yet again, to Dacula. But why? How such a name? Easy, in the end, to explain: it's an amalgam of the two cities it's close to: Atlanta, 32 miles away and Decatur, 27 miles away. Trey King, the Mayor (as of 2020) of the around 7,000 population town, confirms what everyone discovering there is a town by that name thinks. "The town's name is sometimes mistakenly pronounced 'Dracula' by people passing through or new to the area. But if someone is having difficulty spelling Dacula, we just tell them it's spelled like Dracula but with no R." And about the town with the intriguing name, he says: "We pride ourselves on maintaining a small-town feel."

DASH: the "Dracula Dash" is a well established event, held in South Jordan, Utah, USA, around Halloween. The run – 5k for adults and half-a-mile for kids – with everyone in spooky, scary costumes, benefits children in Romania, who are orphaned, disadvantaged or abandoned. The run has been held for 11 years and is organised by Bridge of Love, a non-profit run by Laurie and Scott Lundberg of South Jordan who, on a visit to Romania in 2001, were horrified by the plight of so many needy babies and youngsters. The tagline promoting the run goes: "Dracula is out to change his reputation of doom and gloom by helping to raise donations."

FYFI: https://www.raceentry.com/dracula-dash/race-information

DATES: in the book there is, interestingly, no mention of the year the saga unfolds. Each chapter is marked at the beginning with the date of the month. It starts 3rd May and ends 6th November. It's believed Stoker intentionally omitted the year so as to imbue his work with a sense of timelessness, allowing readers to imagine the events unfolding in their own present day. Another reason is because Stoker wanted to dissuade anyone from trying to check the veracity of the story; he wanted it to feel true, and for many – then and now – he succeeded.

DAUGHTER: a classic Dracula genre movie is *Dracula's Daughter*. Released in 1936 it was made by Universal as a sequel to its 1931 *Dracula* with Bela Lugosi. It's always been said that *Dracula's Daughter* was based on Bram Stoker's short story Dracula's Guest, published in 1914, though the film bears little resemblance to it. The film tells the tale of Countess Mary Zaleska who, thanks to her father, Dracula, is also a vampire. On his0020"death", she steals his body in the hope of releasing herself from being a vampire by burning it in a ritualistic ceremony. It fails. And Countess Mary gives into her lust for blood – from women. The film's lesbian overtones are so strong and obvious – its advertising tagline was "Save the women of London from Dracula's Daughter" – many were astounded by how it got past the censors (alive and well in those days) without a double XX certificate.

FYFI: for the trailer, https://www.youtube.com/watch?v=E_2YyzNAT98 ; to rent or buy the movie, https://search.aol.com/aol/search?q=dracula%27s%20daughter&s_it=loki-keyword

DEANE: Hamilton Deane (1880–1958), the Irish actor, playwright and director, was the theatrical talent who brought *Dracula* to the stage (see PLAY–2). His family, and those of Bram Stoker and his wife Florence, were well acquainted, as all three families lived in Clontarf, the well-heeled suburb of Dublin.

DEDICATION: Bram Stoker dedicated *Dracula* to "My Good Friend Hommy-Beg". His "good friend" was the famed Liverpudlian-cum-Isle of Man novelist Sir Thomas Henry Hall Caine, the author of a slew of melodramatic bestsellers. Hommy-Beg is Manx for "Little Tommy". The two met in 1878, when Hall Caine, then 26, went to London to see Sir Henry Irving in his first production at the Lyceum, after the great thespian of his day had reopened the legendary West End theatre under his own management. After the performance, Hall Caine met 31-year-old Bram Stoker, then personal assistant to Irving. The casual meeting turned into a long and close friendship.

DEER: not everything that carries the Dracula name is scary. There is a deer nicknamed the "Dracula Deer". See ZOOS.

DELETED: at the last moment before the novel was published, not only was the name changed (see UNDEAD) but the preface was deleted. Bram Stoker had written: "I want you to believe ... to believe in things that you cannot ... this mysterious tragedy which is here described in my book Dracula is completely true in all its external respects, though naturally I have reached a different conclusion on certain points than those involved in the story." It was removed because of the fear of terrifying the reader! But four years later it was reinstated in the Icelandic edition – the first translation of the novel (see TRANSLATION).

DELIGHT: mix plums, carrots, ginger, sultanas, red wine vinegar, garlic, salt and paprika and what do you get? "Dracula's Delight"! This plum chutney lives up to its name – it is delightful. And it's made by Pivnita Bunicii, a sustainable food business – started by Scot Jim Turnbull – in the Transylvanian village of Saschiz, Romania. The business, which produces a wide range of chutney, relishes, honey and wild-flower cordials, has made such a social, environmental – and tasty – impact that The Prince of Wales (see PRINCE) has visited. As a result he now sells its honey at his Highgrove shop. Can't image why he didn't take a fancy to "Dracula's Delight". Perhaps now, through popular demand, he will!

FYFI: to find out more about the business and to buy its products, www.pivnitabunicii.ro; to see a short documentary about how the company has revived the old traditions of food production in Transylvania and why it named its plum chutney after Dracula, https://www.youtube.com/watch?v=Grv6V3vS2ys&feature=youtu.be

DEMETER: the name of the Russian cargo ship, a major "character" in the novel, which goes aground in Whitby harbour at low tide. The skipper is found dead – tied to the mast, clutching a crucifix. The only survivor is the ship's dog. It bounds ashore and turns into Dracula. For more see DMITRY.

DEMETER-2: Hollywood's take on the *Demeter* has been 18 years in the making, and counting. After many fits and starts *The Last Voyage of the Demeter* is now in the hands of Steven Spielberg's studio, Amblin.

DESK: the desk that Bram Stoker sat at to write *Dracula* is – in its restored state – exquisite. A piece of art to behold. And its background story conjures up an intriguing story of love, coupled with disregard. To start at the beginning. Around 1903 Stoker gave the desk to his good friend J S R Phillips, the editor of the Yorkshire Post. Some years later, Phillips handed it over to his son, E R Phillips, who was assistant editor of the paper. But his wife had no fondness for the desk and relegated it, out of their house in Scotton, near Knaresborough, into the garden. And there it languished – for years. Finally their author/poet son Guy rescued the deskand took it to his London home, where he repaired it and restored it into a "working" desk.

Guy eventually moved back north and bought a house in Hartlepool. When, in 1975, he sold the house, he abandoned the desk – leaving it to the new owner, Gillian Broderick, to deal with. She had a vague inkling of the desk's heritage and got Guy to confirm its history in a letter. But despite that, and not caring too much for the way Stoker had scrawled "Dracula" on the desk, she allowed her young son Andrew to use it – and he virtually destroy it. In 1995, Mrs Broderick moved and, rather than just dumping the beat-up old desk, gave it to her neighbour, author Billy Yull. Finally, in early 2012, Billy sold the desk to Belgravia art dealer Andrew Lamberty when he appeared on the British TV show Four Rooms – where owners of the rare and unusual offered their possessions for sale.

Lamberty then quickly sold it on to master furniture restorer Mark Brazier-Jones, who worked his magic to totally transform the desk into a piece of art. In November 2012, he sent the desk off to California to be auctioned. It failed to get its $60,000 price and is now back at Brazier-Jones' home-cum-studio in Buckland, Hertfordshire. Brazier-Jones – who has his work exhibited in some of the world's leading museums, including the Victoria & Albert Museum, London; Musee des Arts Decoratifs, Paris; the Museum of Fine Arts, Boston; and in the Brooklyn Museum and Museum of Art and Design, New York. Brazier-Jones has now decided not to sell the desk where "the best known literary character on the planet" was created.

FYFI: www.brazier-jones.com/#product/bram-stokers-dracula-desk

DIABOLIQUE: for fans of the horror genre – film, books and art – the internet magazine for you is *Diabolique*. And it's ace when it comes to pinpointing specific *Dracula* spin-offs. It's loaded with deeply researched, incisive articles about a ton of Dracula things you know about and a ton you don't. Every now and then a print edition is produced. One was promised for late 2020.

FYFI: https://diaboliquemagazine.com

DIP: one of the most popular recipe websites – cooks.com – has got into the Dracula act. For Halloween they suggest "Dracula's Garlic Dip". The recipe couldn't be simpler: 8 oz cream cheese; 1/8 cup mayonnaise; 1 tbsp Dijon mustard; 1 tbsp dill weed; 1/8 tsp each of celery seed, paprika and parsley, and 1 minced clove of fresh garlic. Combine all ingredients and refrigerate for at least an hour before serving. The recipe doesn't call for this but a sprinkling of "caviar", ie, lumpfish, both red and black, adds that extra-special, tasty Drac touch. The online recipe adds: "… there is enough garlic in this potion to ward off any vampires. Happy Halloween!"

DIRECTOR: so many plays – so, so many directors. There's never a day passes that somewhere in the world a production of *Dracula* is not being staged. From full-scale professional companies to amateur dramatic groups, community theatres along with high school presentations, Dracula is always on offer. Somewhere! In November 2014, it was the turn of St Mark's Players, of Capitol Hill, Washington, DC, to take up the challenge of *Dracula*. They chose Steven Dietz's adaptation of the novel. It was directed by Andrew Curtin, who teaches history at Bishop Ireton High School, Alexandria, Virginia.

His "Director's Notes" in the programme supplied a most readable summary of the desperately complex novel and are well worth repeating. Recalling his first introduction to *Dracula*, when he was in high school, he wrote: "… I was shocked at the depth of the story, the thrill of the writing and the wild sensation of dark fates spinning inexorably out of control. Ultimately, though, Dracula is about the people. The eponymous villain, so desperately seeking the energy of life and community, the one thing that his immortal existence cannot give him. Against his wiles stands a group of haggard people with few weapons but their faith in the goodness of the world and their love for each other. It is a story about the power of human love, sacrifice and devotion, one that in a very visceral way asks if those few treasures are enough to defeat an ancient and terrible creature so much stronger than his foes. It's nothing less than a battle between all that is best in us as humans and that which is worst. It's basically existential pro-wrestling!"

Talking about the production he wrote: "Working on this show has felt, appropriately, a bit like reading Stoker's book at times – the rush of an ever-accelerating rehearsal schedule, surprises and the unexpected around every turn ... and most importantly, the sure knowledge that we took every step alongside a wonderful group of people with whom I've been honored to try our wits against Dracula's. I couldn't have hoped for a more perfect group, a band of once-strangers turned dear friends that I have looked forward to seeing every night at rehearsal. Like our heroes tonight, we've struggled together, laughed together and brought out, collectively, the very best in each other; more than enough to 'stand against the darkness'."

DMITRY: the name of the Russian cargo ship – the real one – upon which the *Demeter* (see DEMETER) was based and which gave Bram Stoker the idea of how to get Dracula into England. Stoker learnt about the fate of the *Dmitry* when on holiday in Whitby in 1890. He was flipping through the files of the *Whitby Gazette* in the town library when a photograph of the beached ship caught his eye. The *Dmitry* was swept into the harbour during a tremendous storm on October 24th, 1885, ending up grounded on the town beach. The photograph of the beached ship – taken by the pioneer photographer Frank Meadow Sutcliffe (see SUTCLIFFE) – was to provide a crucial part of the *Dracula* story.

DMITRY-2: to see the shipwrecked *Dmitry* through the eye of a painter, visit the gallery of Whitby artist John Freeman. If you're lucky he will still have a copy left from the limited edition of 500. His take on the accident that inspired Bram Stoker to bring Dracula into England, via Whitby, aboard an ocean and gale-smashed vessel, is emotive – and conjures up all the mystery and dark charm of Victorian Whitby on a stormy autumn night. With the stark outline of the Abbey, high on the cliff, under a sky racing with dark clouds and a full moon, with the red-roofed cottages clustered below, he has the caught the desolation of the beached ship. Also in the picture, under the broken bow of the *Dmitry* is a black dog – which in the novel turns into Dracula!

FYFI: www.johnfreemanstudio.co.uk/artworks_nocturne_5.html

DINOSAUR: Dracula is not a dinosaur! Yet the two nouns have been coupled together to create the name of the blog *Dinosaur Dracula* – a blog that has little, if anything, to do with either of its names. But the reason it's included here is because it's a perfect example of how the name Dracula is used in so many ways without the slightest link to the book, character or vampires in general. The blog explains itself thus: "Dinosaur Dracula is a series of tributes to things that thrill and excite me, or at least, things that used to thrill and excite me. I very much enjoyed being a kid; in fact, I enjoyed it so much that I never stopped being one. As such, you're not likely to find anything on Dinosaur Dracula that a ten-year-old couldn't comprehend. I like toys, goofy food, horror movies, and roadside attractions with guest appearances by bootleg Power Rangers. Dinosaur Dracula is, if nothing else, my perpetual excuse to enjoy things I'm no longer supposed to enjoy." The creator/editor introduces himself, online, as: "I'm Matt. I'm thirty-something, I live in NY, I work in TV and like Ginga Rale (an experimental rock & new-wave band from Salzburg, Austria). Dinosaur Dracula is just a site meant for fun. I hope you have fun when you visit it."

FYFI: www.dinosaurdracula.com

DOG: the film *Dracula's Dog* was released in 1977. It starred the late American character and voice-over actor Michael Pataki (whose parents, coincidently, were Romanian) and household Hollywood name, the late José Ferrer. In the UK, the film was called *Zoltan – Hound of Dracula*. The storyline – a vampire dog belonging to Dracula is sent to the US to track down unsuspecting Dracula relatives – was based on the book *Hounds of Dracula* by American sci-fi writer Ken Johnson. The book is generally considered a good read, while the film was pretty much rubbished – though it's now considered a cult movie.

FYFI: for the movie, https://www.dvdtalk.com/reviews/74049/zoltan-hound-of-dracula-aka-draculas-dog; for the book, www.goodreads.com/book/show/938622

DOG-2: when Dracula's boat was shipwrecked in Whitby harbor, he bounded ashore as the ship's dog. Bram Stoker got that idea from a local legend that exists to this day. The old-timers of Whitby still warn you to be wary of the "Barghest", the mythical black hound, with big teeth and claws, that is said to roam the narrow passageways and hidden alleys of the historic fishing town. Such creatures – the name comes from the German "bär-geist" that translates as "bear-ghost" – are claimed to have been spotted, over the centuries, in many parts of Yorkshire, but never more so than in Whitby. And the legend, perpetuated in *Dracula*, was sealed in 2011 when the Bradford heavy metal band *My Dying Bride* recorded *The Barghest O' Whitby*, a 27-minute EP (extended play) disc.

FYFI: hear it, https://www.youtube.com/watch?v=dJQYCk6NRg0

DOG-3: in recent years gin has gone viral. There's barely a town that hasn't jumped on the gin-wagon to cash-in on this inexplicable popularity. But at least Whitby Distillery has come up with a unique take on what, since the mid-1700s – because then it was so cheap and strong – has been dubbed "mother's ruin". To celebrate Whitby's connection with *Dracula* they produce "Barghest Gin" – in recognition of the above mentioned legendary dog. But it's not just the name that attracts attention. It's the colour of the gin. It's black! And when diluted becomes blood-red. The gin is "laid to rest" in oak barrels from Transylvania (at least that's what the distillery says). Then, according to the distillery: "The oak-aged gin is then gorged in 100% British blackberries and ginger to create a spirit as impressive in appearance as it is on the palate. Deep red, almost black to the eye but, once diluted, takes on a blood-red hue which would surely tempt even Dracula himself." And for you, the Dracula-cum-gin fans, if you want to knock back a bottle of Barghest it will knock you back a cool £57.

FYFI: https://www.whitbydistillery.com/collections/limited-editions

DOG-4: so easy to dress your dog up as Dracula – if you must – for Halloween, or any other time. Just search "Dracula dog costume" on Amazon and you'll find different sized outfits, priced from £13 to £43. Licensed by Universal's Classic Movie Monsters (makers of some of the best Dracula movies), they come complete with cape, bow tie and medallion.

DONOR: when it comes to persuading people to give blood, Dracula is being invoked all ways up. The American Red Cross leads the way with blood-drives around the country – usually around Halloween – linked to Dracula. Many communities dub the drive "Dracula Day"; in Sacramento, California the slogan is "Drip for Dracula". Typical of the come-ons is: "Join Dracula in a 'spooktacular' blood drive. The Count is hungry and needs your blood! It is easy and rewarding to donate life-giving blood." The Australian Red Cross also makes a big deal out of recruiting The Count to boost the number of donors. And, as in the US, more often than not he's on hand to encourage donors, or the drive is tied in with a local ballet or theatre production of Dracula.

Eire also uses Dracula in a bid to raise the percentage of residents who donate. In October 2018, Dracula pitched-up on behalf of the Irish Blood Transfusion Service. The Irish edition of The Mirror got an interview with Dracula. This is what he had to say: "I haven't left the castle since dabbling in real estate back in 1897, when I got on the wrong side of that Van Helsing guy. Bram Stoker wrote a book about it, but he made a few serious mis-stakes. Anyway, I was planning a trip to Ireland when I heard the Irish Blood Transfusion Service were recruiting and thought I'd be bats to pass it up. After all, who knows more about blood than me?"

Romania has also got in on the act. With only two per cent of residents giving blood, the home of Dracula is now also putting him to life-saving use in the hope of persuading Romanians that "bloodsucking" is not all bad. As for the UK? No sign – at the moment – of Dracula hovering around any National Health Service blood donor centres to work his blood-red magic – although donors have dropped by 40% over the past decade, to a mere four per cent of the population.

DONOR-2: note to all those countries and cities that don't "cash in" on Dracula to boost donor numbers: pick "World Blood Donor Day" to do it. It's June 14th. The bid to get people to donate is a World Health Organisation campaign. It chose the date because it is the birthday of the late Karl Landsteiner, the Austrian scientist who won the Nobel Prize for his discovery of the A, B and O blood group system.

DOODLE: on November 8th, 2012, to mark what would have been Bram Stoker's 165th birthday, Google honoured him and his great creation with one of its famed doodles.

FYFI: www.google.com/doodles/bram-stokers-165th-birthday

DOWD: one of America's best-known newspaper columnists is Maureen Dowd. In May 2020 – at the height of the corona-virus pandemic – she penned a scorching piece, demonizing President Trump and his incestuous White House inner sanctum, by invoking Dracula.

In one piercing paragraph she used a quote from Chapter 6 that goes: "He will not admit anything, and down-faces everybody. If he can't out-argue them he bullies them, and then takes their silence for agreement with his views."

Then, having a go at Trump's son-in-law, Jared Kushner, she wrote: "... the pallid nonentity. Kushner is like Renfield, the 'zoophagous maniac' in Bram Stoker's 'Dracula' who eats flies and does the vampire king's bidding ..."

And finally she recounted a conversation she'd had with David Axelrod, former President Barak Obama's campaign manager. "He told me, 'Trump is like a vampire! You've got to drive a stake right through his heart. He's going to keep coming. There's nothing he won't do. Even in this environment, you can't count on him losing'."

DRACULA: OK, nothing in this entry about the book! All about music and how it takes some nerve to form a band and call it "Dracula". But if nothing else, it's is an attraction getter.

It's certainly worked well for an American folk duo and an Aussie heavy-metal trio. Miami-based Dorys Bello and Eli Oviedo have performed together since they were teenagers, over a decade ago. They sing in five languages. And their melodic, soulful music is in total contrast to the name they play under. So why chose the name of the world's most famed horror character? The reason is quite simple. When they were playing around with names Dorys was reading *Dracula*. And that was it.

Meanwhile a heavy-metal trio from Tasmania, also called "Dracula", is wowing fans of the retro beat. When asked why the name, their reply was it was because of their love for the Hammer horror movies of the 60s–70s. "Back when monsters were threatening and to be feared," they said.

FYFI: to read a 2019 interview with the duo, https://www.wlrn.org/post/live-305-meet-indie-folk-duo-dracula#stream/0; to listen and see them, https://www.youtube.com/watch?v=VF36368pNBQ; to listen to a sample track of the Down Under trio, https://hcrdracula.bandcamp.com/album/open-graves-at-midnight

DRACULIN: is a glycoprotein found in the saliva of vampire bats – hence the name. It's being developed as a drug to treat strokes and high blood pressure. See DRUG.

DREAM: in another A–Z – this one *The Dream Dictionary from A to Z* by Theresa Cheung – "V" is for Vampire. The entry reads: "Dreaming of these parasitic creatures can signify that a part of your existence is having the life sucked out of it, that you need to take a closer look at the more tiresome aspects of your life or that you need to employ some self-preservation. It's also possible that you are the one behaving in the parasitic manner and may subconsciously be disturbed by it."

FYFI: www.goodreads.com/book/show/6137549

DRINK: to get a great Dracula/Halloween concoction, pour an inch or two of white fizzy lemonade, like Sprite, into a glass; top up with red Gatorade (the number one US sports' drink, now available all over the world). The latter, because it has less sugar and is therefore lighter than Sprite, will settle on top – providing impressive red and white layers. Plonk some fancy dress plastic Dracula fangs on the rim and sip through a black-and-white-striped straw. BTW: best savoured with a shot of vodka!

DRUG: a drug extracted from the saliva of vampire bats is being developed to help stroke victims and sufferers of high blood pressure. It's been named Draculin. The saliva contains a unique form of anticoagulant – ie, blood thinners, vital in the treatment of both conditions. Medical researchers zoned in on bats because once the prey has been bitten by a vampire bat the prey's blood flows freely for a long time – allowing the bat to gorge on its life sustaining "food".

And the other great excitement surrounding Draculin is the way clinical trials are showing that it's an effective treatment for stroke victims many hours after the stroke has happened. Currently the only clot-busting drug suitable for treating a stroke has to be administered within three hours of the stroke. This is rarely enough time for victims to realise they need help and get to a hospital. Dr Bryan Fry of the School of Biological Studies at the University of Queensland, Australia, is prominent in the cutting-edge research. He announced the breakthrough in June 2013, in a paper nicely titled, Dracula's Children.

FYFI: https://www.uq.edu.au/news/article/2013/06/dracula%E2%80%99s-children-may-lead-novel-drug-design and https://asknature.org/strategy/saliva-breaks-down-blood-clots/#.XkxFzO5_O70

DUMMY: even baby can get in on the "bloody" act. A big seller, particularly at Halloween, is the Little Vampire Dummy. Advertised as being perfect for the kid who likes to stay up late and "doesn't like milk", it sells for around a tenner. The packaging though does not say "dummy" it says "pacifier" – the name for a dummy in America, where it's also hugely popular. For those who care about such things (like parents!), it's important to note this is not a joke item. It complies with all regulations for dummies/pacifiers and comes with a "silicone orthodontic nipple".

FYFI: get it from Amazon on both sides of the pond.

DUNKIRK: one of the thousands of small boats that took part in the evacuation of British and allied soldiers from Dunkirk in 1940 was the *Count Dracula*. The story of the 50-foot wooden vessel is compelling. In a capsule: it's the only surviving boat that served in both World War I and World War II – on opposing sides! Built in 1913 for the German Navy as an admiral's barge, it was at the Battle of Jutland in 1916 and was salvaged by the British Navy after being scuppered, along with its mother ship, SMS Hindenburg, at Scapa Flow in 1919.

After World War I, the *Count Dracula* was sold into private hands and then, in 1940, "served" in Operation Dynamo – the code name for the evacuation of Dunkirk – where, in multiple trips across the English Channel, it rescued 712-plus trapped soldiers.

After decades of neglect, the *Count Dracula* is back in safe and caring hands – undergoing restoration. In 2014, Kevin Kilkenny bought it. He was motivated to save it by a passion for military history and what he sees as a need for the story of the boat, while just a footnote in both World Wars, to be told. And, as he says: "... by what better means than by preservation." The restoration work is being carried out at Wilson's Boatyard in Hayling Island, Hampshire. Kilkenny's plan is to turn it into a floating museum.

Of course, there's one outstanding question unanswered. How did this little boat with such a big history come by its name? While the original German name is unknown (though it would be nice to think it was *Das Graf*), it was evidently christened *Count Dracula* by a post-World War I owner because of the instructions, in Gothic script, inscribed on the controls. And how appropriate, how serendipitous – in light of the fact that, just like Dracula, it refuses to die!

FYFI: http://www.admiralbarge.moonfruit.com/home/4586011604;

https://www.nationalhistoricships.org.uk/register/2834/count-dracula; for countless videos, on the restoration, search "count dracula admiral's barge Dunkirk little ship" on YouTube.

DYEING: there are times – like Halloween or when throwing a Dracula party – you'd love to dish up black food. Well, apart from burning something to a crisp, it's not a cuisine colour easily found. But "activated charcoal" will come to the rescue for your flamboyant plan. It sounds a disgusting idea, pouring ground-up charcoal into your cake, your mash. But it's 100 per cent tasteless – and harmless. In fact, in some cases it's beneficial to wellbeing and health. Its biggest use is medicinal – given to patients who have ingested poison, overdosed on drugs or are in pain through diarrhoea, excess gas or indigestion.

FYFI: buy from, https://www.specialingredients.co.uk/ingredients/activated-charcoal-powder

E

EBAY: in July, 2020, there were a mind-boggling number of items listed for sale – on the global selling site – with "Dracula" in the name. In the US there were 65,869. The UK site had fewer, with 56,287. On both sides of the Atlantic the items run the true gamut from a first edition for £37,158.00 ($42,00.00) to a toilet roll holder for £28 ($36). Whatever your Dracula heart desires – dark or light-hearted – it's there. For example, dart flights, golf club covers, a skateboard, an inflatable drinks' cooler, a table lamp, a tissue box cover, mugs, dinner plates, jewellery, not to mention vintage movie posters and magazines and ... well the choice is endless and if it's out there it's invariably for sale on eBay.

ELECTRICITY: in a fascinating twist on the original story, a 2013 TV take on *Dracula* had The Count posing as an American entrepreneur, out to convince the rich and powerful of Victorian Britain that as that new fangled commodity electricity was emerging, they should invest in the free sort: electricity pulled from the magnetosphere. However, his real purpose for invading Victorian society was to exact his revenge on those who ruined his life, centuries earlier. But his plan is complicated when he falls in love with a woman who appears to be the reincarnation of his dead wife. The 10-episode drama was shown by Sky

Living in the UK and NBC in the US. But despite the lavish settings and fine acting, led by Irish actor Jonathan Rhys Meyers, it was cancelled after the first season.

FYFI: to see the trailer, https://www.youtube.com/watch?v=ztME-XRR76Y

ENCYCLOPEDIA: you want a reference to everything and everyone with a link to vampires and vampirism? Then *The Vampire Book: The Encyclopedia of the Undead* is for you. It's hardly a "handy" reference as it runs to 919 pages (use it as a doorstop if your bookshelf sags under it). Authored by American J Gordon Melton, a minister in the United Methodist Church and prominent religious scholar specialising in new religious movements, the third edition was published in 2010.

The *Publishers' Weekly* review read, in part: "... this comprehensive encyclopedia of vampires and vampire lore is exhaustive, covering vampire esoterica, vampire novelists, historical figures like Vlad the Impaler, and much more ... It allows Melton to incorporate the Twilight phenomenon and acknowledge the cultural importance of Buffy the Vampire Slayer and other developments in the bloody field. Melton's research is meticulous and readers with even a passing interest in vampires will be amazed by the staggering wealth of information presented. However, Melton's volume is redundant in the extreme and some of what he includes (such as entries like the London of Dracula's time) are only tenuously related to vampires. At times, it's difficult to tell if Melton has an extremely dry sense of humor or none at all, since his entries are so obsessively single-minded. Ultimately, readers who really want something to sink their teeth into will find this indispensable, but more casual enthusiasts will likely be overwhelmed ..."

FYFI: https://www.goodreads.com/book/show/607090

EPISTOLARY: the novel *Dracula* is written in an "epistolary" style – told through letters and other documentation. The word comes from "epistolaris", the Latin for letter. According to the *Encyclopedia Britannica*, such a novel is: "told through the medium of letters written by one or more of the characters." And the advantage of a novel in this form is "that it presents an intimate view of the character's thoughts and feelings without interference from the author and that it conveys the shape of events to come with dramatic immediacy. Also, the presentation of events from several points of view lends the story dimension and verisimilitude." Verisimilitude? (I had to look it up) It means: the quality of seeming real. In Dracula's case the story unfolds via a series of letters, diary entries, telegrams and newspaper clippings.

EROTIC: academics and students of literature have spun millions of words as they try to define and wheedle out the hidden sexual undertones of the novel. There are tomes by the dozen, countless theses and learned papers on how Bram Stoker skillfully used the power of euphemism and innuendo to highlight the restrictive mores of the Victorian era and the challenges of sexual repression. And how they impacted the lives of both men and women. One of the best papers and easiest to understand is by Dr Elizabeth Miller, the famed *Dracula* expert (see MILLER). As she so bluntly points out: "... it would be folly to deny any erotic content in a novel about biting and sucking ..."

FYFI: www.erudit.org/fr/revues/ron/2006-n44-ron1433/014002ar

ETSY: the international website for hand-crafted goods and collectibles is a treasure trove for Dracula-linked accessories and rare memorabilia. In July, 2020, it had 13,144 items listed. Among them a letter written by Bram Stoker; Bram Stoker's autograph, in a second edition of his 1881 short story collection *Under the Sunset* for £3,172.59 and a first edition of Dracula for £5,155.46. But for the most part Etsy is jammed with an eclectic Dracula collection of everything from hand-crafted wearables; earrings; bags; pendants; brooches; to gosh, even a bra and panties, made from *Dracula* movie poster fabric.

FYFI: in the UK, https://www.etsy.com/uk/search?q=Dracula; in the US, https://www.etsy.com/search?q=Dracula

EXAM: pupils at a sixth form college in Newmarket, Suffolk, studied *Dracula* for their 2013 A-level English Literature exam. But they were horrified. Not at the content but at the way, with just days before sitting the vital exam, they discovered that they should have been studying *Frankenstein*! Their English Literature teacher had not realised that, after several years on the syllabus, the vampire masterpiece had been removed and replaced by Mary Shelley's 1818 classic. Repeated attempts to get the school to reveal how the pupils had done failed to get a response. Embarrassment at the awful gaffe, I guess.

EXPERIENCE: on Whitby's harbourside is the Dracula Experience. When it opened in 1980 it blasted away the town council's resistance to linking Whitby to Dracula (see BENCH). The Experience takes you through a maze of twists and turns, each one telling part of the *Dracula* story – eliciting screams and shouts along the way. Much of the Experience is animated but at peak times, actors take over to play the various characters. As people walk by the Experience, a monologue attempts to draw them in. The scary, deep-toned voice-over is provided by actor Christopher Fairbank – known for his role as Moxey in the long-running British TV comedy series (1983–2004) *Auf Wiedersehen, Pet*. At the end of the Experience, there's a tiny 15-seat cinema where a five-minute film tells the true and fictitious stories via Vlad the Impaler (on who Bram Stoker based his famous character) and Dracula. But even if you're not interested in testing the scariness of the walk through, there's a ton of Dracula souvenirs – from mugs to bumper stickers – to keep the most hardened fan happy.

FYFI: www.draculaexperience.co.uk

FACELIFT: this one is just for suckers! It's amazing how bloody far people are prepared to go to try and iron out their wrinkles and lift their chins. The "Vampire Facelift" – aka "Dracula Therapy" – sucks the blood out of them one moment, injects it back in the next. It's a short process that costs a fortune. Officially called PRP (platelet-rich plasma), several test tubes of blood are drawn, placed in a centrifuge for about 15 minutes, spinning so the platelets can be separated out, then injected back into the "troublesome" area. Not only faces are treated, but shoulders, necks, hands, arms, legs and buttocks. Costs vary but for a teeny amount expect to pay between £650 to £2,500. In Europe, a leading Vampire Facelifter is Dr Jean-Louis Sebagh, who treats women – and men – who fly into his London and Paris surgeries from all over the world. In America the bloody trend was set by (of course) Kim Kardashian. The way she subjected herself to "Dracula Therapy" is featured on the Facebook site (yes, isn't there one for everything now!) for the blood-letting "beauty" aid.

FYFI: https://www.drsebagh.com/clinic/platelet-rich-plasma; www.facebook.com/vampirefaceliftpage

FACELIFT-2: but you don't have to go and see Dr Sebagh in London or Paris. Many plastic surgeons on both sides of the Atlantic now carry out "Dracula Therapy". In the UK a good bet is The Garrett Clinic which is in London's famed Harley Street.

FYFI: www.thegarrettclinic.com; to find the nearest clinic to you in the US, www.vampirefacelift.com.

FANG: the word "fang" came into the English language from the Old Norse word of the same spelling – which meant grasp, hold, capture. Carnivorous animals, venomous snakes and, of course, vampires, have fangs.

FANG-2: it's not just vampire authors who love writing about fangs and incorporating them into their novels. US money guru Jim Cramer, of *TheStreet.com*, a financial news website and CNBC's *Mad Money*, coined the acronym "FANG" – to refer to best-selling tech stock. The term evolved out of the early outstanding stocks of that type, eg, Facebook, Amazon, Netflix and Google. Now "FANG" charts the most popular and best performing tech stocks in the market.

FANGLAND: is the name of a 2008 novel that retells Bram Stoker's *Dracula*, by John Marks, a former producer at *60 Minutes* (a leading American TV in-depth news programme). The promo reads: "... there's always an audience bloodthirsty for quality, page-turning horror. Now, in a marvelously horrifying turn, John Marks sinks his satirical teeth into twenty-first-century media. In Fangland, Evangeline Harker is an employee of a legendary TV news magazine who is sent on assignment to Transylvania. She delivers more than a story when mysterious emails, coffins, and a creepy guy named Torgu descend on the New York office. This darkly funny tale will appeal to vampire and horror aficionados …"

FYFI: a film adaptation of the book is in the works but there has been no news about its progress since 2106 and it's still listed, on IMDb, as "in development".

FARSON: Daniel Farson, the cultural British icon of broadcasting, writing, celebrity and the underground gay scene of the 60s and 70s, was best known, in popular terms, for the music hall pub he ran on London's Isle of Dogs. In that era there was little if any limelight on Bram Stoker. But Farson changed that. Stoker was his great uncle and Farson's 1975 biography of him – *The Man Who Wrote Dracula* – was one of the first out of the blocks. While not the most revealing of reads, compared to the slew of detailed books about Stoker's life published since, it was peppered with family gossip. It was Farson who drew attention to the fact that Stoker's 1912 death certificate stated that the cause of death was "locomotor ataxy" – a euphemism, in those days, for syphilis.

FYFI: info about the book, https://www.goodreads.com/book/show/1311228

FEMALE: will it work? Dracula getting a sex change? The first real signs of gender-bending came with a female Dracula in the massively popular *Van Helsing* – the TV series shown on the cable channel Syfy. *Van Helsing* is set in the near future, where vampires have risen and taken control. Vanessa Van Helsing – daughter of Abraham

Van Helsing, the Dutch vampire hunter in the novel – is humanity's last hope, as her unique blood composition gives her the ability to turn vampires into humans. With this secret weapon, Vanessa becomes a prime target for the vampires. Finally, in the fourth season of the series – premiered in Autumn 2019 – Dracula comes into the picture as he is hunted down. The pivotal role is played by Canadian Tricia Helfer, who is well known for her leading roles in Syfy's Battlestar Galactica and Fox's Lucifer. Announcing the news, Syfy said: "Tricia will be a fierce and unstoppable Dracula ... as the battle between good and evil reaches new heights."

FYFI: www.syfy.com/vanhelsing

FEMALE-2: also getting in on the act, early, was American Payton Core. As a drama student, in May 2019 she won the "best actor" award at Southeastern Louisiana University for her portrayal of Countess Dracula, in a production adapted by James Winter, the university's associate professor of acting and directing.

Payton – who is now pursuing a stage career in Chicago – said: "Being one of the first to play the role of a female Dracula was by far the most extraordinarily empowering experience any actress could hope to accomplish. Not only was I to play the role of a female Dracula, but also a lesbian Dracula. Vampires are, by nature, overtly sexual creatures and playing the role of Countess Dracula consisted of daily work in order to understand, become, embrace, and share the character. There were many nights when I would step out of rehearsals and feel so overwhelmed by the character I could not help but weep. I studied the Countess so extensively that I started to become her in my dreams. She is more than a dark, powerful, hypnotic, sexual force. She is capable of love, tenderness, empathy, and reasoning.

"To convey that fiery sense of passion to audiences was imperative. It became essential that I explored the far depths of my own inner self to bring forth the essence of Countess Dracula. When many people think of Dracula, they think of a character who uses dark, brooding, intense power to meet his personal demands. The Countess, however, is a creature of composure, persistence, intellect, and cunning."

FEMALE-3: in October 2019, Theatre 3, of Dallas, Texas, staged its own gender-bending version of the novel. Both the lead role and Van Helsing were played by women. Alison Pistorius was Dracula and Gloria Benavides the vampire hunter.

FEMALE-4: the central character in *A Girl Walks Home Alone at Night* – a hit of the 2014 famed Sundance Film Festival (the one that bears Robert Redford's name in Utah) – was almost the first female Dracula. But the young, chador-clad, Iranian woman who roams the streets of a largely abandoned town seeking out victims she can sink her fangs into was not identified as Dracula. But despite that, the movie was hailed as "a new vampire classic worth treasuring" by *The Playlist*.

FYFI: to watch it, www1.go123movies.io/movie/a-girl-walks-home-alone-at-night

FEMALE-5: way back in 2014, American broadcaster/film-maker Chris Denmead planned to be the pioneer of the Dracula sexual revolution. He came up with the controversial movie idea of all the major characters undergoing a gender swop. He launched a campaign to raise the $12,000 seed money he needed to start filming. To show that a female Dracula would be a winner, Chris made a short film, *Dracula's Guest* (nothing to do with the Bram Stoker short story with the same title), with actress Rachel Wiese (not to be confused with Rachel Wieze) as his female Dracula. With brutal honesty, Chris, who runs the *Radio of Horror* show out of Worcester, Massachusetts, admits his plan failed. The money didn't come in. But *Dracula's Guest* was selected to be shown at the 2014 International Vampire Films and Arts Festival (see FESTIVAL-2). Chris says: "The short film was part of a movie we didn't end up making." He added: "I like strong female characters and thought, wouldn't it be cool if Dracula was told as a woman instead of a man as he always is?"

FYFI: https://www.youtube.com/watch?v=67rEH4i6zxI

FESTIVAL: the Bram Stoker Festival is held every year in Dublin – his home town. A four-day event, it starts on the long weekend of Ireland's final Bank Holiday of the year, ie, the last Monday in October. It frequently lands on Halloween but is always a run up to the spookiest time of the year. The festival is invariably billed as: "4 Days of Deadly Adventures".

In 2018, the main feature was the Irish premiere of *NYsferatu: Symphony of a Century* (see NOSFERATU-1). The film was shown at St Anne's Church, Dawson Street, where Bram Stoker married Florence Balcombe in 1878. Another main feature was, a Victorian funfair staged in St Patrick's Park. It was promoted thus: "This ghoulish gathering will present street theatre, a performance tent, free face-painting, Victorian funfair rides, macabre thrills and ghoulish games for everyone to enjoy."

For the 2019 festival, Stokerland was brought back and, again at St Anne's, there was another theatrical premiere. This time it was *Sounds of Wood on Muscle*, a disconcerting, funny, contemporary take on the famed Orson Welles' 1938 radio adaptation of *Dracula* (see RADIO). Instead of using a hammer and a water melon (as Welles did) to produce the scrunching sound of a stake through the heart, high-tech equipment was employed to have the audience squirming in their pews.

At the time of publication, the programme for the 2020 festival had not been announced in detail but it promised: "Whether you're a resident vampire or visiting from further afield, Bram Stoker Festival 2020 has something for everyone in its gothically inspired programme of events. Get ready for four days and nights of deadly adventures as Dublin gets gloriously gothic this October Bank Holiday Weekend. The Bram Stoker Festival playfully celebrates the gothic, the mysterious, the after-dark and the supernatural, and delves into the legacy of one of Ireland's most treasured authors. The packed programme of events devilishly mixes family-friendly adventures with late-night antics for mates, dates and everything in between. From unforgettable spectacles on water, to seances in complete darkness, dress-up screenings in the dead of night to daring theatre in evocative churches, pop-up Victorian fun parks to foodie tours with a devilish twist, there's intimate performances in unusual spaces, live music, instagram horrors, literary and once-off events – Bram Stoker Festival is full of surprises."

FYFI: www.bramstokerfestival.com

FESTIVAL-2: the International Vampire Film and Arts Festival – aka VampFest – was first staged in 2016, in Sighisoara, the ancient Romanian city where the real Dracula, ie, Vlad the Impaler, was born. It's become a highlight of the European Halloween calendar. It states its raison d'être as: "… for two hundred years Vampires have remained the most enduring horror genre. Their appeal straddles literature, film, television, theatre, music, gaming, fashion, lifestyle and the afterlife … the Festival combines industry development with a celebration of the genre along with serious partying."

In July 2019, the festival transferred to the Highgate Village and Camden Town communities of London. The move was made to mark the 200th anniversary of the publication of *The Vampyre* (see VAMPYRE) that set the whole vampire ball rolling. The four-day event featured a slew of vampire-based films, plays, seminars and talks, and lot of parties. It returned to Sighisoara in 2020.

FYFI: www.ivfaf.com

FIGURE: there was great excitement in 2014 when a "Funko ReAction Figure" of Dracula was introduced. For collectors of movie character figures it was good news; for Dracula fans it was huge. The 3¾" likeness of Bela Lugois as Dracula with head, arm and leg movements is now a collectible. Mine sits on top of my desk – to inspire me in the writing of this book!

FYFI: to find one search eBay and Amazon on both sides of the pond.

FIGURE-2: and sitting next to my Funko model (see above) is the cutest ceramic Dracula going. It's only 2" high but it packs a walloping "look at me" punch – with its cheeky grin and blood-stained fangs. And it's only available from one of Whitby's greatest gift shops – Incantation, on Church Street. Owner Pete Simpson has an amazing array of unique and charming products, with a fascinating selection of goth – and vampire – inspired items. But his tiny Dracula – yours for a mere fiver – is a constant bestseller.

FYFI: http://wonderfulwhitby.co.uk/incantation.html

FIGURE-3: and for those with pots of loot to splurge on the Dracula rare and vintage, there is a wide range of figures – honouring Christopher Lee, Bela Lugosi and even Luke Evans – up for grabs from £20 to £500. Most can be found on eBay but for all sources search "Dracula rare figures" and dozens will come up.

FILMS: according to IMDb (Internet Movie Database) there are 356 (and counting) movies and TV shows, that have a Dracula character. There are 200 that have "Dracula" in the title. But only 14 are specifically based on Bram Stoker's novel.

FYFI: to see a full list and breakdown, https://www.imdb.com/search/keyword/?keywords=dracula&ref_=fn_kw_kw_1

FILMS-2: for a complete breakdown of all the "real" Dracula films (as of 2011) read *The Romance of Dracula: A Personal Journey of the Count on Celluloid*. By *Dracula* movie buff Charles E Butler (see BUTLER), it's a massively detailed and entertaining run-down of the 14 that, as he says, are "based exclusively on Stoker's creation". And apart from his thoughts about the films, Butler regales his readers with delightful and incisive facts and insights into the novel, its author and the extraordinary encyclopedia of information that surrounds both.

FILMS-3: the latest movie (as of publication date) is *Dracula Untold*. It was released in October, 2014. It was the first big budget *Dracula* movie since 2000 and starred Welsh actor Luke Evans, famed for his roles in the three The Hobbit films and the 2020 eight-part TV series, *The Alienist: Angel of Darkness*. As *Dracula Untold* was filmed entirely on location in Northern Ireland – with £1.6 million in funding from Northern Ireland Screen – it came as a great shock that it was not premiered in Belfast. Universal Pictures took a lot of flack for ignoring Belfast. It was first shown, at a glittering charity event, in Dublin, on September 30th, 2014. Followed, the next night, by an equally grand affair in London.

But extras, from Northern Ireland who worked on the movie were having none of it. They reacted to the slap-in-the-face by staging their own premiere. So on October 3rd – the general release day – they staged their own fundraising screening, in aid of cancer and arthritis charities. A sold-out event, it was one of the grandest – and most glittering – affairs ever staged in Belfast.

And to coincide with the opening, the Northern Ireland Tourist Board produced a map of the film locations. It included Divis Mountain, the Giant's Causeway, Scrabo Country Park, Roe Valley Country Park, O'Cahan's Rock and Mount Stewart House and Gardens. Divis Mountain hosted battle scenes, the Italian Garden at Mount Stewart acted as the grounds of Dracula's castle, and the world-famous stones of the Giant's Causeway doubled as a fictional Transylvanian mountain – with a little CGI (computer generated imagery) assistance. NI Tourist Board Marie-Therese O'Neill said: "It is very exciting that Dracula Untold was exclusively filmed in Northern Ireland. Many of the locations were utilised to resemble the eerie Transylvanian setting in which the story takes place." Sadly the *Dracula Untold* location map has now disappeared from the tourist board's website – supplanted by the filming spots for the massively popular *Game Of Thrones*.

FYFI: www.nationaltrust.org.uk/features/our-places-in-dracula-untold-2014

FILMS–4: the most obscure movie based on the novel is *Son of Dracula*. Not the original one, made in 1943 and starring Lon Chaney Jnr. This virtually forgotten one, from 1974, has a cult following, not by those who love all things Dracula or vampire, but those who are dedicated and devoted fans of Ringo Starr and the late American singer-songwriter Harry Nilsson. The Beatles' drummer produced and starred in it. Nilsson played the lead role and provided the soundtrack, which was released as an album of the same name. The two were great pals from the moment they met in the early 1960s. Cameo roles were played by other hit-parade rockers, including Keith Moon of The Who, John Bonham of Led Zeppelin and Peter Frampton.

At the time, the American magazine *TV Guide* dismissed the movie with a curt: "A confusing, flat, and utterly misguided attempt to blend horror, comedy, and rock 'n' roll, this bizarre curio offers nothing to the average moviegoer and extremely little to the most ardent fans of its two leads, Ringo Starr and Harry Nilsson." The movie was not widely released and has never gone to DVD although VHS copies were available at the time, mainly to those involved in the making. So anyone with a copy of the panned movie could be sitting on a small fortune. It's said that Ringo does have a copy – but that he can't bear to look at it!

FYFI: thanks to the way things are these days, it can now be seen in its entirety by going to, www.youtube.com/watch?v=cfkHN_QxNcw; also check eBay for rare copies, along with the LP of the soundtrack and posters of the movie.

FILMS-5: yes, you can watch *Dracula* – well, vague versions – in the magnificence of the, never-really-caught-on, "real-life" cinematic technique of 3D. There are two versions: first out of the Transylvania coffin, in April, 2012, was *Dracula 3D*. In November of the same year, *Saint Dracula 3D* was unleashed.

FYFI: https://www.rottentomatoes.com/m/dracula_3d and https://www.youtube.com/watch?v=LPfsINRyO_M

FIRST: there are first editions of *Dracula* out there – all with varying auction estimates or prices (at publication time) ranging from £1,560 to £75,000 (see ABEBOOKS). In 2002, one was sold, by the international auction house Christie's in New York, for a record $47,800. But it was inscribed with Bram Stoker's signature. A couple of years later, a first edition, also sold by Christie's, went for only $28,800. But it did not have Stoker's signature. The latest offering, in October, 2019, was sold for only $8,125, again by Christie's. The low, winning bid, was a surprise as included in the book were letters from Bram Stoker to Hall Caine, aka "Hommy-Beg" (see DEDICATION) to whom Stoker dedicated the book.

FYFI: for first editions on the market, check, AbeBooks, eBay, Etsy, Christie's and Sotheby's.

FIRST-2: the first film based on the novel is *Dracula's Death* – or, to give it its correct name *Drakula Halála*. The Hungarian-made silent movie was released in 1921, a year before *Nosferatu* (see NOSFERATU). It enjoyed a highly successful and long run in Europe. Not surprising, as the screenplay was written by Michael Curtiz who went on to become one of the best known directors of the golden age of Hollywood – he won an Oscar for directing the classic *Casablanca*. Amazingly his *Dracula* movie was never shown in the US. And sadly, it's presumed all copies of *Dracula's Death* are long lost.

FISH: of course there is a Dracula Fish. Isn't there a Dracula everything! The toothless, teeny-weeny fish – more of a minnow actually as it only grows to 0.67" (17 mm) – is only found in one particular freshwater stream in Myanmar.

It got its name because of the teeth-like bone fangs that protrude from the jaws of the male. The fangs are used to fight and fend off other males. The rare fish – which is scaleless and therefore translucent – was discovered in 2009 by Dr Ralf Britz, of the Natural History Museum in London. He is one of the world's leading ichthyologists (the study of fish science). He came across it when a shipment of rare fish he'd ordered from Myanmar for study purposes, unintentionally included several fish he could not immediately identify. He says: "The Dracula Fish is one of the most extraordinary vertebrates discovered in the last few decades." And Britz, who has been researching and searching for fish for over 25 years, counts its discovery as one of the stand-out moments of his career.

FYFI: keen to see one? Visit the Natural History Museum on Cromwell Road, London. Learn more at, http://news.bbc.co.uk/2/hi/science/nature/7935482.stm

FLOWERS: Dracula – be it the book or the character – a thing of beauty? Yes, a resounding yes, when it comes to flowers. There are three plants that have taken the name and – understandably – they are all dramatic, stunning examples of foliage. See CELOSIA, KISS and ORCHID.

FONT: it was only when this book was about to be published I discovered – to my utter delight – that there is a "Dracula" font. I shouldn't have been surprised. But I was. Why should the world of printing be untouched by our man! As a result, part of the book title is in "Dracula" font, along with the capital letters from A to Z and the name of each entry.

FOREST: in Ecuador there is a magnificent stretch of astounding beauty and wildlife resources called Dracula Forest Reserve. It gets its named because it's home to one of the world's rarest blooms – the Dracula Orchid (see ORCHIDS). The Reserve, which is a 20-mile valley on the west slopes of the Andes, just south of the Colombian border, is under threat by road development, mining, logging and conversion to agriculture.

FYFI: to see how you can help preserve the Reserve and the Dracula Orchids, https://reservadracula.org/reserve.html and https://www.rainforesttrust.org/projects/dracula-orchid-reserve

FORGERY: in 1910, Bram Stoker's last book (he wrote 13 novels, six non-fiction and three short-story collections) was published. It was *Famous Imposters*, which explored the con artists and hoaxers that had made historic headlines. As Goodreads (the online book encyclopedia) says: "... an amusing survey of the charlatans, rogues, and other practitioners of make-believe who bedevil and delight us. With a cheerfully withering eye for their cons, Stoker introduces us to many famous fakers including: royal pretenders (such as Perkin Warbeck, who claimed King Henry VII's throne) magicians (Paracelsus, Cagliostro, etc), witches and clairvoyants, women masquerading as men, hoaxers and others."

And now, the latest novel (as of publication of this A–Z) inspired by *Dracula* is also inspired by Stoker's analysis of forgery and its impact on life. *A Talented Man* by Belfast writer Henrietta McKervey, is a psychological suspense about literary forgery. It tells the tale of how, in 1938, a down-on-his-luck scion forges the sequel to *Dracula*.

In April 2020, when her novel was published, McKervey wrote an article in *The Irish Times* in which she talked about Stoker's final book. "When I began A Talented Man I discovered that Bram Stoker had published a book of essays called Famous Impostors ... his classifications included 'Pretenders', 'Practitioners of Magic', 'Witchcraft and Clairvoyance', 'Women as Men' and, my favourite, the giddy catch-all, 'Hoaxes, etc'. In the introduction he noted, 'Impostors in one shape or another are likely to flourish as long as human nature remains what it is, and society shows itself ready to be gulled'. And, boy, are we gulled."

The foreword to *A Talented Man* reads: "Ellis Spender, only son of a once-esteemed society family, believes money, success and the high life are his birthright – only prevented by a cruel trick of fate. Struggling to stay ahead of his creditors, the dejected writer decides to forge a sequel to one of the most famous novels of all time, Bram Stoker's Dracula. Its remarkable 'discovery' will create the lifestyle he believes is his due. But as his scheme begins to bear fruit, others who stand to gain become obstacles. And Ellis will stop at nothing to achieve his desires ..."

The Irish author Joseph O'Connor – whose own 2019 book based on Stoker's was a bestseller (see O'CONNOR) – was full of praise for McKervey's book. He said: "The atmosphere of pre-war London is evoked with skill in this spirited story of literary skulduggery."

FYFI: to buy, https://www.goodreads.com/book/show/52645401; to read McKervey's article, https://www.irishtimes.com/culture/books/fake-blood-what-inspired-a-novel-about-a-forged-dracula-sequel-1.4219168

FORGOTTEN: Bram Stoker penned many stories and poems that were not so much "forgotten" as never really known. The previous entry is a good example. But in December 2012, the spotlight was finally put on many of his other literary works. *The Forgotten Writings of Bram Stoker*, edited by John Edgar Browning (see BROWNING), is a treasure trove of Stoker's work. It got enthusiastic reviews. The *Washington Post* said: "In The Forgotten Writings of Bram Stoker, John Edgar Browning gathers Stoker's early poetry, some of his journalism, several interviews, a number of trivial short stories, the catalogue of his library, and many other odds and ends. Yet what surprises most in these pages is the humor, sometimes sentimental, sometimes macabre, sometimes utterly fanciful."

The *Guardian* reported: "For more than a hundred years the name Count Dracula has struck a chill into the hearts of readers. The original Bram Stoker novel has spawned countless imitation stories and a rich tradition of vampire films that still thrill audiences today. Now a discovery of lost work by him has shed fresh light on a great horror masterpiece . . . the writings reveal much about the style and background Stoker would re-use in his classic vampire story."

FYFI: https://www.goodreads.com/book/show/13722412

FRUIT: love going to the arcade or the pub and pulling the handle of the fruit machine? If you're lucky you might find a retro-Dracula version in one of your haunts. Or, if you're even luckier, you might find one for sale for around £250. Otherwise, being the age we live in, just go to Google Play and download the app for the Dracula Fruit Machine – along with dozens of other Drac-related offerings.

FYFI: best bet to find a renovated Dracula fruit machine, https://www.fruitmachineworld.com/ooh-aah-dracula----250-club-fruit-machine-1274-p.asp

G

GAME: *The Fury of Dracula* is a board game, designed and produced by the Games Workshop, a British company, based in Nottingham, with a global customer base. First introduced in 1987, an updated version of the game was released in 2006, followed by a third edition in 2015, then finally, when fans were in despair, the fourth edition came out in 2019.

The description of the game, as it appears on the website Board Game Geek, reads: "In this game of Gothic adventure, one player takes the role of Dracula while up to four others attempt to stop him by controlling Vampire hunters from the famous Bram Stoker novel. Dracula has returned, and is determined to control all of Europe by creating an undead empire of Vampires. Dracula uses a deck of location cards to secretly travel through Europe, leaving a trail of encounters and events for the hunters that chase him ... to rid the world of Dracula's foul plague, the hunters must destroy Dracula before he earns enough victory points to win the game ... will they have enough wit and bravery to defeat the dark count?"

The verdict of Anthony J Gallela, a leading expert in board game design and role-playing games, is: "The Fury of Dracula is a breakthrough title that introduced cooperative and deductive elements to the adventure board game sub-genre, while managing to retain the feeling of breathless excitement that players seek in an adventure game."

FYFI: for all editions, search eBay and expect to pay up to £120 for a first edition; for the latest edition, https://boardgamegeek.com/boardgame/181279/fury-dracula-thirdfourth-edition

GAME-2: the first Dracula board game came out in 1963. *The Dracula Mystery Game* is now firmly in the vintage-rare category, with – if you can find one – a selling price of around, give or take, £200. Made by Hasbro – the world's biggest toy and game-board provider (eg, Monopoly, My Little Pony, Transformers, Twister, Scrabble, etc) – it's come-on title was: "Will the Vampire Catch You?"

FYFI: to search for one for sale go to eBay and check the site for "collectible" toys.

GAME-3: then in 1981 Hasbro, again, brought out *I Vant to Bite Your Finger*. It was a huge hit – even though tons of kids were too terrified to play it. The game involved trying to get round the board by choosing the number of steps you wanted to make. Then you turned the clock, next to a caped Dracula, by that number of hours. If the cape opened you had to stick your finger in Dracula's mouth. If you were unlucky he would "bite", via his red, felt fangs – that were drenched in marker ink. Then you had to go back to the beginning of the board. Surely Hasbro know how big the Dracula, vampire thing is? Why don't they bring this game back? Until then, they do crop up on eBay for around the £200 mark. Though the ink will have dried up!

FYFI: to see the original TV advert, https://www.youtube.com/watch?v=PkbgypiAZ3k and the plea to bring it back, https://www.youtube.com/watch?v=JxAhMe86OS4

GARLIC: long before the novel was written, garlic had a worldwide reputation and folklore hold as a protector against evil and medical maladies. Romania was no exception and Bram Stoker undoubtedly picked up on garlic's reputed powers via his reading of *Account of the Principalities of Wallachia and Moldavia* (see WILKINSON) which he found in the Whitby library. It was confirmed for him in two books about Transylvania by Emily Gerard (see GERARD).

GARLIC - 2: every garlic bulb, now and then – if it's not going to be thrust in the face of a vampire – needs something to crush it. Try the "Graluca". Shaped like a cartoon-image of Dracula, this garlic press comes from the innovative Israeli OTOTO studio of design. As its marketing blurb goes: "Any other vampire would run a mile at the sight of garlic. But not Gracula – one twist of his head and he will crrrush your garrrlic to smithereens …" The perfect gift – useful too – for that Drac-fan building a memorabilia collection.

FYFI: search "Gracula garlic" for UK and US retailers; the lowest price around (£9) seems to be from UGC (Unusual Gift Company) of Cheshire, www.theunusualgiftcompany.com/search.php?search_query=Gracula&section=product

GEICO: one of America's leading car insurance companies has used Dracula several times in its TV advertising. In 2013 they had Dracula working at a blood donor centre. The premise is that he looks like he's in hog heaven as he prepares to draw blood from a donor, but not as excited as someone who saves money by switching their car insurance to GEICO.

FYFI: watch the commercial at, www.ispot.tv/ad/7oXR/geico-dracula-at-a-blood-drive#actors

GERARD: the works of Scottish writer and author Emily Gerard (1849–1905) had an enormous influence on Bram Stoker and his writing of *Dracula*. Stoker, despite his detailed and colourful depictions of Transylvania, never visited the region. Much of his research came from two of Emily's many publications: *Transylvania Superstitions* (1885) and *The Land Beyond the Forest: Facts, Figures, and Fancies from Transylvania* (1888). Her marriage to a Polish cavalry officer in the Austro-Hungarian Army, who was based for some time in Sibiu (which is now part of Romania) allowed her to become familiar with Transylvanian folklore stories. One of them she related was how Romanian peasants believed in vampires they called "nosferatu". She went on to reveal that the traditional mythical way to get rid of a nosferatu was to wave garlic in front of it and/or drive a wooden stake through its heart. This was obviously a belief Stoker clearly grabbed and ran with.

FYFI: search for both books at AbeBooks; to get both as a free e-book, http://www.gutenberg.org/ebooks/52165 and https://www.gutenberg.org/files/57168/57168-h/57168-h.htm

GIN: Dracula gets everywhere – even into your cocktail cabinet (do people still have them?) and onto the gin shelf of your local pub (well, particularly those in Whitby). See DOG–3.

GLASGOW: every year the Glasgow School of Art presents the Bram Stoker Medal. It's awarded to the graduating student who has produced the most "imaginative" work of the year. The award dates back to 1903. The big question is: what was the link between Bram Stoker and one of the most prestigious art colleges in the world? Well the obvious way to find out is to contact GSA.

But – and this is hard to believe – they don't know. The best anyone could come up with was that, possibly, Stoker was friendly with the painter Francis "Fra" Newbery, who was the school's director from 1885 to 1917.

Several recipients of the award were also contacted but none knew the backstory, although they did reveal that the medal is no longer a "medal" but a certificate. 2015 recipient, Glasgow-based American painter Heather Lander, was so disappointed – despite the £100 cash that came with the award – she asked for a photograph of the first medal awarded. The school gave her a photograph of a brass-rubbing of it they found in the archive. Edinburgh ceramic artist Sandra Brown, who won the award in 1984, said: "I am proud of the award as I think the imagination is undervalued in mainstream education." She added: "I don't know what the connection is with Bram Stoker though." The winner in 2008 was the, now, leading animator and graphic designer James Houston who revealed: "Receiving the award was a surprise. I had no idea it existed until graduation day and my name was read out." Despite a bid to find out, James, like all the other winners, has no clue why Stoker founded the award.

The 2019 winner was Ashley "Ash" Morgan, from Saline, Fife, who didn't even get a certificate – he just got an email saying he'd won, along with £100. But in an interesting twist, Ashley, who lives in Pollokshields, Glasgow, did not read *Dracula* until he went to GSA. As he says in relation to his win: "What a coincidence". And his favourite film version? "I am a massive fan of Francis Ford Coppola's film adaptation of the book. Gary Oldman's portrayal of Dracula terrifies me." And although he was aware of the award he reveals that, until he won it, he thought it was for writers. As it was, he got it for a documentary he made about *Third Lanark*, a once-respected Scottish football team which, although it went bankrupt 50 years ago, still has a strong fan base that connects through memorabilia.

FYFI: bizarrely, just before publication, the photo of the medal vanished off the internet; to catch up with some of the recipients named here, Sandra Brown,

www.creativeceramics.biz; Heather Lander, www.hrlander.com; and Ashley Morgan, https://vimeo.com/ashleymorgan23

GODALMING: as in the novel's Lord Godalming, who was Arthur Holmwood before his father died and he inherited the title. This, by the way, is a totally fictitious title which comes as a surprise, especially as Godalming is one of the "poshest" little towns in Britain. It dates back to 899 and with its cobbled streets, quaint shop fronts and Charterhouse, one of the country's most prestigious public (for American readers, that equates to expensive, private) schools, it is consistently voted as one of the best places to live "the good life". Without a doubt it's one place in Britain where one would expect to come across a Lord of the Manor.

GOLF: the easiest way to find out where a particular golfer is in the PGA rankings is to consult the Dracula Emoji. Every Sunday night, the golf-obsessive compiler of results – who chooses to stay anonymous – posts via twitter, with the handle *Nosferatu*. He's been doing this since March 2011 and consistently beats the weekly projections issued by the Official World Golf Ranking (OWGR). In a May 2019 interview with NBC Sports, he revealed: he lives near Dublin and that his first name is Vince but he wants to stay anonymous to protect his day job – which is in academia and research. The only clue to his sought-after success he was prepared to reveal was: "Whatever I do, it involves a lot of maths."

FYFI: https://twitter.com/vc606 and to read the NBC piece https://olympics.nbcsports.com/2019/05/16/nosferatu-golf-rankings

GOODREADS: is the website to find information about virtually every book ever published. It lists over 2,900 with "Dracula" in the title. After a synopsis and reviews of the book, along with a biography of the author, it has links to all outlets selling it, as well as the library nearest to you that has it.

FYFI: https://www.goodreads.com

GOOGLE: want to keep up with everything *Dracula*? Then sign-up for *Google Alert*, citing Dracula as your area of interest. The result will be a dozen items, or more, a day from publications around the world relating to or invoking Dracula, in some way or another. This internet "tool" is a dream for writers. Or, as I can attest to, a nightmare. One of the reasons this book took a long time to put together was because I discovered something new about the subject in hand every day.

FYFI: https://www.google.com/alerts

GOREY: Edward Gorey, the famed American illustrator, writer and poet (1925–2000) known for his macabre and surreal imagery, gained cult following when he got involved in the 1977 Broadway production of *Dracula* (see PLAY–2). His innovative set and costume designs – which were basically all black and white with scarlet flashes – had an enormous impact. They brought him a Tony Award for costume design and a Tony nomination for set design. In 1979 he added to his Dracula portfolio by producing *Dracula: A Toy Story*, a four-page pop-up book, that – with simple assembly – shows three stage sets from the Broadway production, with 15 cut-out figures. And fans can stock up on all manner of goods – from totes to serving trays – bearing some of his iconic Dracula illustrations, that are sold by The Gorey Store.

FYFI: for the pop-up book, www.goodreads.com/book/show/645888, and for souvenir items, https://goreystore.com

GOTHS: a concise explanation as to who the Goths were was published in March 2016 by the web-magazine *Life Science*. It reads: "The Goths were a people who flourished in Europe throughout ancient times and into the Middle Ages. Referred to at times as 'barbarians' they are famous for sacking the city of Rome in A.D. 410. Ironically, however, they are often credited with helping preserve

Roman culture. After the sacking of Rome, a group of Goths moved to Gaul (in modern-day France) and Iberia and formed the Visigothic Kingdom. This kingdom would eventually incorporate Catholic Christianity, Roman artistic traditions and other aspects of Roman culture. The last Gothic kingdom fell to the Moors in A.D. 711.

Today, the meaning of the word 'Goth' has evolved beyond any direct relationship to the ancient Goths. In the late Middle Ages, a style of architecture arose, characterized by large, imposing cathedrals and castles. The term 'Gothic' was applied to the style as a critique, the word even at that time being a synonym for 'barbaric'. During the 18th and 19th centuries, a genre of dark, romantic literature called 'Gothic fiction' flourished. Characterized by novels such as Bram Stoker's 'Dracula', Mary Shelley's 'Frankenstein' and the works of Edgar Allen Poe, the genre got its name from the Gothic locations in which the stories took place – for example, Dracula's dark, foreboding castle. In modern times, 'Goth' has been used for a subculture with its own style of music, aesthetic and fashion. The dark, often gloomy Goth imagery was influenced by Gothic fiction, particularly horror movies."

FYFI: to read the whole article, https://www.livescience.com/45948-ancient-goths.html

GOTHS-2: as for the Goths associated with Dracula and the vampire world in general, they are totally different creatures from the ones detailed above. The best way to get close to them, find out what makes them tick and even join their ranks, is to go to Whitby in April or October. Twice a year the Goths pay homage to their main man, Dracula, as they promenade around the historic seaport-cum-seaside town – where in the novel he arrived in Britain. Clad in Victorian or Edwardian grandiose costume, outrageous over-the-top garb where anything goes, and de rigueur accessories including giant crucifixes, black hair, pale-painted faces, ruby-red lips, embroidered corsets, lots of lace, cravats, capes, top hats, ostrich-plumed hats and kick-arse boots, they attract as many sightseers as there are of them. The weekends started in 1994, first just in October (for obvious reasons) then, in 1997, the April event was added. Both weekends now attract Goths from all over the world.

FYFI: http://www.whitbygothweekend.co.uk and for a manual on how to be a Goth, www.wikihow.com/Be-Goth

GOUT: if it hadn't been for a debilitating bout of gout, Jonathan Harker (major character in the book) would not have made the trip to meet The Count. He was dispatched to Transylvania because his boss, London solicitor Peter Hawkins, was felled by the condition. In Chapter 2, this is revealed when Jonathan, on his arrival, hands a letter from Mr Hawkins to Dracula that, in part, reads: "I must regret that an attack of gout, from which malady I am a constant sufferer, forbids absolutely any travelling on my part for some time to come. But I am happy to say I can send a sufficient substitute, one in whom I have every possible confidence."

GRAPHIC: tons of excitement were generated over the latest graphic novels based on *Dracula*. In late 2020, two hit the bookstores. One was, *Bram Stoker's Dracula Starring Bela Lugosi*, from Legendary Comics and the other, *Dracula, Motherf##ker!*, from Image Comics.

The first one combines Lugosi's (see LUGOSI) famed portrayal of Dracula with the novel. It was produced in cooperation with the Lugosi Estate. His granddaughter, Lynne Lugosi Sparks, said: "Bela Lugosi created his unique portrayal of Count Dracula on the Broadway stage and has become a cultural icon for his performance in the 1931 film. This graphic novel beautifully answers the question: What would Lugosi's performance look like in a direct interpretation of Bram Stoker's novel? We believe Legendary Comics has proven what fans already know – Bela Lugosi is Dracula."

Robert Napton, Senior Vice President of Legendary Comics, said: "There have been great Dracula graphic novels, but to unite Bram Stoker's novel in a faithful adaptation with the definitive Dracula in the form of screen icon Bela Lugosi is a dream come true."

Dracula, Motherf##ker! starts in 1889 Vienna as three of Dracula's brides nail him down in a coffin in a bid to see him disappear from the world. But to no avail. The story jumps to 1974 California, where an ageing starlet finds a way of resurrecting him. Written by British-American Alex de Campi and illustrated by Erica Henderson – both leading comic book award winners – it's tipped as the pulp-horror offering of its age.

FYFI: to buy and find a comic shop near you, https://www.comicshoplocator.com/StoreLocator. To see images from both books, https://movieweb.com/bela-lugosi-bram-stoker-dracula-comic-book and https://www.cbr.com/dracula-motherfker-image-vampire-graphic-novel

GUEST: in 1914 *Dracula's Guest* – a short story by Bram Stoker – was published, two years after his death. It was originally written as the first chapter for *Dracula* but was removed by the publishers. In gripping, frightening detail, it tells the story of an English man (presumably Jonathan Harker but never named) and his terrifying coach journey from Munich to unknown Transylvania territory. It involves him being led to a ghost town, during a monumental thunderstorm, where women, bleeding from the neck, lie – neither dead or alive – in forest graves. The young man is set upon by pack of wolves before being miraculously rescued by a team of men dispatched by, it turns out much later, Dracula.

FYFI: https://www.goodreads.com/book/show/10511555

HARVARD: even it – one of the world's greatest seats of learning founded in 1636 – is not immune to the lure of the vampire. Dr Susan Weaver Schopf, formerly associate dean and director of the Master of Liberal Arts Program at the Harvard Extension School, is Distinguished Service Lecturer in Extension at the university, teaches a class called 'The Vampire in Literature and Film'. It's not always on her agenda – as it has to alternate with other courses she's famed for. But when it is her Harvard website says: "The vampire story has been used by authors and filmmakers alike as an encoded way of talking about a lot of things besides vampirism. It's been a useful metaphor for a whole variety of anxieties that are inherent in the age."

When Dr Weaver Schopf is not sinking her academic teeth into *Dracula*, her writing-intensive literature courses run the gamut from English romantic poetry to Irish literature, orientalism in British literature to literary criticism and theory.

Strongly committed to the idea that walking in the footsteps of writers and artists is important to understanding their work, Schopf has created a number of spring break tours for her literature students in England, Ireland, Greece, and Egypt. After her first visit to Romania she reported:

"I wanted to know whether Bram Stoker – despite never having traveled there – had managed to research the geography, history, & culture sufficiently to capture these with some accuracy. I'm happy to report that he did. Dracula came fully to life for me while traveling in the region."

In her introduction to her vampire course – which is one of the most popular ones she teaches – she says: "The vampire is everywhere in popular culture in novels, young adult literature, television series, short fiction, comic books, graphic novels, and film. Although this mythic creature has occurred in diverse mythologies for thousands of years and occupied the literary imagination of authors and audiences for more than two hundred, at no other time has it been represented in such an intriguing variety of ways. How can we account for the popularity, adaptability, and unique appeal of the vampire figure? With what fears and fantasies in the human psyche does it connect? Do people in diverse cultures interpret the vampire story in different ways? And in terms of literary genre, how do we classify these increasingly diverse works? In addition to their expected place in the horror genre, vampire stories have been used as code to address a host of provocative topics, including sexuality, death, disease, addiction, adolescence, immigration, religious doubt, and diminishing energy resources.

"Most surprising, in recent years the vampire has morphed from a terrifying figure of pure evil to a handsome, self-hating outsider who only seeks community with humans. The course explores vampire literature's evolution, from its origins in the Gothic tradition to its recent incarnation as urban fantasy and paranormal romance. Students also consider the implications of the vampire myth from anthropological, psychoanalytical, and socio-political perspectives. A number of films that present unique approaches to the vampire myth are likewise viewed in class so that we can explore the public and private anxieties that they embody."

FYFI: www.extension.harvard.edu/faculty-directory/sue-weaver-schopf

HARVARD-2: in 1999 "GradeSaver" was founded by two Harvard students, to help English literature students edit and revise their essays before submitting them to the intense scrutiny of their professors and teachers. As the number of essays edited by "GradeSaver" – now operated by other Harvard graduates and students – increased, it became obvious that many students needed good literature resources on the internet to help them with their essays. As the website, under "about us", states: "GradeSaver soon decided to create classic literature study guides and put them on the internet for free." With millions of users each month and over 400 titles, it ranks among the largest academic resources available online.

FYFI: to see all it has to say about *Dracula*, www.gradesaver.com/dracula/study-guide/summary

HEAVY METAL: in January 2015, Norwegian heavy-metal heroes Jorn Lande and Trond Holter released a concept album based on the story of *Dracula*. According to the PR blurb for *Dracula – Swing of Death*: "It's inspired by the life of Count Vlad III, Prince of Wallachia, widely known as Vlad the Impaler – or Dracula. His backstory formed the basis of countless vampire tales." Lande impersonates Dracula on the record, while the female parts are sung by Norwegian singer Lena Fløitmoen. According to those behind the project, "The drama of the story reveals Dracula's inner battle, where he still remembers what true love was, and as he wandered the earth for centuries with a thirst for blood, his loneliness and desire to be able to love again has led him to the brink of insanity." Lande and Holter say the album is influenced musically by 1970's-era Meat Loaf, Queen and Alice Cooper and features some other classic and more contemporary hard rock elements.

FYFI: to listen to a short track, www.youtube.com/watch?v=Q4iPn1k9aZw

HILL: the novel mentions Shooter's Hill (chapter 13) in connection with Hampstead Heath, which is in north London. But the location is wrong. Shooter's Hill is in Greenwich, which is in the south-east of the city. The thinking is that Stoker meant Shoot Up Hill, which leads to the Heath. And note, it's not named for drug use, but because it "shoots up" steeply.

HILL-2: if you're into the risqué, slapstick comedy that was once the staple of British telly, then you've got to check out Benny Hill's take on *Dracula*. Even if you've no idea who Benny Hill was, still check it out. The seven-minute 1979 sketch, with him racing around with fangs trying to sink them into every pretty girl he spies, while a granny-figure (who looks like Old Mother Riley – a Hollywood character only remembered by the over 70s) chases after him trying to stop him, is hilarious. Totally un-PC and so back-in-the-day humour.

FYFI: https://www.youtube.com/watch?v=T23Js8rE_P4&list=RDT23Js8rE_P4

HISTORIAN: the bestseller, *The Historian*, by American author Elizabeth Kostova, is a riveting read for anyone – but particularly *Dracula* fans. A dark, multi-generation family mystery, it gives new life to *Dracula* as it explores medieval Europe and its grim lust for blood-thirsty activities. Published in 2005, the reviews were enthusiastic about the new take on *Dracula*. The *Observer* said: "A spirited update of Bram Stoker's classic, with a vastly ingenious plot in which Dracula has developed a mysterious penchant for librarians." The *Miami Herald* echoed the thought with: "Impossible to resist ... Kostova blends fact and fantasy to remind us that the original Dracula legend is rooted in monstrous acts of unblinking evil."

FYFI: https://www.goodreads.com/book/show/30236962

HITLER: Hollywood writer, film director and producer, Patrick Sheane Duncan, has unleashed one monster to stop another. In his novel *Dracula vs Hitler* (2016), the Romanian Resistance calls on the vampire powers of The Count to see off Hitler, who in 1941 is poised to ravage their country via the Nazi Secret Service. As the blurb enticingly points out: "Resistance forces turn to the one-time ruler of Transylvania, Prince Vlad Dracula, who is, above all else, a patriot. He proves more than willing to drive out his country's invaders. Upshot: no one minds if he drinks all the German blood he desires. In Berlin, when Hitler hears about the many defeats his forces are suffering at the hands of an apparent true vampire, he is seduced by the possibility of becoming immortal. Thus two forces are set upon a collision course, the ultimate confrontation: superpower against superpower."

FYFI: https://www.goodreads.com/book/show/29241335

HORSE: when it comes to dressage, Dracula is the horse to beat. Owned and ridden by top Californian equestrian Seelchen Feibush, his reputation as a Friesan show horse is formidable. His list of wins and awards is long. And you've only got to take one look at Dracula and you know how he got his name. His totally, glossy, all-jet-black coat, says it all. On her website, Seelchen describes him as: "a very fancy fairytale-type Friesan".

FYFI: to see him in action, https://www.youtube.com/watch?v=OOB3ZgwpvpQ; to check his record, http://friesiandressage.com/HOME.html

HOTEL: the animated movie franchise *Hotel Transylvania* was launched in 2012, followed by two sequels in 2015 and 2018 with the fourth coming in 2021. The films star Dracula in a novel role – as a hotel keeper and a father. Both those roles are pivotal to the action. He operates a high-end resort – for fictional monsters only – away from the human world, helped by his teenage daughter Mavis. In the first movie he goes into overprotective mode when a human boy discovers the resort and falls for Mavis. In *HT-2* the hotel has opened to humans and Mavis is married to one. Their son lacks vampire abilities which sends his great-grandfather Vlad into overdrive concern. In *HT-3,* the family take a break from welcoming guests and goes on a family holiday aboard a Monster Cruise Ship.

As for the storyline in *HT-4*? The drama starts as the Dracula family is on a train, crossing Europe on its way to Transylvania – to celebrate Mavis's 127th birthday. Terror strikes when vampire-hunter Van Helsing suddenly turns up and Dracula pleads to be left alone. *HT-4* was originally slated for a Christmas 2020 release but the corona-virus crisis delayed production and the premier was shifted to August 6th, 2021.

The voice-overs are supplied by a galaxy of stars. Featured in all four are Americans Adam Sandler (stand-up comic, film star and screenwriter); Selena Gomez (singer/actress); Fran Drescher (TV actress) and David Spade (comedian–actor). Legendary filmmaker Mel Brooks joined the cast in 2, 3 and 4. A new addition to the Hotel family in 4, is American late-night TV star, Jimmy Fallon.

FYFI: for the *HT-4* trailer, https://www.youtube.com/watch?v=81J4KxaibWw

HULL: John Wedgwood Clark, an acclaimed poet and creative writing lecturer at Hull University, featured Bram Stoker and *Dracula* in a BBC TV series *Books That Made Britain*. His 30-minute programme – one of 11 – aired in November 2016. He travelled from Whitby to Hull, pinpointing various neighbourhoods and areas and describing their influence on a group of iconic poets and writers which, apart from Stoker, included Philip Larkin, Anne Brontë and Winifred Holtby. About his part in the series he said: "It's a combination of literary pilgrimage and investigation and an entertaining view of how writers have left their mark on this wonderful stretch of coastline."

FYFI: to see a clip from the programme, www.bbc.co.uk/programmes/p04c052s

HYPODONTIA: is the rare and unsightly dental condition that inflicts missing, along with fang-like, teeth on sufferers. The poor people who have this congenital, dental anomaly invariably suffer bullying as kids and are given the not surprising nickname of "Dracula". One young woman, from Southend-on-Sea, Essex, made the headlines in December 2019 when she "cured" the curse of her vampire-like teeth for £200. Selina Warren, 21, ended the daily ridicule with clip-on veneers.

FYFI: for Selina's story, https://www.echo-news.co.uk/news/18128355.mum-nicknamed-dracula-school-finally-feels-beautiful-thanks-199-veneers

ICE CREAM: not everybody's idea of a treat, but garlic-laced ice cream is out there. Naturally, it's called "Dracula". It's only available (at the moment) in Shingo – the Japanese town where it's made. The ice cream brings together two of Shingo's claims to fame: the biggest garlic producer in Japan and the bizarre claim that Jesus settled in the town and is buried there. So Dracula's enemies – garlic and a crucifix – come together with tasty ease. Gold images of both adorn the black tub of ice cream. At first the ice cream was marketed simply as Garlic Ice Cream. Sales were OK but not that good. But once the "Dracula" moniker was added – along with the advice to "avoid leaving Dracula ice cream in direct sunlight and it survives best in the darkness of your freezer" – sales soared.

FYFI: https://soranews24.com/2013/05/19/shingou-town-claims-spiritual-enlightenment-for-many-of-the-worlds-mysteries

ICE CREAM - 2: black pudding ice cream? Please say it's not so. But it is. And Dracula would love it! So would anyone with a taste for the unusual. Made by Salt & Straw – probably the most inventive ice cream makers in America – Dracula's Black Pudding is available for a month around Halloween. They have 19 "scoop" shops on the West

Coast, in Los Angeles, Anaheim, San Diego, San Francisco, Portland and Seattle, with two about to open in Miami. The website proclaims: "this is the most intoxicatingly, impelling ice cream flavor we've ever featured! We've taken careful measures to balance both delectable and frightful. A heady combination of warm spices and cream into pig's blood ... then a spin in our ice cream laboratory. It'll make you squirm with delight."

FYFI: www.saltandstraw.com

ICE CREAM-3: one of the best ice creams in the world is made in Whitby – and sold only in Whitby and other parts of North Yorkshire and the North East. Trillo's history stretches back almost as long as *Dracula*, the book, had been around. Founded by an Italian family that moved to Whitby over a century ago, it stayed as the Trillo's family business until 2006, when it was bought by local farmer, David Stevenson. He and his team have stayed faithful to the name and the quality of their product, using only locally sourced milk and cream. But one change they have made is acknowledging the *Dracula* phenomena, and the lure of jet, the semi-precious stone – both of which owe so much to Whitby – by serving up a black cone of totally black ice cream.

In the end, after a lot of discussion, the name of the grim-looking but tasty offering favoured the "jewel" and was named "Whitby Jet", as opposed to something that invoked Dracula, such as "Blacula". The ice cream is vanilla that has been dyed, along with the biscuit cone, with charcoal. Charcoal? Hang on, are we talking about the ashes left over from that barbeque? No. It's "activated charcoal" that has a multitude of uses (see DYEING). The other Dracula-related ice cream Trillo's has come up with is a nod to the Goths that flood Whitby twice a year (see GOTHS–1). Called "Gothic" it's blood-red in colour, with black streaks. It's made with blackcurrants and liquorice.

Such is the uniqueness of these icy treats that Mary Berry, the queen of British TV food programmes, turned up in Whitby, in November 2019, to sample Trillo's "grim" offerings. Her visit was to be featured in a show. But like so many programmes, the corona-virus held up production and it's still (at the time of publication) not been screened. Of course the fact filming took place during an icy rainstorm might have something to do with that!

FYFI: https://www.trillosofwhitby.com

ICE CREAM–4: see LOLLIES.

ICED EARTH: the massively popular American heavy metal band paid tribute to Dracula in a track on their 2001 album Horror Show. One verse goes:

> *There are far worse things awaiting man than death.*
> *Come taste what I have seen.*
> *I'm spreading my disease,*
> *I will feed upon His precious child.*
> *The human race will bleed,*
> *They will serve my need.*

FYFI: www.youtube.com/watch?v=tUIHTX-uE_Y&list=PLEA41C84EF43E965F and http://icedearth.com

ICELAND: amazingly, the first translation of *Dracula* was into Icelandic, in 1901. The Icelandic version – which was compiled by Icelandic publisher and writer Valdimar Asmundsson – was renamed *Makt Myrkranna*, ie, "Powers of Darkness". For decades even the most earnest *Dracula* afficionados had no clue that Makt Myrkranna was anything but a pure, straightforward rendition of *Dracula* into Icelandic. But no way. The first surprise came in 1986 when it was discovered that Stoker had written a preface. Up until that time no one had bothered to check on the translation. Then in 2014, *Dracula* scholar Hans de Roos took the time to investigate and actually read the translated work. Shock, horror and delight. It was barely recognisable as the original.

In 2016, the "new" *Dracula* was unleashed on the world – as *Powers of Darkness: The Lost Version of Dracula*. The publishers pointed out the Icelandic version – apparently with Stoker's blessing – was not just a mere translation but an entirely new version of the story, with all-new characters and a totally reworked plot. They said: "The resulting narrative is one that is shorter, punchier, more erotic, and perhaps even more suspenseful than the original. Powers of Darkness will amaze and entertain legions of fans of Gothic literature, horror, and vampire fiction". And the *Guardian* said: "Our familiar, beloved Count has a wintry doppelgänger, thanks to this strange, pleasing curiosity of a book."

FYFI: www.powersofdarkness.com

ICELAND-2: in February 2017 it was reported that two of Iceland's major film-makers were working on bringing

Powers of Darkness to TV. Movie producer Sigurjón Sighvatsson (best known outside Iceland for the 1990s "cult" TV series, *Twin Peaks*) and scriptwriter Ottó Geir Borg were seeking funding for their English-language project. But over three years on there's been no further news.

ILLUSTRATIONS: the first editions of the novel had no illustrations. It wasn't until 1901, four years later, that illustrations were included. One of them, in Chapter 4, showed Dracula, portrayed as a bat-like creature with bare feet, crawling head-first down the castle wall – as Jonathan Harker looked on in horror from a window. This image was a highlight of the exhibition *Terror and Wonder: the Gothic Imagination* staged by the British Library from October 2014 to January 2015. The exhibition was the biggest ever put together around Gothic literature.

About the 1901 Dracula illustration, Greg Buzwell, curator of the exhibition observed: "At this stage, the count genuinely does resemble the description of the character in the book: tall, thin, pale, old – although he looks younger after feeding – and mustachioed. The more glamorous renderings of the count, portraying him as a suave and sophisticated figure with a dangerous sexual magnetism – such as those given in the famous Hammer films by Christopher Lee, for example – were still many years away."

FYFI: to see the illustration, www.pinterest.com/pin/302726406176531665

IMAGES: there are a handful of powerful images traditionally associated with *Dracula* – both the character and the book. They all have their own entry – see: ABBEY, BATS, BLOOD and FANGS.

INTERVIEW: a couple of months after the publication of *Dracula*, author Bram Stoker gave his only known interview about the book to journalist Jane "Lorna" Stoddard. It was published in the *British Weekly*, on July 1st, 1897. A couple of weeks later it was published in America in the *Daily Tribune*, Salt Lake City, Utah. In the interview, Stoker revealed that the storyline had been "a long time in my mind" and that it took him over three years to write it. He said he'd always been interested in vampires, adding: "It is undoubtedly a very fascinating theme, since it touches both on mystery and fact. In the Middle Ages the terror of the vampire depopulated whole villages."

Asked if there was any historic basis to the legend he replied: "It rested, I imagine, on some such case as this: a person may have fallen into a death-like trance and been buried. Afterwards the body may have been dug up and found alive and from this a horror seized upon the people and in their ignorance they imagined that a vampire was about. The more hysterical, through excess of fear, might themselves fall into trances in the same way; and so the story grew that one vampire might enslave many others and make them like himself. When once the panic seized the population their only thought was to escape."

FYFI: www.bramstoker.org/nonfic/dracula.html

IRVING: Sir Henry Irving, the legendary Victorian thespian for whom Bram Stoker worked as his business manager for almost 30 years. Stoker took Sir Henry, with whom he had a rather difficult master–servant relationship, as part of his inspiration for Dracula. That was probably why Irving dismissed the novel as "rubbish" and refused to play Dracula – although it was staged at the theatre he made his own, The Lyceum, in London. Stoker went on to write a biography of Irving. *Personal Reminiscences of Henry Irving* was published in 1907, two years year after Irving's death. In the preface to the book Stoker writes: "I was an intimate friend of Irving; in certain ways the most intimate friend of his life. I knew him as well as it is given to any man to know another."

FYFI: the book is available in many forms, including a free download:
http://bramstoker.org/pdf/nonfic/03irving03.pdf

J

JACKET: fancy a jacket like the one worn by Dracula – ie, Luke Evans – in the 2014 movie *Dracula Untold*? The black leather replica is yours for £199.00 from Jackets Creator, which specializes in exact copies of gear sported in movies and TV series.

FYFI: see it, buy it, www.jacketscreator.com/product/luke-evans-dracula-untold-jacket

JAPAN: has a massive interest in *Dracula* and all genres linked to the novel and the person. In May 2018, a bloodthirsty trilogy of films made by Japanese film director Michio Yamamoto was released on DVD by Arrow Home Video, which specializes in restoring classic/horror/cult movies. The trilogy features the 1970s movies that made Yamamoto famous, ie, *Vampire Doll*, *Lake of Dracula* and *Evil of Dracula*. The DVD was welcomed by cult horror film fans. As BMD (Birth.Movies.Death) said on its website: "For years, Yamamoto's vampire films toiled away in obscurity, only known commodities to the hardest core cult film fans. Thankfully, Arrow Home Video has restored and released these curiosities for a new generation of crate diggers to discover and evangelize about, in hopes of spreading the gospel regarding this bizarre, beguiling trio of horror films."

FYFI: www.youtube.com/watch?v=4ZJkLZfC5YA

JEWELLERS: in Chapter 13, Bram Stoker makes mention of a real jewellery shop. It's Giuliano's in London's Piccadilly. The name crops up when Jonathan Harker and his wife Mina spot Dracula gazing at a pretty girl in a horse and carriage outside, what was in those Victorian days, one of the most prestigious jewellers in the country. In the book, Bram Stoker spells the name incorrectly. He transposes the "i" and "u" and calls it "Guiliano's". Italian Carlo Giuliano opened his shop at 115 Piccadilly in 1875. Sadly he died in 1895, two years before the book was published – so he never knew how his name (even if spelled wrongly) and business were immortalized in what was to become one of the most legendary works of literature. The business was carried on by his sons, but closed in 1914. Giuliano pieces are among the most collectable and fetch huge prices at auction, often in excess of hundreds of thousands of pounds.

FYFI: https://www.langantiques.com/university/giuliano/

JEWELLERY: no excuse for *Dracula* fans not to be adorned with all manner of trinkets celebrating, well, just about everything to do with the character, the films, the stars that played Dracula – even a locket with a photo of Bram Stoker. The best place to seek out the ghoulish earrings, rings, bracelets, chokers, necklaces cufflinks (have I missed anything?) is the internet site Etsy. It is the global home of the hand-crafted. At the time of going to print, there were 1,825 Dracula, vampire jewellery items posted for sale.

FYFI: http://www.etsy.com/uk/search?q=dracula+jewelry

JET: in Chapter 6, when the narrative of the novel has moved to Whitby, there is a reference to visitors buying jet. In the 1800s, the "mining" of jet and the conversion of it into jewellery and ornaments, stood alongside fishing as the main industry of the historic seaport. In simple terms, jet is not a gemstone but an organic material that comes from fossilized wood, mainly from the monkey puzzle tree. In its original state, jet is dull and dark brown but it polishes to a gleaming black. Inferior jet is found in parts of Spain, South America and Siberia, but the finest quality is found – in the cliffs or deep into the beach – within a 10-mile radius of either side of Whitby harbour.

Queen Victoria popularised the wearing of jet. After the death of her husband Prince Albert in 1861, it was the only jewellery she wore. It was a rewarding industry for those who could master the skilled craft of carving jet, which under careless hands is prone to splintering. The work finally tailed off but in the past couple of decades the working of jet has returned to Whitby in style.

FYFI: to see and buy the finest examples of Whitby jet, Robinsons,
https://www.facebook.com/Robinsons-Jet-419275182175734; One O' Five,
https://www.visitwhitby.com/one-o-five; Heritage Jet,
https://www.whitbyjet.co.uk; Aurora Jet,
https://www.whitby-jet-jewellery.com; Ebor Jet, https://eborjetworks.co.uk

JOKES: there are so many, most of them playground standard, such as:

- # What coffee does Dracula drink? Decoffinated.
- # What does Dracula say at Christmas? Best vicious for the season.
- # What does Dracula get when he's anaemic? Batfatigue.
- # What sort of dog does Dracula own? A bloodhound.
- # Why does Dracula have no friends? Because he's a pain in the neck.
- # What's Dracula's favourite fruit? A blood orange or a neck-tarine.
- # Why did Dracula go into hospital? To have his ghoulstones removed.
- # What do you get if you cross Dracula with Al Capone? A fangster.
- # In America what day is dedicated to Dracula? Fangsgiving Day.
- # What is Dracula's favourite song? Fangs for the Memory.
- # What's the difference between Doc Martin and Dracula? One faints at the sight of blood.
- # Where in New York does Dracula hang out? The Vampire State Building.
- # What is Dracula's favourite circus act? He always goes for the juggler.
- # Where does Dracula have lunch? In the casketeria.
- # What does Dracula do to a pint of beer? He necks it.
- # What is Dracula's favourite mode of transport? A blood vessel.
- # Which song does Dracula hate most? You Are My Sunshine.
- # Where does Dracula keep his money? In a blood bank.

- # Why is Dracula like false teeth? Because he comes out at night.
- # If Dracula is crossed with a snowman what do you get? Frostbite.
- # Why did Dracula split up with his girlfriend after she had a blood test? She wasn't his type.
- # Why did Dracula always read the best-selling newspaper? Because it had a good circulation.
- # Dracula was on one of those DIY TV programmes recently. His castle was getting a revamp.
- # A friend of mine has boxed Dracula a few times and keeps losing. He can never beat the count.
- # Why does Dracula never attack chickens? Their blood is fowl.
- # What's Dracula's favorite dessert? I-scream
- # What kind of ice cream does Dracula eat? Veinilla.
- # What's Dracula's favorite cocktail? Bloody Mary.
- # Why does Dracula like tapas restaurants? Lots of platelets.
- # What's Dracula's favorite cereal? Bran, of course.
- # Who's Dracula's favorite action character? Batman.

What do you think of these Dracula jokes? They're bloody awful!

JOURDAN: the late French actor Louis Jourdan – he of *Gigi* fame – played Dracula in the 1977 BBC film, *Count Dracula*. It's considered one of the best adaptations of the novel and Jourdan's performance – with his famed suave persona – one of the finest depictions of The Count.

FYFI: watch it, https://www.youtube.com/watch?v=co0sLSf1Boo

JOURNAL: getting on for 100 years ago, a slim, unmarked notebook was passed down through various relatives of Bram Stoker. It finally ended up with his great-grandson, Noel Dobbs, where it was hidden away for decades, forgotten about, in his Isle of Wight home. Not until Stoker's great-grand-nephew Dacre Stoker contacted Noel about the idea he had for a book, and asked if he knew anything about a journal in which their literary iconic relative made notes and jotted down thoughts, did Noel pay attention to the fragile notebook. After he dug it out from its buried place among forgotten family "heirlooms", he discovered to his astonishment – and the delight of *Dracula* academics and fan base – that he had discovered the notebook, signed by Stoker, that was a handwritten blueprint of what was to become the phenomena, *Dracula*.

It contained 305 entries dating from 1871. Some of the "notes" are pages long. Others are just scribbled, barely decipherable, sentences. And here and there are love poems. As Dacre Stoker said at the time: "When I saw it I was amazed. I thought, 'The Holy Grail' – we've found it." You can see for yourself exactly what Stoker's *Dracula* thought process was: in 2013 it was published as *The Lost Journal of Bram Stoker: The Dublin Years*.

FYFI: https://www.goodreads.com/book/show/12995873

JOURNAL-2: once a year, the North American Chapter of the Transylvanian Society of Dracula produces *The Journal of Dracula Studies*. It's edited and published by Kutztown University, Pennsylvania.

FYFI: www.facebook.com/Journal-of-Dracula-Studies-1732548426803201

JUG: in 1997, Royal Doulton produced a Dracula Toby Jug. It was designed by David B Biggs, whose ceramic artistry dominated Royal Doulton products for years. His Dracula jug – which features garlic bulbs at the top of the handle and a crucifix as part of it – won the prestigious "character jug of the year" award. Produced as a limited edition of 2,500, it now sells, on eBay, Etsy and other sites, for around £300.

KILMARNOCK ARMS: in 1893, while on a walking holiday, Bram Stoker visited Port Erroll, now better known as Cruden Bay, on the north-east coast of Scotland (see CRUDEN BAY). A year later he returned, with his wife and son, and stayed at the *Kilmarnock Arms*. He wrote in the guest book. His message, which is on display in the hotel, reads: "Second visit to Port Erroll. Delighted with everything & everybody & hope to come again to the Kilmarnock Arms." The next year, he and his family did return and he started writing *Dracula*. Finally, in February 2019, the *Kilmarnock Arms* was recognised with a plaque, for the support and succor it supplied to Stoker. It is simple but direct in its inscription: "Bram Stoker wrote the early chapters of 'Dracula' here in 1895."

FYFI: all about the hotel, http://www.kilmarnockarms.com/bram-stoker-kilmarnock-arms-hotel.html

KING: the mantle for number one horror-writer lies on Stephen King's shoulders. And one of his bestsellers (to this day) is one of his earliest novels – *Salem's Lot*, which was inspired by King's love of *Dracula*. On his website, King – who back-in-the-day was a high school English literature teacher – acknowledges his admiration for the novel. He writes: "One of my high school classes was

Fantasy and Science Fiction, and one of the novels I taught was *Dracula*. I was surprised at how vital it had remained over the years; the kids liked it, and I liked it, too. One night over supper I wondered aloud what would happen if Dracula came back in the twentieth century, to America. 'He'd probably be run over by a Yellow Cab on Park Avenue and killed,' my wife said. That closed the discussion, but in the following days, my mind kept returning to the idea. It occurred to me that my wife was probably right – if the legendary Count came to New York, that was. But if he were to show up in a sleepy little country town, what then? I decided I wanted to find out, so I wrote 'Salem's Lot'."

FYFI: https://www.goodreads.com/book/show/11590

KISS: any kiss linked to Dracula has got to be deathly. Right? No, not always. There is a delightful one. *Dracula's Kiss* is a type of iris. It stands out from all other iris because of its vibrant black-purple petals that turn even darker in the autumn, along with a caterpillar-like, bright tangerine beard. Strangely, although widely on sale in America, it's difficult to track down in the UK.

FYFI: to buy in the States go to the iris specialists, Schreiner's. They ship world-wide.

https://www.schreinersgardens.com/search?noheadings=1&keywords=Dracula%27s+Kiss0

KNIT: yes, forget woolly caps, socks, sweaters, scarves … knit a Dracula, for yourself or another Drac-lover. The pattern – for the cutest, six-inch-high soft-toy Dracula around – will set you back a "massive" £1.20. Then there is the magnificent shawl/wrap that, by using silk and alpaca yarns in various shimmering reds, blacks and greys, tells the story through motifs of castles, hearts and bats, woven into the pattern. A showstopper of a pattern for a fiver.

FYFI: download both, plus dozens of others, https://www.ravelry.com/patterns/search#query=Dracula

KODAK: in Chapter 2, the iconic camera gets a good mention. Introduced to the world in 1888, Jonathan uses a Kodak to take photos of the London property Dracula wants to buy. When Bram Stoker put a camera in Jonathan's hands, he would have had a "Brownie" in mind. It was the camera that took photography out of a specialised world, only accessible by professionals and the wealthy. It allowed everyone to take photographs with a simple click. Introduced in 1900, it was a camera staple used into the 1950s. If you like the idea of ditching your mobile for taking photos and snapping away Dracula-style, there are plenty of Brownies – named because it came in a brown canvas case – of all vintages, on sale online.

FYFI: if you are really, really interested, make that fascinated, by the camera that put the "snap" into our lives, http://www.brownie-camera.com/index.shtml

L

LAMENT: how sad that Dracula was desperate to repent and change his ways – but couldn't. That is the theme of *Dracula's Lament*. It's a poignant, moody song written and sung by Jason Segal, the multi-talented American entertainer who is best known for his role as Marshall in the TV situation-comedy *How I Met Your Mother*. He penned the *Lament* when he wrote and played the lead in the 2008 movie *Forgetting Sarah Marshall*. In it his character writes, and stages, a *Dracula* musical that is performed by puppets. On December 16th 2009, Segal performed the song live on CBS's *The Late, Late Show*, then hosted by Scot, Craig Ferguson. The lyrics are:

> *"It's getting kind of hard to believe things are going to get better.*
> *I've been drowning too long to believe that the tide's going to turn.*
> *And I've been living too hard to believe things are going to get easier.*
> *I'm still trying to shake off the pain from the lessons I've learned.*
> *And if I see Van Helsing, I swear to the Lord I will slay him.*
> *Ah ha ha ha! He taketh from me, but I swear I won't let it be so.*

Ah ha ha ha! Blood, will run down his face, when he is decapitated.
Ah! His head on my mantle is how I will let the world know
How much I love you.
Die, die, die (pause) I can't."

FYFI: to hear Segal sing *Dracula's Lament* go to, www.youtube.com/watch?v=Gq1vikN3XLM

LANGELLA: deemed by many critics as the "classiest" of all the Draculas, Frank Langella holds a unique – well, almost – position when it comes to the role. Apart from Bela Lugosi, he's the only actor to play Dracula on stage and on film. He was nominated for a Tony Award for his 1977 Broadway portrayal. He reprised his role in the 1979 film *Dracula*, which, while not the biggest hit of all time, won him best actor in the Saturn Awards (given by the Academy of Science Fiction, Fantasy and Horror Films). Legendary producers, brothers Marvin and Walter Mirisch (of *Some Like it Hot*, *The Magnificent Seven*, *West Side Story* and *The Pink Panther* fame) decided to make the movie after seeing Langella's Broadway performance. Walter said: "I truly had no idea what to expect. But I found that Frank Langella had created a completely different character from the accepted sinister one – a character with charm, sex appeal, and most important of all, he endeared himself to the audiences. I decided right then to make the film!" Director John Badham (whose break-out movie was *Saturday Night Fever*) picked up the best director Saturn Award for *Dracula*. Before offering Langella the role, he went to see his Broadway performance four times. But before accepting, Langella obtained the assurance that there would be no scenes with his fangs dripping blood.

At the time of his Dracula roles he said: "I don't play him as a hair-raising ghoul. He is a nobleman, an elegant man with a very difficult problem ... a man with a unique and distinctive social problem: he has to have blood to live and he is immortal."

FYFI: the film is available as a DVD from Amazon UK; to watch/buy/rent, in US, https://www.vudu.com/content/movies/details/Dracula/5550

LATEST: the newest crop of books, vampire movies and TV series is a massive indicator that the horror genre, sparked by *Dracula*, is more than alive and well, and not going anywhere but up, up, up. The big – make that huge – news is that the massively talented duo Steven Moffat and Mark Gatiss (the writers behind *Sherlock* and *Dr Who*) made a *Dracula* mini-series. The three-parter – co-produced by the BBC and Netflix – brought telly 2020 in with a bang. It premiered over three consecutive nights, starting on New Year's Day.

The star role is played by Danish actor Claes Bang. Before becoming Dracula he was best known to English-speaking audiences for his 2018 role in *The Girl in the Spider's Web*. On landing the coveted role, he said: "I am thrilled to be taking on the role of Dracula, especially when the script is in the hands of the incredible talents of Steven Moffat and Mark Gatiss. I'm so excited that I get to dig into this iconic and super-interesting character. Yes he's evil, but there's also so much more to him. He's charismatic, intelligent, witty and sexy. I realize that there's a lot to live up to with all the amazing people that have played him over the years." As for the writers they said: "Who else could it be than Claes! He has it all. Brilliant, gorgeous, charismatic, lethal. Tall, dark and gruesome all at once. Hell has a new boss." And about their mission: "To reintroduce the world to Dracula, the vampire who made evil sexy." Other members of the cast include John Heffernan (*Collateral, The Crown*), Joanna Scanlan (*Hold the Sunset, No Offence*), Dolly Wells (*Can You Ever Forgive Me?, 45 Years*), Morfydd Clark (*His Dark Materials, Patrick Melrose*), Lujza Richter (*Phantom Thread*) and series co-writer Mark Gatiss, who like Alfred Hitchcock always makes a cameo appearance in all his productions.

In March 2019 as the script was being written, Gatiss told the *Radio Times*: "We sort of made a promise to ourselves and the people who are making it, paying for it, that we'd make Dracula the hero of his own story, and less of a shadowy presence. And that's a really clever idea, but we had to make good on it!" He added: "There's lots of things that are challenging about Dracula. Having an evil lead character is actually really difficult. That's been the main challenge. We quickly found out why he's often kept as a shadowy presence. So it's hard work, but I think it's worked." In a joint statement the pair said: "There have always been stories about great evil. What's special about Dracula is that Bram Stoker gave evil its own hero."

Surprisingly, much of the filming was not in Romania but in Slovakia, which is separated from Romania by Hungary. And most scenes were shot in the medieval, UNESCO world heritage city of Banská Štiavnica. A prime reason for the choice was that the city's old castle makes a perfect Dracula lair.

FYFI: watch, https://www.netflix.com/title/80997687

LATEST-2: no sooner had this "new" *Dracula* aired than there was talk and predictions about a second round from Mark Gattis and Steven Moffat. After all, The Count cannot be killed. Weighing in on the possibility, Claes Bang – who was deemed a charismatic and sinister Dracula – said: "I would be super happy to do one more season. It was really fulfilling and lovely, and really, really cool to do."

LATEST-3: to coincide with the debut of the above mini-series, on January 4th, 2020, the BBC showed the documentary *In Search of Dracula*. In it Mark Gatiss – co-writer of the series – explored what inspired Bram Stoker to create *Dracula*, along with tracking the world's number one vampire from printed page to his many celluloid reincarnations. Speaking to the *Radio Times* about the documentary, Gatiss said: "As a lifelong horror fan – and of Dracula especially – this was a wonderful chance to get back to the vampire's roots, examine the strange character of Bram Stoker himself and immerse myself in the vast and joyous cinematic legacy of the Count. Dracula, to my delight, has once more risen from the grave!" Along with delving into Stroker's inspirations for the character, Gatiss looked at Dracula's journey from book to screen, discussing the various actors who have played him – from Bela Lugosi to newcomer Claes Bang, who stars in his, Mark Gattis's, BBC series.

FYFI: https://www.bbc.co.uk/programmes/m000cs1t

LATEST-4: some of the filming of *Dracula* upset the good folk of Caversham, near Reading. The last scenes to be shot (December, 2019) were in the town's cemetery – which sparked fury among those whose relatives are buried there.

The filming was slammed as "totally disrespectful". They feared the graves of their loved ones would be seen in a *Dracula* film. The production company assured them that only outlines of tombstones would be seen.

LEATHERDALE: probably the most prominent British *Dracula* academic is Clive Leatherdale. After getting a PhD in Arabian history he turned his scholarly mind to the book that, as a teenager, had grabbed his attention and never let go. The result, in 1985, was *Dracula: The Novel and the Legend: a Study of Bram Stoker's Gothic Masterpiece*. He followed it up with *The Origins of Dracula: the Background to Bram Stoker's Masterpiece*, in 1995, and three years later with his tome *Dracula Unearthed*, which was the novel with over 3,500 textual notes and annotations. In 2012, he penned the introduction to *Dracula: Sense & Nonsense*, an extremely informative read about the myths, untruths and misconceptions about the book and its author Bram Stoker, by the world's number one expert on *Dracula*, Elizabeth Miller (see MILLER).

FYFI: to check on all his books, https://www.goodreads.com/author/list/74116

LEE: Christopher Lee made 250 movies – both big screen and TV – but he will be forever associated with the nine times he played the role of Dracula for Hammer Films. Born in Belgravia, London, in 1922, he first wrapped himself in the Prince of Darkness's cape and sported the bloody fangs in 1958. He made his last *Dracula* movie in 1973. But in a 2005 interview, he complained about how little dialogue he was ever given. "I pleaded with Hammer to let me use some of the lines Bram Stoker had written. Occasionally

I sneaked one in." Even so, *Dracula* movie expert Charles E Butler (see FILMS-2) dubbed Lee, who was knighted in 2009, the "definitive" Dracula. A sentiment echoed countless times – especially when he died in June 2015.

LEEDS: the Yorkshire city's University Library has, in its Special Collections, a wonderful array of Bram Stoker letters, manuscripts and speeches. Altogether there are 3,411 letters and notes, sent and received, along with three volumes of manuscripts. But, surprisingly, there's nothing about *Dracula* – except words of thanks from those to whom he sent a copy of the book. The library's website mentions the lack of *Dracula* material. When the library staged an exhibition of all the Bram Stoker material, to mark Halloween 2014, the website introduction to the collection pointed out: "It's a running joke that we have a Bram Stoker collection with no reference to *Dracula*, except for letters of thanks from friends and associates for their copies of his book."

One such letter enthusiastically describes the effect the book had on them: "... there isn't a drop of blood in my body that doesn't feel as if it has been in a cold-storage closet." Sadly – because it has so many wonderful items, covering so many genres, to show off – the library has no plans to stage another Halloween exhibition. The collection was bequeathed to Leeds University in 1935 by Lord Brotherton of Wakefield, Yorkshire. An industrialist, he was a philanthropist of the first order and in 1927 he founded the venerable Brotherton Library at the University with a £100,000 donation.

FYFI: https://library.leeds.ac.uk/special-collections-explore/7381

LEHRER: the wonderful creative genius Tom Lehrer – he of the finest black humour/satirical/pithy song lyrics – gave Dracula a nod in 1972. Dracula appears at the end of the song *L-Y* which he wrote and sang for *The Electric Company*, an American children's TV show that ran from October 1971 to April 1977. It was aimed at "graduates" of *Sesame Street*. The song displayed all the ways "ly" can be used in a word. The song was not released on record until it showed up in 1990 as a bonus track on the CD of *Tom Lehrer Revisited*, then again, in 2010, on *The Tom Lehrer Collection*. The Dracula verse goes:

> *You enter a very dark room,*
> *And standing there in the gloom,*
> *Is DRACULA!*
> *Now how do you say goodbye?*
> *Immediately, Immediately,*
> *Immediate L-Y!*
> *Bye-Bye!*

FYFI: listen to the original, www.youtube.com/watch?v=dB2Ff8H7oVo

LENNOX: *Love Song for a Vampire* is a song composed and recorded by Scottish singer-songwriter Annie Lennox. It was recorded as the theme song to Francis Ford Coppola's 1992 film, *Bram Stoker's Dracula* (see COPPOLA). The song is used in the end credits of the film. The first two, of the seven, verses go:

> *Come into these arms again*
> *And lay your body down*
> *The rhythm of this trembling heart*

Is beating like a drum
It beats for you. it bleeds for you
It knows not how it sounds
For it is the drum of drums
It is the song of songs.

FYFI: to listen and buy, https://www.discogs.com/Annie-Lennox-Love-Song-For-A-%20Vampire-From-Bram-Stokers-Dracula/release/2925778

LIBRARY: amazingly, it wasn't until late 2018 that it was known Bram Stoker had consulted more books than he acknowledged in his research for *Dracula*. His omission only came to light when the London Library announced that it had suddenly discovered six books that Stoker had borrowed but never admitted using. In his notes he listed 34 books that helped him come to grips with the country (Romania) and the subject (vampires) he was writing about. His intensive work at the library came to light when staff realised that Stoker had committed the most heinous of library crimes – using pages, in borrowed books, as jotting pads. He made margin notes, underlined passages and turned down pages.

This discovery led to the Library – established in 1841 –staging its first play. It brought the villain, created within its eminent walls to "life" where it all began. In February 2019, the Creation Theatre of Oxford staged a month-long presentation of *Dracula* – with just two actors playing multiple roles and an innovative audio-visual aide providing a cyber Dracula. For the theatre company, which since 1997 has turned classic books into plays and staged them in unusual spaces (anywhere but in a theatre), it was the first time it had tackled *Dracula*.

FYFI: www.londonist.com/london/books-and-poetry/
london-library-discovers-bram-stoker-s-dracula-notes-
scribbled-in-margins-of-their-books

LITTLE: kids are entranced by *Little Dracula*, an eight-book series that personifies spooky silliness just for the sake of it. Written by Martin Waddell and illustrated by Joseph Wright, *Little Dracula* has youngsters in stitches as he goes bowling with skulls, eats a hearty breakfast of brains and has a glass of bedtime blood before going to sleep in his miniature coffin. *Little Dracula* also had a short life as an animated TV show. Made by Fox Family Channel, it enjoyed a short season in 1991, with an equally limited revival in 1999. See also: CHRISTMAS and WADDELL.

LIQUEUR: "Dracula's Blood" is a German-made schnapps. Ginger-based, it's laced with cherry. It's been produced by Alcomix Marken of Essen, since 1982. It's currently only available in Germany although the company is looking for an importer in the UK. The name came about very simply, says co-owner and general manager Fritz L Brüggemann. "It tastes like a vampire bite. First it is sweet, because of the cherry, and then comes a hard, sharp taste in the throat, because of the ginger."

FYFI: www.dracula.de and to buy, https://www.wine-searcher.com/find/dracula+original+liqueur+germany

LOLLIES: for Halloween 2013, Wall's (the British food company that's been making ice cream since 1922) brought back its "Dracula Lolly". It was similar to the original Wall's 1976 product but not as much fun. Like that one, it had a black cola coating and a blood-red strawberry filling inside vanilla ice cream, that changed the colour of your tongue. But, unlike the original (which was produced for several Halloweens), there was nothing special about the stick. Originally there were a host of different stencils on the stick, depicting bats, fangs, a droopy Dracula moustache, etc. Sadly Wall's has not brought it back at Halloween – or any other time – since.

FYFI: watch the TV advert for the 1981 version, https://www.youtube.com/watch?v=k05F76K4lEY

LUGOSI: Bela Lugosi immortalised the role of Dracula – both on stage and on the silver screen. He was born in 1882 in – can you believe it? – Transylvania. His home town was then part of the Austro-Hungarian Empire and was known as Lugos. Now that has a familiar ring? Lugosi's family name was Blasko but he adopted his stage name in honour of his birthplace. At the end of World War I it became part of Romania and the name changed to Lugoj. He once said: "I was born in almost the exact location of the Dracula story. I know that certain things which are looked upon as mere superstition are really based on fact."

At first Lugosi could barely speak English and learnt his lines phonetically. Before finding fame, via the 1931 Universal movie, he played the lead role in the first Broadway stage production of *Dracula*, in 1922. After each final curtain he would suddenly reappear to utter these words: "Just a moment ladies and gentlemen. Just a word before you leave. We hope the memories of Dracula won't give you bad dreams – so just a word of reassurance. When you go home tonight and the lights have been turned out and you are afraid to look behind the curtains and you dread to see a face appear at the window – why just pull yourself together. Remember, that after all, there are such things!"

Although Lugosi made scores of movies he is best remembered for his one-time-only Dracula role. But despite having played the role on stage he only got the film part because Lon Chaney Jnr (a Hollywood horror-movie fixture), who'd already been cast as Dracula, died suddenly, at age 47, of a throat hemorrhage, caused by complications from pneumonia.

Lugosi died in 1956, at age 74, from a heart attack. He was buried in full Dracula regalia, including the trademark black cape. In 1997, his Dracula role was further immortalised when the US postal service issued a commemorative stamp featuring Lugosi as his famed character.

FYFI: the movie is available as a DVD from Amazon; for a condensed version in the UK, https://vimeo.com/14517008 and for the trailer in the US, www.youtube.com/watch?v=wDg7Mjd3BXE

LUGOSI–2: a good indication of the massive impact Lugosi had on the genre are the prices paid for *Dracula* movie-memorabilia featuring him. An original poster for the 1931 *Dracula*, which shows a glowering Lugosi, sold for – wait for it – an unbelievable $528,800. That was in November 2017.

A couple of years later, in November 2019, what is known in the movie industry as a "lobby card", ie, a poster designed to be shown in the cinema foyer, usually near the ticket booth, went for $160,000. It showed Lugosi, with his Dracula cape wrapped around his co-star Helen Chandler, who played Mina. Universal Studios, who made the original 1931 *Dracula* movie, printed a very limited number of the promotional posters. Lugosi had retained one and it was kept in the family until it came on the market.

Both items were sold by Heritage Auctions at its Dallas, Texas, location. The auction house, which is the world's largest "collectibles" auctioneer, has salerooms around the world. Its London office is in Shepherd Market, Mayfair. Of the half-million-plus sale, the company's vintage poster specialist Grey Smith said: "Considering the sheer beauty of the poster and the timeless popularity of the film, it's not a surprise that the demand was so high." And of the other he pointed out: "We knew collectors were going to be excited by this particular piece. Not only is it of unquestionable rarity, the fact it came from Lugosi's private collection makes it a true piece of cinematic history."

LUGOSI-3: in a 2009 auction in California, the sale of a unique item also highlighted the massive interest in Lugosi. It was a plain visiting card that was hand-signed *Count Dracula*. Revealing the story behind the card, the anonymous seller said: "Lugosi was appearing at a theater in San Francisco, in the early 1930s, and I wrote to him care of the theater, and asked him to send me an autograph but to sign it 'Count Dracula'. About a week later I received the autograph in the mail." It sold for $4,250 – four times the estimated price.

LUGOSI-4: want to adopt the Dracula likeness of Bela Lugosi? Buy the officially licensed (by the Lugosi family)

$60 mask. The makers claim it is the most accurate one ever produced, saying: "It's an amazing replica of the one true Creature of the Night." One look at the latex, over the head, mask and it's a hard claim to dispute.

FYFI: to buy in the US, https://trickortreatstudios.com/bela-lugosi-dracula-mask.html; in the UK try eBay, search for "mask head Bela Lugosi Dracula".

LUNATIC: a certified lunatic is a major character in the book – ie, Renfield (see RENFIELD). Now there is *Lunatic*, a play based generally on the book but primarily on Renfield. It's the 2016 work of London-based American writer and director Whit Hertford, who is a leading figure in London's fringe theatre and initially shot to fame in 1993 as a child actor in *Jurassic Park*.

FYFI: https://vimeo.com/187577175

LYCEUM: in 1897, Bram Stoker gave a reading of a condensed *Dracula* as a play (see PLAY) at the Lyceum Theatre. It was an obvious choice as it was the "home" of Sir Henry Irving – the great British Victorian thespian, for whom Stoker was theatrical manager. Their relationship was not the easiest. Stoker was for ever trying to win the respect of his "master". He hoped *Dracula* – after a series of "went nowhere" short stories – would win him the respect and praise of the man he served and so admired. But Irving was not to be swayed by his "servant's" literary talent and callously dismissed the reading as "dreadful". But then Stoker, it is widely claimed, based the character of Dracula on Irving – inspired by his mannerisms and stature – so maybe that was the problem!

M

MAASAI: you don't have to be vampire to drink blood. The Maasai of Kenya and Tanzania include freshly drawn blood from cows in their daily diets. To get the blood, the jugular vein of the cow is nicked. No harm is done to the animal. Until recent times every young child and breastfeeding mother was given a daily ration of blood. Although the tradition of blood-drinking has declined it is still an important part of the Maasai diet and is believed to be a major reason – along with their other staples of milk and raw meat – why the Maasai are largely disease free. Frequently the blood is mixed with milk to provide a bloody but healthy milkshake.

MAMMOTH: For Dracula fans in particular and all-round vampire lovers in general, *The Mammoth Book of Dracula* is a must read. First published in 1997, the 520-page book with more than 30 short stories by a galaxy of well-known fantasy writers, has undergone several revisions since. Edited by British author Stephen Jones, one of the leading writers of the horror genre, it was last updated in 2017 under the title *In the Footsteps of Dracula*. All the stories have Dracula as the central character, as he traverses the world spreading his evil.

FYFI: for info on all the editions, www.stephenjoneseditor.com

MANUSCRIPT: the tale of the original *Dracula* manuscript is worthy of a book itself. To start at the end of the story, the manuscript belonged to a man who nobody, probably never in as many years as *Dracula* has been published, would guess was the owner. But being wealthy brings surprising, wonderful rewards. Paul Allen, co-founder of Microsoft (along with Bill Gates) bought the manuscript, in 2002, for £914,000. No further information about its whereabouts, or how it is used or stored, can be revealed. Sadly, in October 2018, Allen died, at the age of 65.

It is known that while under his ownership the manuscript was rarely shown or allowed to be used for research. But Leslie S Klinger got lucky. Allen allowed him a precious, hard-paced two days to study the 541-page typed manuscript. The result, in 2008, was *The New Annotated Dracula*. Among the dozens of academic tomes devoted to *Dracula* and Bram Stoker it still stands as one of the best and most insightful. But mystery surrounds the "lost" years of the manuscript. For that see PHILADELPHIA.

FYFI: https://lesliesklinger.com/books/the-new-annotated-dracula

MARKLE: yes, even she – ie, Meghan, aka Duchess of Sussex – has a *Dracula* connection! No, it's nothing to do with the way many Brits feel she's sucked precious lifeblood out of the Royal Family. So how, why? See PHILOSOPHICAL.

MAY: the month. It has a very special significance for *Dracula* enthusiasts. In 1897, on Tuesday the 18th, the world got its first hint of what was to come. Bram Stoker read extracts from his yet-to-be-published novel to an audience at the Lyceum Theatre (See LYCEUM), in London's West End. Then on the 26th it was published. See WORLD

McCALLUM: as in that wonderful Scottish actor, David McCallum. He's best remembered for his celebrated TV roles, first in the long-running series *The Man from U.N.C.L.E.*, which in one episode and in a novel based on the series, drew heavily on *Dracula*. Currently McCallum still makes guest appearances, as the medical examiner Ducky in the hit, *NCIS* (see UNCLE). But *The Man From U.N.C.L.E.* is not McCallum's only link to *Dracula*. In 1992 he narrated the novel for an audio-book, which is still available from The Book Depository or Amazon. And back in 1975, along with the late British-American actress Carole Shelley, he recorded an LP (ie, a vinyl long-player) of four scenes from the novel. It was later available as a cassette. Both are hard but not impossible to find. Search eBay or Amazon or by putting "David McCallum and Carole Shelley" into a search engine.

McKELLEN: why, oh why, has Ian McKellen (he of British thespian fame and a knight of the realm to boot) never reprised his Dracula role? Reprised? You mean he's already played him? Yes, not that you would have noticed unless you were a huge fan of *The Pet Shop Boys* (the Brit pop duo who dominated the charts in the late '80s and are still very much around) and took close note of the video that accompanied *Heart*, their number one hit. It was a song all about love and romance and marriage – and in a maniac twist the video featured a gnarled, poignant, pathetic Dracula seducing the bride at the altar. In a surprise – even shocking – move, McKellen was Dracula. And a knock-out one at that. Please Sir (Ian) some of us want more ...

FYFI: https://www.dailymotion.com/video/xy1g4u

McKELLEN–2: in February 2006, Sir Ian unveiled the plaque on the outside of the Lyceum Theatre (see LYCEUM) that commemorates the centenary of Sir Henry Irving's (see IRVING) death. The plaque also marks Bram Stoker's pivotal connection with both Irving and the theatre. It says: "... Whilst working at the Lyceum as Irving's acting manager, Bram Stoker wrote Dracula."

FYFI: to see the plaque, https://www.londonremembers.com/memorials/lyceum-theatre

MEAD: there's nothing sweet and palatable about Dracula but that hasn't stopped an American mead-maker calling its top seller "Dracula's Pie". The Dizzy Bee Mead Company of Chattanooga, Tennessee, specializes in traditional and experimental batches of the ancient, fermented honey-based tipple. Dracula's Pie is described as having: "Honey and Cherry sweetness on the nose and palate with notes of cinnamon & vanilla". One fan described it as: "16% cherry pie in a glass."

FYFI: https://untappd.com/DizzyBeeMeadCo

MEDAL: there are two Bram Stoker Medals. One is awarded by the Glasgow School of Art (see GLASGOW) and the other by the Philosophical Society of Trinity College, Dublin (see PHILOSOPHICAL).

MEDALLION: the one Bela Lugosi wore in the 1931 film *Dracula* marked him as an "aristocrat". It was worn as part of his formal evening attire as a "neck order" which, in the early 1900s, denoted rank, status and achievement, as it does today. A "neck order" is worn around the neck with evening dress, as opposed to a ribbon on the chest, which is traditionally worn with a uniform. Hollywood lore has it that Lugosi was buried with the medallion. But, if you've got $249 going spare, a replica is yours. Produced by Factory Entertainment – which specialises in reproducing movie props and ships overseas – it's a masterful copy (as it should be at that price) of the original. The design is a sunburst with six crescents and star finials.

FYFI: https://www.factoryent.com/Universal-Monsters-Dracula-Medallion-p/408177.htm

MICROSOFT: why shouldn't the humongous software company that dominates so many aspects of daily life have a *Dracula* connection? But its link is nothing to do with electronically accessing archives, cyber-probing museums or allowing *Dracula* fans around the world to communicate in seconds. It's all to do with the wealth generated for those behind the company. As in the late Paul Allen, co-founder of Microsoft. For his connection see MANUSCRIPT.

MIGNOLA: in 1992 the most successful spin-off from Francis Ford Coppola's *Bram Stoker's Dracula* was a comic-book version of the movie. It was the work of one of the leading exponents of the genre, Californian Mike Mignola.

This "treasure" was out of print for years but in late 2018, by massive popular demand, it was re-issued. "I cannot tell you what a relief it is to have this book back in print," said Mignola. "People have been asking about this one for ages – more than any other book of mine – and I honestly didn't think it was ever going to be possible to see an edition, but here it is."

His world-renowned, award-winning bibliography is enormous, with his creation *Hellboy* – the half-demon occult detective – being top of the list. His passion for things that go bump in the night, and worse, began as a young teen. His website reveals his "... fascination with ghosts and monsters began at an early age. But reading *Dracula* at age 12 introduced him to Folklore and Victorian Supernatural literature from which he has still never recovered."

FYFI: www.artofmikemignola.com

MILLER: Canadian Dr Elizabeth Miller is a leading *Dracula* expert. She started her academic, university teaching life specialising in Newfoundland literature at the province's Memorial University. But from 1990 she's concentrated on Bram Stoker and *Dracula* and has carved out a prized niche. Dr Miller, who lives in Toronto, travels throughout Canada, the USA and Europe, giving lectures and interviews and taking part in documentaries about *Dracula*, the meanings behind the work and the impact on society today.

Explaining her interest, Dr Miller, who is honoured with the title Professor Emerita at Memorial University, has said: "I am a scholar whose interest in Dracula is academic.

First and foremost there is the novel itself, one of the most influential books ever written. As a professor of literature, I am interested in how it came about, its author, and its aftermath as an influence on literature and popular culture. Another area in which I have done considerable research is the historical Dracula – Vlad Tepes – whose name Bram Stoker borrowed for his vampire Count. I am especially interested in the Romanian connection: how Romanians view the two Draculas and the contrast between Western and Romanian perceptions. While my focus is primarily on Dracula, this naturally expands to the vampire figure in general, including the vampires of folklore, vampires in literature, and vampires in popular culture."

Miller won the Lord Ruthven Award (see RUTHVEN) for *Dracula: Sense and Nonsense* (2006). The preface to the book says: "Literary sleuth Elizabeth Miller exposes popular misconceptions, distortions, and fabrications that have plagued our understanding of Stoker and his famous novel. Where is this nonsense coming from? This book will tell you."

FYFI: https://en.wikipedia.org/wiki/Elizabeth_Miller_(academic)

MILLION: it's no surprise that *Dracula* – with all the connections to the book and the main character – is a multi-million-dollar business. So, of course, there is a million dollar bill honouring him. Great fun to have a stash and hand them out – prankster-style – to fellow Dracula fans. They're produced by American Art Classics, the headquarters of novelty money which has over 35 categories of fun bills – from animals to zodiac signs – in its extensive repertoire. Frank Makan, President of AAC, introduced Dracula to the collection in 2012. It was an easy decision. "Who doesn't love Dracula and all that mystery that abounds?" he says. "We sell a ton, particularly around Halloween and whenever a new Dracula movie comes out."

FYFI: get your Drac-bills from Amazon (both sides of the pond) or order direct from: www.americanartclassics.com/index.php?p=catalog&mode=search&search_in=all&search_str=Dracula

MINNEAPOLIS: the lake-filled American state, that shares a border with Canada, hasn't really anything to do with *Dracula*. But it gets a mention (not just because the "lovely Gary" – see the dedication – was from there) but because Bram Stoker first travelled to the States, in October 1903, on board the *SS Minneapolis*. He made the transatlantic crossing in the company of his boss, Sir Henry Irving, the Victorian thespian, and 80 members of the Lyceum Theatre Company, which toured in the US several times. The British-built ship, launched in Belfast in 1900, was sunk during World War I when, en-route to Egypt, it was torpedoed by a German submarine.

MISTRESS: novels based on the original *Dracula* keep on coming. One of the latest (March 2017) is *Dracula's Mistress* by Carmen Stefanescu. As a Romanian, she has a head start in coming to grips with the vampire myths of Transylvania. "I was born in Romania, the native country of the infamous vampire Count Dracula, but where, for about 50 years of communist dictatorship, just speaking about God, faith, reincarnation or paranormal phenomena could have led someone to great trouble – the psychiatric hospital if not to prison. I survived the grim years of oppression by escaping in a parallel world, that of the books. I have dreamed all my life to become a writer, but many of the things I wrote during those years remained just drawer projects. The fall of the Ceausescu regime in 1989 and the opening of the country to the world meant a new beginning for me."

FYFI: www.goodreads.com/book/show/34608806

MOCKUMENTARY: in the movie *What We Do in the Shadows* – made as a spoof documentary – the *Dracula* saga is wonderfully mocked. Released early 2014, it did the rounds of film festivals around the world – including Sundance, Berlin and Toronto – before finally going on general release a year later. The movie revolves around four vampires who become housemates in Wellington, New Zealand. Written by New Zealanders Jemaine Clement and Taika Waititi, who also play lead roles, it gives a hilarious glimpse into the daily woes of the undead. Like all people living under the same roof they squabble about who does the washing-up, what they're going to have for dinner, despair where the rent's coming from, criticize what the others are wearing and argue about how to spend the evening. And, of course, all this is compounded by the fact they cannot go out of the house until it's dark. The *Guardian* proclaimed it "the best comedy of the year", while *The Telegraph* dubbed it: "desperately funny".

FYFI: watch the trailer, www.youtube.com/watch?v=Cv568AzZ-i8

MOCKUMENTARY-2: in 2019, *What We Do in the Shadows* (made by FX Networks in the US) debuted as a ten-part TV series on BBC-2. The setting was switched from New Zealand (see movie above) to Staten Island, New York. A second season started airing in June 2020 and a third season is in the can and scheduled for release Spring 2021. Announcing that the series would continue, FX's original programming President Nick Grad, said, "Week in and week out, the producers, writers and our amazing cast continue to make one of the funniest and best comedy series on TV."

MORPHING: start with a black beaker, add hot liquid and watch it morph into a likeness of Dracula, or something associated with the book. In the UK, the image that appears is the signature of Bram Stoker, author of *Dracula*. The beaker is – or was – on sale at The Whitby Museum.

FYFI: to check if it's still available, https://whitbymuseum.org.uk

MORPHING-2: thanks to Morph Costumes (on both sides of the pond), change your whole body into Dracula with a one-piece polyester and spandex suit, that includes the head.

FYFI: in the UK, www.morphsuits.co.uk/dracula-morphsuit; in the US, www.morphsuits.com/dracula-morphsuit-us

MUNCH: the legendary Norwegian artist Edvard Munch is, in popular terms, best known for *The Scream*. But one of his enduring paintings is *Vampire*, which he did in 1893.

The painting shows a flaming red-head with her face down into a man's neck. He is pressed against her breast. Munch, who died in 1944, aged 81, named the work *Love and Pain*. But some years later, at the urging of the well-known Polish novelist and poet, Stanislaw Przybyszewski, he changed the title to *Vampire*. In doing so Munch was falling in line with the Vampire trend and genre that was sweeping Europe with the publication of *Carmilla* by Sheridan Le Fanu in 1870 (see CARMILLA) and, of course, *Dracula* in 1897. And while the painting clearly depicts a woman dominating a submissive man, there might have been a more personal reason behind Przybyszewski's choice of name. It's believed the woman who modelled for the painting was the Norwegian writer Dagny Juel, who was Munch's lover before marrying Przybyszewski.

FYFI: https://www.edvardmunch.org/vampire.jsp

MUSEUM: there are several museums devoted to Dracula. There is one housed in a 1700s mansion in Bucharest, the capital of Romania. The museum – which unsurprisingly is called The Dracula Museum – has come up with an interesting concept. Its aim is to present the story of the two Draculas: the historical one, Prince Vlad Dracula of Wallachia, aka the Impaler, and his Gothic alter ego, Count Dracula. The website says: "Our goal is to bring our cultural and historical project to life, by mobilizing financial resources, materials, and volunteers, in order to open a museum dedicated to the history of Dracula from a double perspective, both as a historical character (Vlad III Dracula, a.k.a. Vlad the Impaler, the ruthless 15th century Prince of Wallachia, present Romania) and the Gothic myth of Dracula (directly derived from the real-life Vlad Dracula), as featured in films and literature."

The museum, which opened in August 2019, was founded by the Ordo Draconum Foundation, a group of Romanian history enthusiasts. It was closed over the following winter for extensive restoration work to the historic building. Just as it was about to re-open it was hit by the global coronavirus lockdown but was finally back in business in time to celebrate its first anniversary.

Dr Marius Vasile, the museum's manager, hopes that Dracula fans from around the world put it on their Romanian "to do" list. Particularly those from Britain. As he says: "The gothic myth of Count Dracula, the vampire, inspired from the real-life one, is a genuine part of the British culture."

FYFI: https://www.dracula-museum.com

MUSEUM-2: Dublin, Bram Stoker's birthplace, has what is claimed to be the biggest and the best. It's part of Castle Dracula (see CASTLE-4) and tracks Bram Stoker's life with an eclectic collection of memorabilia, much of it unique and exclusive to the museum. Among the items is a gold pendant that holds a lock of Stoker's hair. It was cut while he was on his death-bed by his wife Florence. It was donated to the museum by Stoker's great-grandson, Noel Dobbs, who along with Stoker's great-grand-nephew Dacre Stoker, has visited the museum.

MUSEUM-3: once-upon-a-time there was The Dracula Museum in Germany. It was only around for four years before, sadly, closing in 2007. But it's still going – sort of – on Facebook. During its short existence it was, first of all, inside a part of the Castle of Laubach in Hesse. The museum attracted visitors from all over the world. One of the most prominent was *Dracula* expert, Professor J Gordon Melton – author of the monumental *The Vampire Book: The Encyclopedia of the Undead* (see ENCYCLOPEDIA). When the Count zu Solms-Laubach needed the rooms back, the museum relocated four miles away to Buseck, where it stayed for another year before closing for good.

FYFI: https://www.facebook.com/The-Dracula-Museum-110889415608130 and https://www.youtube.com/watch?v=v_M2JHyCjfc

MUSIC: *Hand Drawn Dracula* is a leading independent record label. The Toronto-based outfit got its catchy name when founder James Meja was travelling with a friend, in 2007, to watch a band in Montreal. Telling the tale behind the name he says: "On the drive he complained about the trend of indie album artwork being all badly hand-drawn. 'Hand-drawn birds, hand-drawn flowers, hand-drawn Draculas, etc', he moaned. For some reason I stopped him mid-tangent and said that when, if ever, I started a label of my own I would call it *Hand Drawn Dracula*. I liked how it sounded. The name seemed to pretty much encompass a lot of what I'm drawn to as an artist and as a fan. It also had the potential for a branding that I found interesting." A year later, when Meja started his company, he recalled what he'd said and fulfilled the pledge. And his choice of name has never let him down. It's a constant source of interest – backed up by bands of interest.

FYFI: www.handdrawndracula.com

MUSICAL: In 2001, *Dracula, the Musical* premiered in La Jolla, California. The work of a trio of award-winning, international talent – score by American Frank Wildhorn, lyrics by Brits Don Black and Christopher Hampton – it should have been a resounding success. But it took some time to make its mark, and then not in any flash-bang-wallop way. After many revisions it opened on Broadway in 2004. With a lacklustre welcome from critics it only lasted 157 performances. But, after more revisions and reworking it's done much better outside the US. It was first seen in St Gallen, Switzerland, in 2005, followed by a season in Graz, Austria. But it was not produced in Britain until 2010 and then only in Lancashire, first in Lytham St Annes, then Lancaster. However, on mainland Europe it's always being staged somewhere. And since 2010 it has been in the repertoire of Theatre Dzep in Novi Sad, Serbia.

FYFI: to obtain the licence to stage it, https://www.mtishows.com/dracula-the-musical; download the soundtrack, https://globalvisionrecords.com

MUSICAL-2: in 2006 a French–Canadian musical – *Dracula: Entre L'amour Et La Mort* (Dracula: Between Love and Death) was staged in Montreal, starring its creator, Quebec singer Bruno Pelletier. It ran for a year. In 2008 it was revived at the Maison de la Danse in Lyon, France, and the DVD was released.

FYFI: to buy, https://www.discogs.com/sell/list?artist_id=1263331&ev=ab&q=Dracula%3A+Entre+L%27amour+et+la+Mort

MUSICAL-3: another one with a similar title is *Dracula, L'amour plus fort que la mort* (Dracula: Love Stronger than Death), produced by French choreographer Kamel Ouali. It was his debut production and was first performed on 30 September 2011 at the Palais des Sports de Paris and continued until 1 January 2012. A filmed version of the work was also shown on widescreens throughout France between 20 and 22 July 2012.

FYFI: www.youtube.com/watch?v=Yl6o0QTy8EU

MUSICAL-4: and yet another simply called *Dracula*. Written and scored by the late, prolific Czech composer, Karel Svoboda. It had its world premiere in 1995 in Prague and has been staged, mainly throughout Europe, many times since.

FYFI: to hear extracts, to get detailed information about tracks, and to buy, www.discogs.com/Karel-Svoboda-Zden%C4%9Bk-Borovec-Richard-Hes-Dracula-Komplet/release/5106671

MUSICAL-5: yet again, exactly the same title as the first one but this time with a colon, ie, *Dracula: the Musical*. A 2010 Swedish production, it pretty much follows the plot of the novel. It had a very limited run in Stockholm but a video – now out of print – was made by splicing together extracts from three live performances.

MUSICAL-6: another *Dracula the Musical* (this one without any punctuation) was staged in the run up to Halloween 2015, by the Dallas Theater Company. It was a spoof on the novel, described as an "unparalleled romp" from start to finish.

MUSICAL-7: and yet another variation on exactly the same theme. Only this time *Dracula – The Musical* is separated from the others by including a hyphen in its name. Sadly it is only a soundtrack – recorded in 2007 – starring the great Irish singing star Michael McCarthy, known around the world for his role as Javert in *Les Miserables*. The Welsh duo, composer Christopher J Orton and lyricist Gareth Evans, have long planned to bring their version of a musical *Dracula* to the stage. But the fans are still waiting!

FYFI: buy the soundtrack,
https://www.amazon.co.uk/gp/product/B000T5MX9W?
and https://www.amazon.com/Dracula/dp/B000T5MX9W

MUSICAL-8: finally one based on the 1922 silent movie, *Nosferatus*. The work of author and composer Bernard J Taylor, who has converted dozens of classicals – eg, *Wuthering Heights*, *The Pirates of Penzance*, *A Christmas Carol*, *Pride and Prejudice,* etc – into musicals, *Nosferatu the Musical* was premiered at the Madison Theatre, Peoria, Illinois, USA, in September 1995. It had its first European staging a month later in Eastbourne. The work has been translated into German, Spanish and Hungarian.

FYFI: to listen to an extract, www.youtube.com/watch?v=IsYWmV2xYU4; buy the CD from Amazon.

N

NARVA: the Baltic port from which the *Dmitry* (the cargo ship that ran aground in Whitby harbour in 1885 and inspired Stoker to write *Dracula*) sailed. In the book, Stoker changed the name of the home port to Varna and the name of the ship to *Demeter*. When Stoker penned the book, Narva/Varna was in Russia. It's now a part of Estonia. Just. It sits on the border between the two countries. Amazingly, in response to an e-mail, the Narva Tourist Information Centre revealed they had no clue about its city's connection to *Dracula*, the novel. That should change now!

NEVER: Bram Stoker never went to Romania. Although the country, particularly Transylvania, is described in meticulous detail, all his research was via books. See GERARD, ONWARD, SAMUELSON, WILKINSON.

NEWMAN: for author and broadcaster Kim Newman's links to *Dracula* see: QUEEN.

NIELSEN: *Airplane!* (1980) was not Canadian film star Leslie Nielson's only spoof movie. In 1995 he starred in *Dracula: Dead and Loving It*. Written and directed by the legendary Mel Brooks it was a parody on the novel. Unlike award-winning *Airplane!* it was greeted with a widespread thumbs down by the critics and was pretty much a total flop.

FYFI: to watch it online, https://bflix.to/film/dracula-dead-and-loving-it-m2v2x

NILSSON: the late American singer, song-writer Harry Nilsson caught *Dracula* fever. See FILMS–4.

NOSFERATU: this is the film that the law tried to get rid of. But happily the bid to confine it to the rubbish bin failed – and now it's in the top ten of cult movies. Made in 1922, it's hailed as the first movie based on *Dracula* but in fact there was an earlier one called *Drakula Halala* (see FIRST–2). *Nosferatu – A Symphony of Horror* was made by the silent-movie master German F W Murnau and starred famed German actor Max Shrek as Count Orlock – who differed from the now popular image of Dracula in that he was repulsive, charmless and killed his victims.

The widow of Bram Stoker – *Dracula's* creator – was so angry at the way Murnau plagiarized her husband's novel that she sued. All copies were ordered destroyed. But a copy sent to America survived. Now it's shown, all over the world, regularly.

The late, legendary American film critic Roger Ebert included it in his *Great Movie List*. In his 1979 review he said: "To watch 'Nosferatu' is to see the vampire movie before it had really seen itself. Here is the story of Dracula before it was buried alive in clichés, jokes, TV skits, cartoons and other films. The film is in awe of its material. It seems to really believe in vampires ... And 'Nosferatu' is more effective for being silent. It is commonplace to say that silent films are more 'dreamlike' but what does that mean? In 'Nosferatu' it means that the characters are confronted with alarming images and denied the freedom to talk them away. There is no repartee in nightmares. Human speech dissipates the shadows and makes a room seem normal. Those things that live only at night do not need to talk, for their victims are asleep, waiting."

FYFI: to check if and where it's being screened in the UK, www.britinfo.net/cinema (put in "London" for location and anywhere being shown in UK will come up); in the US it's screened, every Halloween, at the American Film Institute in the Washington, DC, suburb of Silver Spring, Maryland. And to read Ebert's thoughts on it, www.rogerebert.com/reviews/great-movie-nosferatu-1922

NOSFERATU-2: in 1979 there was a remake of the 1922 film – again a German production. *Nosferatu the Vampyre* was directed by Werner Herzog and starred Klaus Kinski. Herzog made the film as a tribute to F W Murnau, saying that *Nosferatu* (see previous entry) was the greatest film to ever come out of Germany. Unlike its predecessor it was not restricted by copyright so the names of the major characters could be used. Filmed in the Baltic Sea city of Wismar and in Transylvania, it was a critical success and also (like its predecessor) made Roger Ebert's *Great Movie List*. In his review he said: "*Nosferatu the Vampyre* cannot be confined to the category of 'horror film'. It is about dread itself, and how easily the unwary can fall into evil. Here is a film that does honor to the seriousness of vampires. No, I don't believe in them. But if they were real, here is how they must look."

FYFI: to read his review in full, www.rogerebert.com/reviews/great-movie-nosferatu-the-vampyre-1979; to buy www.vermontmoviestore.com/products/nosferatu

NOSFERATU-3: in 2017, the stunning animated film *NYsferatu* was released. Based on *Nosferatu* (see previous entries) it has the subtitle of: *Classic Tale, New Interpretation*. Set in present day New York City, *NYsferatu* turns the original film on its head, and uses it as a dramatic metaphor for what is happening to society as it struggles to cope with strangers in our midst. In *Nosferatu,* the vampire character arrives in town and wreaks death and destruction. In the Big Apple, he is the ultimate outsider – a migrant, escaping from a war-torn country only to be confronted with all the modern-day fears that are so often whipped up by refugees and asylum seekers.

The roto-scoped film, which comprises 35,000 hand-drawn images, replicates the eerie, flickering shutter effect of the silent movie era and is the work of Italian-American multimedia artist, Andrea Mastrovita. It's accompanied by a specially commissioned musical score. During the summer and autumn of 2017 it was shown on multiple occasions at public screenings in various venues all over New York City. Since then it's been seen in Rome, Switzerland and Germany. And in October 2018 it was a major attraction at the annual Bram Stoker Festival (see FESTIVAL) in Dublin.

FYFI: www.nysferatu.org

NOSFERATU-4: an opera and two musicals have also been based on the film, see MUSICAL–8 and OPERA–3.

NOSTRUM: is an old name for a questionable patent medicine – of which there were many in Victorian days, the era of the novel. In a brief moment of sanity, the spider/

fly-eating lunatic Renfield recalls his thwarted attempt to kill Dr Seward in a bid to consume his blood and so be revitalised. He cites the Biblical phrase "For the blood is the life" for his grisly goal. Then adds: "Though, indeed, the vendor of a certain nostrum has vulgarized the truism to the very point of contempt." With that comment, Stoker is drawing attention to a very popular nostrum of the day – "Clarke's World-Famed Blood Mixture". In its advertising it claimed: "For the blood is the life".

FYFI: http://thequackdoctor.com/index.php/for-the-blood-is-the-life

NOT: if you didn't know about *Dracula* and its Whitby connection before you picked-up this book, don't worry. You're not alone. Actor Ralf Little – of *The Royle Family* TV fame and now back in British living rooms with his lead role as the inspector in *Death in Paradise* – has admitted that he had no clue until filming in Whitby. In 2019 he teamed up with Ricky Tomlinson, his *Royle Family* dad, to go touring in a camper van to make the six-part TV series, *Ricky and Ralf's Very Northern Road Trip*.

As they travelled the length and breadth of Lancashire, Yorkshire and the Lake District, the Lancastrian duo hit places and sights, known and unknown to them. And a highlight of their very funny – and informative – "staycation" was their stopover in Whitby.

Afterwards Ralf, who grew up in Ramsbottom on the edge of the Pennines, revealed: "I'm a little embarrassed to admit it but I only learnt on this trip that *Dracula* was partly inspired by Whitby Abbey. I think I went to the town once, as a boy, and had fish and chips. That is my only memory of it – no recollection of Dracula at all."

FYFI: the show aired in May 2020 on Gold UK. To see the pair in Whitby, https://gold.uktv.co.uk/ricky-ralfs-very-northern-road-trip/article/about-ricky-ralfs-very-northern-road-trip

NOVELS: apart from *Dracula*, Bram Stoker wrote 12 novels, four published before the one he's remembered for. His first book was the first in his three collections of short stories. Published in 1881, it was *Under the Sunset*. It could not have been any more different from *Dracula*. The eight stories were fairytales for children!

FYFI: https://www.goodreads.com/book/show/782552

NOVELS - 2: there's a slew of fiction out there, all invoking *Dracula* or using the original story to new ends. There's a fulsome list, compiled by *Goodreads*, amounting to 157 titles.

FYFI: www.goodreads.com/list/show/11284.Best_Books_Featuring_Dracula

NOVEMBER: how about this for an eerie coincidence. November 8th is the birthday not only of Bram Stoker but Vlad the Impaler on whom Dracula is based. Serendipity at its best! Though at the risk of spoiling a good story, I have to point out that most biographies, references, etc, only say that Vlad was born in November. I guess records were not that well kept in 1476. But, according to *OnThisDay.com* there is no doubt. It states unequivocally that he was born on the 8th.

OBITUARY: in this day and age its hard to understand ... but when Bram Stoker died on April 20th 1912, the many obituaries barely mentioned *Dracula*. If at all. It had been published 15 years earlier. The report of his death in the *London Evening Standard* was typical. On page eight of its April 23rd edition, it devoted just 19 lines, at the bottom of a page, to Stoker's death. It started: "The death is announced of Mr Bram Stoker, who was for 30 years intimately connected with Sir Henry Irving. Mr Stoker, who was an invalid for six years, was in his 65th year. Born in Dublin and educated at Trinity College, he was for some years in the Irish Civil Service as Inspector of Petty Sessions. In 1876 he met Sir Henry Irving and two years later became his manager and confidential secretary ..." It ended with: "Mr Stoker wrote the biography of Sir Henry Irving on the death of the latter, and for a time devoted himself to fiction, producing several novels."

The *London Daily News* (which closed in 1930) also concentrated on Irving, with a headline that read: "Sir Henry Irving's Friend and Manager". After detailing Stoker's involvement with the great thespian it did find space to mention several of his novels by name, including *Dracula*, adding: "They introduce weird improbabilities and are particularly lurid."

O'CONNOR: in his highly acclaimed, 2019 book *Shadowplay*, award-winning novelist Joseph O'Connor paid tribute to his fellow Irishman, Bram Stoker. In a gripping read, he uses the real-life stories of three famed Victorians to weave an ingenious yarn that provides luring insights into the "birth" of Dracula. The trio is Henry Irving and Ellen Terry, the leading thespians of those days, along with Bram Stoker, who was Irving's personal assistant and manager of his London theatre, the Lyceum (see LYCEUM).

As the preface to *Shadowplay* says: "In 1878 three extraordinary people start their life together, a life that will be full of drama, transformation, passionate and painful devotion to art and to one another. Henry Irving is the volcanic leading man and impresario; Ellen Terry is the most lauded and desired actress of her generation, outspoken and generous of heart; and ever following along behind them in the shadows is the unremarkable theatre manager, Bram Stoker. Fresh from life in Dublin as a clerk, Bram may seem the least colourful of the trio but he is wrestling with dark demons in a new city, in a new marriage, and with his own literary aspirations. As he walks the London streets at night, streets haunted by Jack the Ripper and the gossip which swirls around his friend Oscar Wilde, he finds new inspiration. But Irving is determined that nothing will get in the way of his manager's devotion to the Lyceum and to himself. And both men are enchanted by the beauty and boldness of the elusive Ellen. This exceptional novel explores the complexities of love that stands dangerously outside social convention, the restlessness of creativity, and the experiences that led to *Dracula*, the most iconic supernatural tale of all time."

On publication of *Shadowplay*, O'Connor (who by the way is the brother of Sinead) talked about Bram Stoker's influence. He told *The Irish Times*: "Bram Stoker has been with me from when I was six or seven. He is the first Irish author I ever heard of, the first Irish author I loved ... the first fiction I tried to write was influenced by Stoker, very Gothic. I love Dracula ... one of the really striking things about it is its modernity. Dracula includes telephones, sound recordings, blood transfusions, women's magazines, you can see Stoker trying to make it as up-to-date as possible. It's so brilliant that he sets the vampire in the world of the reader. We often think mistakenly that it is set in Transylvania but most of it is set in England. It's marvellous how Stoker teaches you to vary the texture. It doesn't have to be one authorial voice, you can have newspaper articles, ballads, songs, diaries. Stoker taught me that the music of a novel is as important as the plot. It should be like a concert, some moments are guitar solos, some are silence, some should be a symphony but use them all. Hence the title, it's more about what's happening in the shadows, not the limelight."

FYFI: goodreads.com/book/show/41723505

OLDMAN: another one-time-only Dracula was Gary Oldman. *Dracula* movie expert Charles E Butler (see FILMS–2) pulled no punches about what he thought of the performance of the British actor in the 1992 Francis Ford Coppola's *Bram Stoker's Dracula*. Butler says, in his book *The Romance of Dracula: A Personal Journey of the Count on Celluloid*, published 2010: "... not the best Count Dracula ... his bravely attempted Dracula is tucked away as a lucrative but painful memory ..."

But despite that, Oldman's performance went down well with the Academy of Science Fiction, Fantasy and Horror Films (who knew) who gave him the best-actor nod. He also, along with Winona Ryder who played Mina, won the "best kiss" in the MTV (Movie and TV) Awards.

OLIVIER: even the greatest thespians have made their mark via *Dracula*. Sir Laurence Olivier played Van Helsing, the Dutch vampire-catcher, in the 1979 film *Dracula*, alongside another great veteran actor, Donald Pleasence, who was Dr Seward and a newcomer to movies, Trevor Eve, who went onto international fame for *Waking the Dead*. He played Jonathan Harker. The star role of The Count was played by Frank Langella (see LANGELLA).

OPERATION: not surgical but military. In May 1945, *Operation Dracula* was launched – by British and Indian forces – to push the Japanese invaders out of Rangoon (now known as Yangon). A pivotal part of World War II's famous Burma (now known as Myanmar) Campaign, it was an airborne and amphibious attack, ordered by Louis Mountbatten, then Supreme Allied Commander South-East Asian Command, and led by the legendary Field Marshal William Slim. So what is the backstory to why the mission was given the Dracula moniker? In the absence of a response to repeated requests for information from the Imperial War Museum and Department of War Studies, King's College, London, it would seem safe to assume it was because all the action was carried out under the cover of darkness. But not so. It took place in daylight.

FYFI: to see the *Pathe News* coverage go to, www.facebook.com/BECFFESEA19371946/videos/2263381780396466

OPERATION-2: no surprise here … there is an *Operation Dracula* video game. It's got "gold award" status from *Pocket Gamer*, the world's leading website for mobile, handheld, portable games and is considered a number one player in the shump (shoot 'em up) genre.

FYFI: to buy it, https://apps.apple.com/us/app/operation-dracula/id980540474, to see a clip, https://www.youtube.com/watch?v=OI82RgwS2So

ORANGES: if you're in Australia or America keep an eye out for "Dracula Blood Oranges". They're marketed under the Dracula moniker, in eye-catching black and red boxes, and mesh bags, with a cartoon Dracula sinking his fangs into a sliced orange in a bid to grab attention. They are the product of Pinnacle Fresh, an Australian fruit company, based in Melbourne, that now has an office in Kingsburg, California. The company turned to Dracula to boost sales – not just because they were "blood" oranges – but research revealed that blood oranges are a high-antioxidant fruit and have the capacity to boost metabolism, improve the immune system, stimulate collagen and act as a natural anti-inflammatory. Sounds like useful protection from the harm inflicted by any vampire!

FYFI: http://www.pinnaclefresh.com.au

ORCHIDS: there are 118 orchids which carry the name "Dracula"! How did such a beautiful, evocative bloom end up with a name that translates to such gore and horror? The name was acquired in 1978 when they were separated from the large orchid group, *Masdevallia*. The Dracula Orchids – which are native to Central America and the north-west Andes – did not acquire their name, as might be assumed, because the orchids all sport a slash of red. Which they don't. No, it's because the positioning of the triangle petals and the downward-looking flower give the appearance of a flying bat. And the appearance reason is compounded by the way Dracula Orchids masquerade as mushrooms – and so lure flies. Bit like Dracula posing as a suave lover and drawing young beauties into his clutches.

FYFI: an easy way of buying a Dracula Orchid is from eBay, both UK and US sites. They have dozens on offer. To see 47 of them, in glorious colour, www.pbase.com/glazemaker/dracula

ORCHIDS-2: if you're in, or visit, San Francisco, see as many as a dozen or so Dracula Orchids in their decadent beauty in the Conservatory of Flowers in the Golden Gate Park (see BALLS).

OREO: in 2013 a cheery cartoon image of Dracula was used to promote the sale of America's favourite cookie, the Oreo. To a jaunty tune, the jingle ponders the question, what would happen if a vampire was given an Oreo. "Would he act less undead? Would he thirst for milk instead?" The famed Oreo is two chocolate biscuits sandwiched together with a white cream filling. It's been a pantry staple in the US since 1912. It was finally made available in the UK in 2008 and since 2013 has been made in Sheffield.

FYFI: to see the TV ad, www.youtube.com/watch?v=43YAc20tAog

ONESIE: deck the babe at Halloween – or any time of year – in a Dracula onesie. There are dozens out there, many of the best on Etsy, the global site for hand-crafted goods. A favourite is the one emblazoned with a cartoon-like Dracula – black and scarlet cloak spread aloft – with the moniker "Handsome Devil". Pair with that other baby essential, referenced in entry DUMMY.

FYFI: for the "Handsome Devil", https://www.etsy.com/listing/556663261/handsome-devil-dracula-onesie-funny?ref=hp_rv-1&pro=1

ONWARD: as in *Onward Christian Soldiers*. What on earth could this iconic hymn have to do with Dracula? Well, frankly, nothing. Except the man who wrote it has. He was the Rev Sabine Baring-Gould, who apart from being a vicar was a prolific author. Among his most popular works was *The Book of Werewolves*, which documented the ghoulish lust for blood across the ages, from Medieval to Victorian times. Published in 1865 – 12 years before *Dracula* – Bram Stoker acknowledged, in notes attached to the original manuscript, consulting Baring-Gould's werewolf book when he was researching *Dracula*. While Dracula was not portrayed as a werewolf (which also survives on blood) there are constant references to wolves, as in the wolves are "children of the night" and the way Dracula is described, early in the novel, as having pointed ears, hairy palms and nails sharpened to a point.

FYFI: search AbeBooks.com

OPERA: in October 2000, an operatic version of *Dracula* premiered at the Lancaster Opera House, in New York state. By composer Paul Ziemba (see ZIEMBA), the score includes a waltz, a polonaise, a mazurka, several romantic arias and a lively gypsy number.

OPERA-2: in late 2005, the opera *Drácula*, by the Colombian composer Héctor Fabio Torres Cardona, opened in Manizales, Colombia.

FYFI: https://www.youtube.com/watch?v=_iW95dE_8XM

OPERA-3: there have been two operas based on the 1922 silent movie, *Nosferatus*. First was the 1993 Canadian Opera Company's production by Canadian composer Randolph Peters. In 2004, the Rimrock Opera Foundation, of Billings, Montana, staged the world premiere of the version by Americans Dana Gioia, composer, and Alva Henderson, librettist. It was performed again in 2018.

FYFI: to buy the CD or MP3 of the latter go to Amazon.

ORIGINALLY: Stoker's original manuscript ran to 529 pages – and was named *The Undead*. The title was switched to *Dracula* at the very last moment – just as it went to the printer. And the manuscript was reduced to 491 pages.

P

PACIFIER: for the Dracula link to that American thing designed to soothe babies see DUMMY.

PALANCE: probably the last name to fall off the lips when thinking of film actors who have played Dracula is that of Jack Palance, who had the lead role in the 1973 TV movie Dracula. But note well, the *Dracula* movie afficionado Charles E Butler (see FILMS–2) has no doubt that Palance turned in the best of the Dracula performances. He says: "He won hands down ... only Jack Palance has been able to imbue the Count with the required menace of Stoker's imagination ..." Palance, who died in 2006, aged 87, said he was glad when filming was finally over. He said that as a method actor he felt he was "becoming more Dracula" than he wanted. And despite several more offers to play The Count in subsequent movies he always declined.

FYFI: to buy in the UK, go to Amazon; in the US, go to Vudo, https://www.vudu.com/content/movies/details/Dracula/27732

PANTOMIME: of course there's a pantomime! The script is available from Limelight Scripts, the Sheffield-based outfit that supplies panto scripts to professional and amateur theatrical companies all over the world. *Dracula the Panto* is described thus: "... traditional British pantomime, incorporating visual comedy, slapstick and audience participation ..." And the synopsis reads: "Count Dracula arrives in England in search of the key to his hoard of stolen treasure. Assuming the guise of property tycoon Major Artery, he crosses paths with Duffy the Vampire-slayer, whose mother rents a house from him. Dracula escapes back to Transylvania, but is pursued by Duffy, who in turn is followed by her mother, Dame Plasma. A terrific gothic-style panto, which contains all the elements needed to keep your audience spellbound. Suspense, mock horror and heaps of tongue-in-cheek humour."

FYFI: www.limelightscripts.co.uk/product/dracula-the-panto-perusal

PARKING: there's no end to the ways in which Dracula is used. To mark Halloween 2014, Tesco (the giant British supermarket) reserved a parking spot for The Count at its store in Wembley, London. They painted a cartoon-like Dracula in a space. And they used glow paint – so customers got quite a fright once darkness descended. But there was also a real purpose among the fun. Because of the glow paint, customers had no problem in knowing which way the store's entrance was. Dracula's illuminated left hand pointed them in the right direction.

FYFI: https://www.mylondon.news/news/local-news/dracula-parking-spot-wembley-tesco-8017797

PARKING-2: fancy a "Dracula Parking Only" sign? For $20 you can get one from Monsters in Motion. It's made from weatherproof aluminum, with an antiqued finish, thanks to the simulated rusted edges and faded paint. It carries the message, to non-Dracula parkers: "All Others Will Be Bitten and Drained". If you're anywhere near Placentia, California – 30 miles south of Los Angeles – pick one up from the MiM bricks and mortar shop. But not to worry, wherever you live, you can get one. MiM ships worldwide.

FYFI: https://www.monstersinmotion.com/cart/item-list-d-c-303_315/dracula-parking-only-metal-sign-9-x-12-p-25967.html

PARROT: on the basis there are so many animals called "Dracula" because of bodily features that remind people of our man, it's hardly surprising that there is a "Dracula parrot". It's only found in the cloud forests of New Guinea, where its main diet is figs. It got its name because of its brilliant red plumage – which stands out against its dark-grey body and makes it a target for poachers. Hence the dangerously low numbers.

FYFI: https://allthatsinteresting.com/dracula-parrot

PEN: in December 2012, a collectors' pen was created – by the globally famed pen designers, ACME – to commemorate the 100th anniversary of Bram Stoker's death. It was commissioned by the Bram Stoker Estate. The fountain pen, uniquely, converts to a roller-ball. It comes in a satin-lined coffin-box, enclosed in what appears to be a bound copy of the novel, along with a bottle of specially formulated red ink and a refill for the roller-ball. And when the coffin is opened, the haunting tones of Bach's *Fugue in D Minor* play. The pen is decorated with a blood-red-on-black Dracula logo on the cap and dribbling "blood" on the barrel. Only 999 were produced and, yes, there are some still left for sale – for £400.00 and upwards.

The limited-edition number is stamped in gold on the end of the cap. Next to it is Bram Stoker's signature replicated in gold. All-in-all a stunning piece of Gothic-looking, functional, memorable art. The logo was designed by award-winning American Michael Doret, who is world renowned for his artistic lettering and illustrative talents. He described his Dracula pen work as "decayed elegance". ACME – based in Hawaii – was founded, and is operated by husband and wife, American Adrian Olabuenaga and New Zealander Lesley Bailey. At the launch of the Dracula pen they said: "We are so thrilled and honored to translate Bram Stoker's classic tale into a limited-edition pen for our collection."

FYFI: to buy a pen in the UK search eBay; in the US go to Fahrney's, Washington, DC's legendary pen shop, https://www.fahrneyspens.com/Item--i-16289;

to get details of Michael Doret's Dracula design process, www.michaeldoret.com/blog/2412; to see a beautifully captivating video of the pen, http://youtu.be/TfCj-tkpVlA

PEN-2: another customised Dracula pen is not as dramatic as the one above but just as appealing. It's made from wood reclaimed from Whitby's famed 17th-century church, St Mary's – which figures heavily in the novel. Manufactured by the family-run firm of York and Beyond, the £44 fountain pen comes with a certificate of authenticity signed by the rector of the church and a 32-page booklet about Whitby's connection to the novel.

FYFI: to buy, www.yorkandbeyond.com

PENCE: the current (as of 2020) vice president of America, Mike Pence, has been likened to Dracula. At an infamous – off-the-wall – December 2018 White House meeting between the Democratic leaders in Congress, Nancy Pelosi and Charles Schumer, Pence just sat there not saying a word, not making any movement of any sort, bar the occasional blinking. His bizarre behaviour was pilloried and made fun of. The best line came from The Pittsburgh Courier. In an editorial it said: "Was that the vice president sitting there? Or was it someone auditioning for the role of Dracula? My god man, get some sun. And open your mouth every now and then."

PENGUIN: no, not the animal but the publisher. For true *Dracula* fans, there is no finer edition of the book than the 2003 edition put out by Penguin Classics. It's jammed with much more than the book itself. It has an introduction, with very illuminating notes by Maurice Hindle and a preface by Sir Christopher Frayling. The former is renowned as one of Britain's foremost authorities on Gothic writings, Shakespeare and John Lennon (who he met as a student). The latter has held many positions within the arts and is the author of *Vampyres: Lord Byron to Dracula* (1992). The Penguin edition has a lot of information about Dracula and other works by Stoker that throw a revealing spotlight on Stoker the man. Namely, the correspondence between Bram Stoker and the legendary American poet Walt Whitman; the published interview Stoker conducted with a young Winston Churchill; the article Stoker wrote on *The Censorship of Fiction*; the account of the Stoker family's ordeal with the Irish outbreak of cholera in 1875, detailed by his mother Charlotte in a letter to Stoker, then safely living in London; and a chronology of Stoker's life.

FYFI: to find a copy go to AbeBooks.com and search "Dracula (Penguin Classics)".

PEPPERS: as the selling slogan goes: "Beware – they have a big bite ..." "Count Dracula Peppers" got their name because, unlike all other peppers, they are not red, green or orange. They have jet-black leaves and flowers that start out purple, then turn black before finally ripening into deep blood-coloured fruit. On the Scoville Scale (ie, the measurement of spicy heat) they rate 25,000 – which sounds mighty hot but in fact is in the mid-range, the same category as Tabasco. A great use for them is to add "grim" colour to dips/chili, etc.

FYFI: https://www.pepperscale.com/count-dracula-pepper; although not available from every garden centre or nursery, an internet search will throw up suppliers.

PERSONALISED: fancy starring as a character in the novel? Easily done. Just contact U Star Novels and pick who you want to be. The British-based company will then print a special copy with your name in place of the chosen character. There are six principals to chose from – Dracula, Jonathan Harker, Professor Van Helsing, Mina Murray, Lucy Westenra and Dr John Seward – so you can include family and friends in one personalised version. The spider-eating, madman Renfield is not included. So no chance of offending anyone by making them him!

FYFI: www.ustarnovels.co.uk/personalised-classic-novels/dracula

PERU: a massively strange vampire story links a weaver from Blackburn, Lancashire, to Pisco, Peru. Somehow the wild tale circulated that 51-year-old Sarah Ellen Roberts was executed in her home town for being a "bride of Dracula". It was said she had been seen biting the neck of a child and sucking its blood – which she then spat out over a bowl of ice cream before slurping it up. And as the town refused to allow her to be buried in consecrated ground, her husband roamed the world looking for a place that would accept her body. Finally he found her a final resting place in Pisco.

How the crazy myth was hatched is just as big a mystery as the story itself. But it's one that the good – if crazed – folk of Pisco still cling to. To the extent that her grave (yes, she was buried in Pisco) is revered to this day and is visited by a constant stream of people who believe the daft story or are just plainly intrigued. The real story is very simple and bland: her husband went out to Peru to join his brother who had set up a cotton factory in Pisco. Eventually Sarah joined him. She died unexpectedly, in June 1913, at age 41. In 1993, a South American TV programme about vampires announced it had uncovered the horrific truth about Sarah. It spread like wildfire, all round the world. These days it would be dismissed as "fake news".

The story and belief took such a hold that the, then, Mayor of Pisco, Edgar Nunez, wrote to the town of Blackburn, suggesting the towns should be "twinned". Blackburn's, then, Mayor, Paul Browne, was swift in his put down. He said: "This vampire lark will do our town no good at all. People around the world will think we are bloodsuckers."

FYFI: http://cottontown.org/Names%20of%20Note/
Notorious%20Names/Pages/Vampires.aspx

PHILADELPHIA: is home to the Rosenbach Museum, which boasts one of the finest collections of original documents linked to some of the world's best known literature. One of its prized collections is a wonderful assortment of Bram Stoker items, including his notes for *Dracula*. See ROSENBACH.

PHILOSOPHICAL: the world's oldest student society is The University Philosophical Society of Dublin. Since 1683 it's brought world-class debates and speakers to Trinity College, where Bram Stoker was a student. During his time there he served as President of the Society, which is why the Society has a Bram Stoker Club and a Bram Stoker Medal. The Club meets weekly and is devoted to student paper readings. Recent readings have included papers on artificial intelligence, nightclubs and the history of bottled water. As for the medal, which was started in 2011, it is awarded for "cultural achievement".

The medal is not awarded annually but as frequently as merit dictates – which doesn't seem to be very often! Among recipients is the Duchess of Sussex – who received it in 2013, for her role in the Canadian TV series Suits when she was simply Meghan Markle, actress. Other recipients are the late Christopher Lee (see entry LEE), who was the first to get it in 2011; followed by American late-night comic Conan O'Brien in 2012 and the Hollywood acting duo of Channing Tatum and Jonah Hill, who picked up their medals in 2014 when they were in Dublin for the Irish premiere of their movie, 22 Jump Street.

PINBALL: there are two Dracula electronic pinball machines out there. The earliest one was produced in 1979 by Stern – the famed US arcade game creators. The other came out in 1993 – to coincide with the movie *Bram Stoker's Dracula*. It was made by the other renowned US pinball manufacturer, Williams Electronics. Marketing slogans used to sell the latter included: "This will really slay the pinball pro!"; "It has a killer feature!"; "Players will be 'coffin up' quarters …" and "A game you can really sink your teeth into!" Now and then one or the other hits the market – either "as is" or "refurbished" – with a price tag of around $1,000, for a very used one, or close to $6,000 for one in mint condition.

FYFI: for British buyers, Home Leisure Direct is the company to contact, https://www.homeleisuredirect.com; for Americans it's The Pinball Company, https://www.thepinballcompany.com
Also, search "Dracula pinball machine" on eBay.

PIPES: smoking a pipe is, without a doubt, a back-in-the-day thing. But there are still the diehard users out there. And many of them love the Dracula Range, produced by the world's oldest pipe makers, Peterson's of Dublin. The Irish company has been making pipes since 1845. In 2012 it introduced its Dracula pipes – there are four styles – to mark the 100th anniversary of the death of Dublin-born Bram Stoker. All the pipes have a jet-black bowl and blood-red stem, etched with black swirls. They're finished off with a nickel band, with "Dracula" engraved on it, that, as Peterson's point out, "lends the pipe a touch of elegance that would surely meet with approval from that most aristocratic of monsters." They sell for €93.

FYFI: go to, https://www.peterson.ie; and to buy in US, www.pipesandcigars.com/p/peterson-dracula-pipes-pipes/1473940

PLAID: no our anti-hero didn't wear one. But a trio of Brooklyn, New York-based punk-rockers have coupled the word with Dracula to come up with a name for their band. *Plaid-Dracula* carries the tag-line: "loud like plaid – pale like Vlad". The two guys and a gal, who make up the band describe themselves as "glampires". A word of explanation here for Brit readers: in American-English the word "plaid" is not used correctly. Americans call any tartan-like pattern "plaid" – ignoring that "a plaid" is the tartan shawl that is an integral part of Scottish traditional dress, worn over the left shoulder.

FYFI: to listen to and buy tracks from the band, https://plaiddracula.bandcamp.com/releases

PLANE: there is a plane called Dracula! It's an aerobatic biplane designed, owned and flown by the world's number one flying-circus master, Kyle Franklin of the famed Franklin's Flying Circus. It made its debut in December 2012. It was an event dreamt of by Kyle's late father, Jimmy – who died in a mid-air plane crash in 2005. The idea for the Dracula plane, with its blood-red slashes of paint, was his. But despite the ghoulish moniker, the plane has a unique life-saving device. It has what Kyle calls an "Amanda Switch". It automatically switches off the fuel supply if the plane crashes. The "Switch" is in memory of his wing-walking wife Amanda who died, aged 25, from burns suffered when the plane he was piloting crashed and burst into flames, in March 2011.

FYFI: http://franklinairshow.com/index.html

PLAY: There are many stage adaptations of the novel. The first bid was a disaster, even though it was the work of the author himself. Just eight days before publication of *Dracula*, in 1897, Bram Stoker did a hasty adaptation of his own. He rushed it off to the Lord Chamberlain's Office, a requirement under the Stage Licensing Act of 1737, in order to protect the dramatic rights to the book. He arranged for his version of *Dracula* as a play to be performed, with barely two hours notice, at London's Lyceum theatre, which was owned by his mentor and boss, Sir Henry Irving. A handwritten poster outside the theatre, saying the performance was open to the public for free, attracted two customers. It was Stoker's adaptation's one and only airing. Sir Henry, who was the third member of the almost non-existent audience, announced his thoughts of the play in one withering word. He pronounced it "dreadful". Stoker was so discouraged by the destroying one-word verdict of Sir Henry, that he tore up the script and threw it into the wastepaper basket.

FYFI: to check where there is a UK stage production of *Dracula*, or any plays with the name in its title, go to: http://www.whatsonstage.com

PLAY-2: surprisingly, after Stoker's own abortive attempt, it took 27 years before *Dracula* took to the stage, again. The first production of *Dracula*, the play, was on August 5th, 1924, at The Grand Theatre, Derby. This time the novel was adapted (with the blessing of Stoker's widow) by Irish writer actor-director Hamilton Deane (see DEANE). It was Deane who created the sartorial image of the Dracula we all know – by dressing him in a dinner jacket (ie, for American readers, a tuxedo), stand-up collar and flowing cape. Deane wanted to make him a more urbane character, one who would be welcomed into Victorian society. The play toured provincial theatres for three years – with each performance having a nurse on standby, equipped with copious amounts of smelling salts, in case anyone fainted – before finally transferring to the West End and then Broadway.

It made its West End debut, significantly on Valentine's Day, at the long-demolished Little Theatre, which was on John Adam Street, just off The Strand. Deane, whose parents knew both the Stoker family and that of Florence Balcombe, Stoker's wife, in Dublin, played the part of Van Helsing in the play. Later, in 1927, the play – again revised, in partnership with Deane, by American journalist turned playwright John L Balderston – opened to massive plaudits on Broadway. In New York, Deane had planned to play Dracula. But in the end the part went to the unknown Bela Lugosi (see LUGOSI). It made him a star – particularly after the release of the first movie in 1931. In 1977, the play enjoyed a huge revival success on Broadway. It ran for two-and-a-half years. This time Frank Langella (see LANGELLA) played the lead and, just like Lugosi, he went on, in 1979, to star in a movie version.

PLAY-3: the play most staged in the UK and around Europe is *Dracula: the Bloody Truth*. It's the work of the Exeter-based theatre company Le Navet Bete – which translates to "daft turnip". The name pretty much sums up what the company gets up to. Gales of laughter, produced via silliness and daftness, abound. Their take on *Dracula* – along with other shows based on the *Wizard of Oz*, *Dick Tracy* and *A Christmas Carol* – has made them a force of jollity to be reckoned with. As the website for the *Dracula* show says: "Le Navet Bete is committed to creating hilarious, physical and totally accessible comedy theatre using creative and engaging storytelling. This comedy theatre show will take audiences on a journey across Europe from the dark and sinister Transylvanian mountains to the charming seaside town of Whitby and into the world of the supernatural, educating us all on the perils of dealing with vampires."

Performed by four actors playing – in whirlwind fashion – 40 characters, *Dracula: The Bloody Truth* is a full-blooded adaptation offering abundant opportunities for any theatre company or drama group to sink their teeth into. It's been translated into French, German and Greek. When it debuted in 2017, *Broadway World* said: "The company, which specialises in physical theatre, has stumbled upon a surefire hit with their Dracula adaptation, coupling ghoulish goings on with hilarious horseplay to make a comedy show worthy of the highest plaudits. It is side-splittingly funny and is, by far, the best new comedy."

In 2018, Le Navet Bete took it on the road throughout Britain. It premiered in the States in May 2018 when it was staged by the famed amateur Nomadic Theater group, of Newton, Massachusetts. Among the reactions it spawned were: "A manic infusion of laughter! Four actors inhabit 40 characters in this batty British farce. This Dracula totally sucks – in all the best ways!" And: "The amazing versatility of the actors plus the absolute silliness and fun of the script makes 'Dracula: The Bloody Truth' quite a unique experience." Since then it's been staged throughout the

US. In June 2019, it had its New Zealand premiere, at the Theatre Royal in Nelson – and it's staged throughout the UK on a regular basis.

FYFI: to see a trailer from the first production, https://www.youtube.com/watch?v=gFbB8Uk3Ep4; for more about Le Nave Bete and its calendar, http://lenavetbete.com

PLAY-4: one of the most recent adaptations is the work of the Alnwick-based Northumberland Theatre Company, which tours Britain using village halls and community centres as venues in small rural towns and villages. From August 2018 to June 2019 it took its *Dracula: The Travesty* on a whistle-stop run through the North East and Aberdeenshire.

Devised and created by NTC actor and writer Stewart Howson (who has appeared in dozens of well-known TV shows from *Coronation Street* to *Silent Witness*), its PR blurb reads: "Light, funny and daft but with strong storytelling and some genuinely scary moments. This is Gothic storytelling at its best: imaginative, atmospheric and physically exciting. Appealing to family audiences it features all the anticipated elements of the story: wolves, bats and the Brides of Dracula with plenty of audience participation, humour and music."

In his review, Peter Lathan of the *British Theatre Guide* said: "Disrespectful to a classic? Of course. That's what a travesty is. And it is hilarious. It takes a lot to make me really laugh out loud nowadays – aged and jaded, that's me – but this show succeeded."

PLAY-5: the newest – and most exciting – *Dracula*-based play was expected to premiere in 2020. But at the time of going to press there was no indication of a date. It's *Dracula The Truth* written by Bram Stoker's great-grand-nephew, Dacre Stoker (see DACRE). The promo for the play reads: "The play is based on an omitted section of the novel 'Dracula' which is the forerunner of horror literature. A section at the opening of the book was removed by the publisher as it was thought to be too frightful for audiences. Stoker had originally written words to the effect that Vampires might exist ... and walk among us and the play is based around this belief."

The script is co-written by Stoker and director Gary Gillies, who is famed for the way he brought an interaction production of *Alien Wars* to the British stage. Thanks to all the latest high-tech "toys", members of the audience were subjected to the virtual reality of being "there".

The same treatment will be dished out to audiences of *Dracula The Truth*. The plan is for Stoker to open the show with a presentation, explaining how he has spent his life researching Bram Stoker's manuscripts and how he believed vampires to exist. He will convey how it has taken him years of dedicated research to uncover and finally meet a vampire and how he has invited the vampire to appear before audiences where he will interview him and discuss how he/they have managed to exist and survive undetected in the world. The preview promises: "The overall look and feel of the performance will be dark, terrifying and it will have an interactive quality, where the cast will at time enter the audience ... it will have realism so the audience will question if what they are experiencing is in fact real."

FYFI: https://www.facebook.com/draculathetruth

PLAY-6: in October 2014 a very special Dracula play premiered. *Jonathan Harker and Dracula* is an adaptation of the novel that is as close to the original as it can be without reciting every word. Written by the prominent British theatrical director Michael Poynor as a one-man show, it starred the award-winning Irish actor Gerard McCarthy. He played every part – including those of Lucy and Mina – with an astonishing range of accents and voices.

Interviewed by Damian Michael Barcroft, the writer and historian who specialises in Gothic literature (as well as detective fiction), Gerard said: "Oddly enough, we've kept it fresh by going right back to the original text and not messing with it. Dracula is not sexy and sparkly, we've not set it in 2014, there are no gimmicks or slants on it. It is a 100-per-cent truthful and honest retelling of Bram Stoker's story which I personally don't think can be bettered."

And about Jonathan Harker he said: "I suppose the main challenge of playing Jonathan is that he is so naive. He doesn't know what a vampire is, he doesn't know why he only sees Dracula at night-time or why he doesn't have a reflection, so the audience is already streets ahead of him! This doesn't make him stupid, he's certainly not that, so it's important to watch him gradually put all the pieces of the jigsaw together and to remember that this is all new to him. Jonathan is actually my favourite character to play because he grows throughout the play, he gets stronger and braver and towards the finale finds the strength to do things that he would never have done at the beginning. I guess, in a way, he has as much of a metamorphosis as Dracula."

FYFI: to read the full interview, http://dmbarcroft.com/tag/michael-poynor

PLAY-7: then we have *Dracula: the Journal of Jonathan Harker*, adapted by Jim Helsinger, the artistic director of the Orlando Shakespeare Company, in Florida. It's been staged in Orlando several times, as well as by theatres all over the United States. In the opinion of American writer and theatre critic Steven Surman, the adaptation "captures the soul of Bram Stoker's legendary Gothic novel without weighing itself down in overwrought theatrics ... there's only one voice in the play – that of Jonathan Harker – and through him we hear the story of Count Dracula and the band of heroes determined to destroy him. Such a simple approach might mislead you, but don't let it. This is one of the best adaptations of Dracula ever."

FYFI: to read the script or buy it, https://www.playscripts.com/play/1907

PLAY-8: in 2013 and 2014, Blackeyed Theatre, based in Bracknell, Berkshire, took its version of *Dracula* on the road, to theatres throughout Britain. The promo for the adaptation of the novel said: "The time is 1897. Mankind is on the cusp of vast technological change, scientific mastery and media innovation. Poised between traditional beliefs, the threat of the unknown and the shock of the new world, an altogether darker fear is emerging. Bram Stoker's timeless Gothic thriller embodies the struggle to break taboos, resist temptation and stop the unknown outside becoming the enemy within. This brilliant, theatrical treatment of Bram Stoker's adventure blends Victorian Gothic with the Contemporary, drawing eclectically on a wide range of forms of popular entertainment that were established or emerging at the time."

The production got rave reviews. *The Stage* said: "There have been numerous productions of Dracula over the years, creatively conceived and generally well staged, but few have drawn so effectively from the timing of Bram Stoker's novel and the Victoria era of change …"

The forte of Blackeyed Theatre, which was founded in 2004, is bringing classic literature to the stage. Its previous adaptations include *Dr Jekyll and Mr Hyde*, *Frankenstein*, *The Great Gatsby*, *Sherlock Holmes* and *Jane Eyre*. While there are no specific plans to re-stage *Dracula*, Artistic Director Adrian McDougall said: "I'd like to produce it again at some point …" Here's hoping!

FYFI: to watch the *Dracula* trailer, www.youtube.com/watch?v=wXFrSl9JCuU; for theatre info, www.blackeyedtheatre.co.uk

PLAY-9: American actress/storyteller/writer Megan Wells has won critical acclaim for her one-woman production of *Dracula*. She adapted the novel for a 90-minute show after re-reading it following her young daughter's *Twilight*-inspired interest in vampires. The adaptation came out of realising "what an amazing" read *Dracula* is and how the movies and copycat books have moved a long way from the original monster that sparked the genre so many years ago. Megan, who lives near Chicago in La Grange Park, Illinois, has a voice rich with deep tones that resonate with which ever part she is playing – be it Dracula or Mina – so has no problem giving voice to all the characters.

FYFI: to check on her schedule for *Dracula* go to, www.meganwells.com

PLAY-10: yet another adaptation of the novel came along in 1985, this time by renowned Scottish writer Liz Lochhead. It premiered at the Royal Lyceum Theatre in Edinburgh. Since then it's been staged all over Britain. And in 2016, the BBC got David Suchet (Poirot) as Dracula and Tom Hiddleston (The Night Manager) as Jonathan to record the play.

The programme notes for the adaptation read: "... this stage version of Dracula marries Stoker's fantastic imagery with modern questions about the battle between faith and reason, sanity and madness, gender roles and women's sexuality. Examining the relationship of women to the vampire legend, and what this means in terms of women's relationship with men in general, is certainly still relevant ... the play shows Dracula's effects on the humans he manipulates, from madman Renfield in a padded cell of an asylum to Lucy in the romantic garden of an estate in Whitby, growing paler by the day. Lochhead's beautiful language, filled to the brim with imagery, wordplay, punning and inarticulate sounds, contributes to the psychological and sociological complexity of the characters."

FYFI: www.youtube.com/watch?v=mqavUvFgZUQ; buy the CD from eBay.

PLAY-11: *Dracula: A Song of Love and Death* was premiered in October 2018 at Kansas City Actors Theatre. It was written by Mitch Brian, a longtime *Dracula* aficionado, who has previously written for the TV show *Batman: The Animated Series and Viper*, in addition to writing scripts for 20th Century Fox, HBO, FX, and other studios.

In addition to its world-premiere status, this production also boasted some bold casting choices, including the casting of not just a black female Renfield, the vampire-sensitive lunatic, but a black Quincy, the cowboy. And, while this remains Bram Stoker's classic story and setting, Director John Rensenhouse was excited about how the story had been updated. "I'm so impressed with how Mitch Brian has made this classic story resonate with modern relevance," said Rensenhouse. "There are gender politics, sexual politics and racial politics all wrapped up in this Victorian, turn of the century piece and we are offered the chance to experience the story through a new lens."

In its review, *Broadway World* said: "With so many adaptations over the years it's difficult to imagine that there is anyone who doesn't know who Dracula is, but for those who don't, this show is the perfect introduction."

FYFI: to listen to a discussion about the play, https://www.youtube.com/watch?v=R_6ccLvxGKo

PLAY-12: and yet another adaptation, this time by South African writer Rosie Fiore-Burt. It premiered at the Bridwell Theatre in Blackfriars, London, December 2018. Asked why she had joined the ranks of playwrights bringing *Dracula* to the stage, Fiore-Burt answered: "Quite simply because I have never yet seen an adaptation which does justice to this remarkable book."

PLAY-13: as said in the first PLAY entry, there are numerous adaptations. To see reviews of many of them go to, www.britishtheatreguide.info/reviews

PODCASTS: there's a whole host of them – honouring *Dracula* in all its forms. From straight readings of the book to spoof plays.

FYFI: https://player.fm/podcasts/dracula

POEMS: in 2014 there was the "To Be Bram Stoker for a Day" contest, organised by Poetry Soup, a website for budding poets. This was my entry:

> *Now then Dracula my man*
> *You really must stop this.*
> *It virtually scares me to death*
> *Every time you nibble my neck.*
> *Why can't you find others*
> *To fulfil your night time larking?*
> *Your nocturnal longings are not for me.*
> *Please visit during the day*
> *So you and I can love in peace.*

Needless to say, it didn't even get an honourable mention.

FYFI: to see the poems that made the cut, www.poetrysoup.com/poems/best/bram_stoker

POMADE: the hair preparation has been around longer than Dracula … the first global commercial brand was launched in London in 1873. And now Dracula has got in on the act of helping men create a slick, shiny hair-do. Suavecito, the US haircare business that dates back to 2009, is now attracting a new generation of pomade-users. And among its biggest sellers is its $12, 4 oz red jar bearing the name Dracula and a sketch of him on the lid, showing off his "slick-back" hair style. Suavecito says: "We thought a monster as classic as Dracula deserved our iconic Original Hold Pomade. This collectible pomade features the fanged fiend himself and a red jar to pay homage to his meal of choice. Get a slickback as sleek as Dracula's with this water-based formula."

FYFI: in the UK buy from, https://slickstyles.co.uk; in US, https://www.suavecito.com

PONTIANAKS: are female vampires – beautiful beings that change into organ-devouring monsters – that are a mainstay of Malaysian and Indonesian folklore. Their origin emerges from the ghosts of women who have died during pregnancy or in childbirth, who claw open humans with sword-like talons in a bid to find their baby. Amazingly, as they are perceived as such harmful and insidious creatures of the night, the capital city of the island of Borneo, Pontianak, is named after them.

PORPHYRIA: is often referred to as the "Dracula Disease". It is an inherited and incurable blood disorder – of which there are eight types – that affects the body's production of haemoglobin in the red blood cells. Victims suffer in many ways but sensitivity to light and shrinkage of skin that makes teeth look canine-like is common – hence the link to vampires. Having said that, porphyria, in all its forms, is very rare which makes diagnosis problematic. It's claimed that it's a medical rarity that has afflicted the Royal Family. Mary Queen of Scots and King George III –

the "mad king" – are said to have been sufferers. The last known member of the family inflicted with the disease was Prince William of Gloucester, who died in 1972, aged 30, when a plane he was piloting crashed.

FYFI: http://www.porphyria.org.uk

POSTCARDS: for the true fan, New Zealander Alex Broome has put together a handmade set of 24 vintage *Dracula* movie posters reprinted as postcards and available on Etsy. They include some of the obvious ones to the less known, like *Guess What Happened to Count Dracula* and *The Seven Brothers Meet Dracula*.

FYFI: https://www.etsy.com/listing/591584892/postcards-set-24pcs-dracula- vampires?ref=related-1

PRECIS: an excellent precis of the book – which includes notes on all chapters and quotes – can be found at, https://www.sparknotes.com/lit/dracula/.rhtml

PRESIDENTIAL: at the height of the 2016 US Presidential campaign – when the Republicans were battling it out whether to pick Donald Trump or Ted Cruz as their nominee – our man Dracula was invoked. In a letter to *The State*, the newspaper of South Carolina, reader Pat Mohr wrote: "What we now have is Republicans running through the woods fleeing from Trumpenstein by falling into the arms of Dracula-Cruz, where they'll only be sucked dry of every vestige of reason and compassion." Of course, many now argue, that's exactly what America has to cope with (at the time of going to press) – after Trumpenstein won out.

PRINCE: as in Charles, ie, the Prince of Wales. He has an attachment to Transylvania – particularly the hamlet of Zalanpatak, with its fewer than 200 residents along with the surrounding, superb undulating, wild flower crammed, meadows. He first visited in 1998. In his own words he was: "totally overwhelmed by its unique beauty and its extraordinarily rich heritage".

Prince Charles owns at least 10 properties in Transylvania. The first place he bought was in the Saxon village of Viscri, now a UNESCO World Heritage Site. The house he renovated there is now the headquarters of the Romanian branch of The Prince of Wales's Foundation. Prince Charles claims distant kinship to Vlad Tepes. "You could say I have a stake in the country," he once said of his love for Romania.

The website for his guesthouse reveals: "The Prince of Wales hopes that his guesthouse will encourage more people to visit Transylvania and in this way promote sustainable development ... his private nature retreat lies nestled amongst the meadows and hills of Zalán Valley. The property has kept its Transylvanian authenticity by having been carefully restored with traditional methods and materials." The price of €129 pp, per day, includes three meals a day and wine, plus guided tours and other activities. Proceeds from the guesthouse go to The Prince of Wales's Foundation Romania.

FYFI: https://zalan.transylvaniancastle.com;
https://www.facebook.com ThePrinceofWalesFoundation inRomania

PRINCE-2: in 2017 Prince Charles was offered the honorific title of Prince of Transylvania. It came from Mircea Hava, then Mayor of Alba Iulia, the ancient capital of Transylvania. The offer was prompted because of the way the Prince, whose passion for Romania and its people is well known (see previous entry), has laid claim to being descended from Vlad the Impaler. He's tracked his bloodline back – via his great-grandmother Queen Mary, wife of King George V, who was born a German princess – to being the grandson of Vlad, 16 times removed.

In his letter to Prince Charles, Mayor Hava wrote: "We know how much you love Transylvania. It has become your second home and you have been the region's most valuable ambassador. Moreover, you claim your roots from our legendary Prince Vlad. As you love Transylvania so much, we thought, what if instead of only being 'The Prince of Wales', you would be known from now on as 'The Prince of Wales AND Transylvania'? You have to admit that 'Prince of Wales AND Transylvania' sounds like a fantastic way to introduce yourself, in addition to being a great conversation starter." There is no indication that the Prince accepted the honour.

PRINT: there are lots of *Dracula*-linked prints out there, to shove in a frame and put on your wall. Many are found on Etsy, the global arts and crafts website. But one of the most popular – and in no way scary – is the quote from the book that reads: "Welcome to my house. Come freely. Go safely. And leave something of the happiness you bring".

FYFI: www.etsy.com/uk/search?q=dracula+quotes&ref=shop_search

PSYCHIATRIST: one of the best spin-offs of the *Dracula* story is *The Secret Life of Laszlo, Count Dracula*. It's the 1994 work of British-American author Roderick Anscombe whose background as a psychiatrist, working with the criminally insane, has provided him with authentic information of just how mad and craved the behaviour of the insane can be. Despite his success as a horror novelist, Manchester-born, Oxford-educated, Massachusetts-based Anscombe still practices psychiatry. The book is based on the provocative premise that there have never been vampires, only tortured human beings. It is the late 1800s and a young aristocrat, Laszlo, is at medical school in Paris. His deadly attraction to a mental patient leads him away from his high-society haunts into the city's dark underworld. Laszlo returns to Transylvania to inherit his Dracula title. There he cultivates his image as a saintly doctor by day – while the savage part of him stalks the night with cunning and ferocity.

FYFI: https://www.goodreads.com/book/show/1123376

PUBLISHED: *Dracula* was published on 26 May, 1897, by Archibald Constable and Company. It sold for six shillings and there was an initial print run of 3,000 copies.

PURFLEET: the Essex village on the River Thames, 18 miles east of London, is the setting for two major buildings in the novel: Carfax Abbey, which Dracula bought, and the "private insane asylum" where Dr Seward treated Renfield. There was a building called Carfax House in Purfleet, but it was not the one featured. The real Carfax House was built several years after *Dracula* was published and it was demolished in the 1880s. Instead, it's believed Bram

Stoker took the mansion Purfleet House – built by famed brewer Samuel Whitbread in 1791 – for his inspiration. The mansion was demolished in the 1920s but many of the stones were recycled to build St Stephen's Church. The church now bears a plaque marking the site's connection with *Dracula*.

As for the asylum, there never was one in Purfleet. But the one Renfield was held in was probably based on the fortress-like magazine complex that stored gunpowder for the Army and Navy. Built in 1765, it was very close to Purfleet House, which fits in with the scene in the book when Renfield escapes and tries to make it the 400 yards to where Dracula is residing. In 1962, the ordnance centre was closed and most of the magazines were demolished. But one was left and it's now the Purfleet Heritage Centre.

Although there is no record of Stoker ever visiting Purfleet, he probably did. In the 1880s, with its Thames-side setting and spa hotels, it was popular with Victorian day-visitors from London, who could get there easily on the train from Fenchurch Street Station.

PUTIN: in 2014, at the beginning of the Russian challenge to Ukraine, President Vladimir Putin was massively ridiculed, particularly in Kiev, the capital. In the tent city that grew up around the scene of the massacre of 53 protestors, there were posters and slogans galore mocking and attacking Putin. One of them read: "Putin = Dracula".

Q

QUEEN: imagine it! A widowed Queen Victoria marrying Dracula! Well in fiction any wild fantasy can be true. And in *Anno Dracula*, by British-born, US-based Kim Newman, that's what happens. A classic in a series of four *Anno Dracula* novels, it was the first, originally published in 1992 then re-issued in 2014. Over the years it's picked up a myriad of awards.

FYFI: https://www.goodreads.com/book/show/8970727

QUEEN-2: in October 2017, *Queen Dracula*, a 53-minute independent horror movie, was released with the plug line "death is the only way out of her fatal embrace". It was panned by the Horror Society, a website that specializes in indie horror films. Its review read: "*Queen Dracula* is nothing short of terrible. It's going to take a lot more than a couple of Bram Stoker and Dracula references to incite the reaction that you want …"

FYFI: www.horrorsociety.com/2018/10/19/review-curtis-everitts-queen-dracula

QUEER: the novel is constantly cited when Queer Theory is debated. The online *Merriam-Webster Dictionary* defines Queer Theory as: "an approach to literary and cultural study that rejects traditional categories of gender and sexuality".

FYFI: for a full explanation and background to Queer Theory, https://www.encyclopedia.com/history/dictionaries-thesauruses-pictures-and-press-releases/queer-theory; for how *Dracula* relates to it, https://phdessay.com/dracula-queer-theory

QUOTES: there are so many great quotes from the book. Here are just a few:

> *Welcome to my house. Come freely. Go safely and leave something of the happiness you bring.*
>
> *Listen to them, the children of the night. What music they make.*
>
> *I have crossed oceans of time to find you.*
>
> *And then there was silence, deep awful silence, which chilled me. Between me and the moonlight flitted a great bat, coming and going in great, whirling circles.*

FYFI: an easy reference to these, along with information of the chapters in which they appear, and the rest of the best can be found at, http://classiclit.about.com/od/dracula/a/aa_draculaquote.htm and at, https://www.goodreads.com/author/quotes/6988

R

RADIO: the power of the novel revealed the awesome power that radio (even in this day) can wield. On the evening of Monday, July 11th, 1938, millions of American listeners, coast-to-coast, were frightened stupid by Orson Welles (then aged 23) and a host of other renowned actors of the time. America's leading station, Colombia Broadcasting System (now known as CBS), launched its legendary *The Mercury Theatre on the Air* series. The first production to be aired was *Dracula*.

The adaptation was done by Welles and his long-time theatrical partner, the multi-talented British-American John Houseman, who – by happy coincidence – happened to be Romanian by birth. As a radio drama it stayed very close to the book. For 60 minutes, Welles and his talented crew scared the living daylights out of a massive number of people gathered in their living rooms, crowded round the wireless (which for readers under 60 years old, families used to do).

In a bid to create the sound of a stake being driven into a heart, the production team first experimented with piercing a large cabbage with a sharpened broomstick. It didn't have the right effect. In the end they cracked open a watermelon with a hammer. Welles approved the sound, saying it was akin to gurgling blood and it was so effective even the studio audience – who could see what was happening – shuddered. In his introduction to the live presentation, Welles said: "... this is the best story of its type ever written ..."

FYFI: to listen, https://www.youtube.com/watch?v=SK4frrg7SyU; to buy the original vinyl, https://www.discogs.com/sell/release/3070980?ev=rb; to get the text of the script, http://www.genericradio.com/files/generic_radio_workshop_radio_script_0cd6ca7e1d5e4e1c.txt

RADIO-2: some good came out of the 2020 corona-virus horror – a "terrorific" four-part adaptation of the novel as a radio-romp. *Dracula: A Comedy of Terrors* – starring a galaxy of Broadway names – was issued as a podcast (see PODCASTS). Available from May 1st, it was produced by Broadway Podcast Network, to benefit several actors' charities.

FYFI: https://www.broadway.com/buzz/199196/christopher-sieber-laura-benanti-john-stamos-more-set-for-dracula-a-comedy-of-terrors-radio-play

RAFTING: another example of how *Dracula* is being linked to all manner of activities. The International Rafting Federation (think whitewater) has designated a course, for competitive use, on the Buzau River in Nehoiu, Romania. They first staged the sprint, head-to-head and slalom events of the Rafting Euro Cup there in April 2018 and again in 2019. The 2020 event was postponed (because of the corona-virus) until October. The plan is to keep the event there for the foreseeable future. No prize for guessing what they promote their one and only Romanian event, as. Yes, "The Dracula Race".

FYFI: www.internationalrafting.com

READ: while not wanting to encourage reading books for free, I have to point out that *Dracula* can be read in full, online, courtesy of *Page by Page Books*, which has hundreds of classics on file.

FYFI: www.pagebypagebooks.com/Bram_Stoker/Dracula

RENFIELD: is a major character in the novel. He's the insane one who eats spiders. In the psychiatric world there is a condition called Clinical Vampirism, ie, someone with the obsession of drinking blood. In popular terms it's referred to as Renfield Syndrome, although in the book Renfield relies on small insects to appease his obsession.

RENFIELD-2: at last a welcome spin-off to the *Dracula* tale is coming our way. Universal, famed for its take on classic monsters, has *Renfield* – a film devoted to his henchman of that name – in the pipeline. Directed by a Brit, Dexter Fletcher, he of *Bohemian Rhapsody* and *Rocketman,* it will not be a period piece but set in the present day. The script is by American Ryan Ridley, of *Rick and Morty* – the adult animated science fiction sitcom fame. In mid-2020, it was widely rumoured that Benedict Cumberbatch – he of TV's *Sherlock* fame – would get the Dracula role. But, as of late 2020, no confirmation of that or word about who would play the title role.

FYFI: https://variety.com/2019/film/news/dexter-fletcher-dracula-henchman-renfield-robert-kirkman-1203410649

RENFIELD-3: a fascinating take on the story of Renfield is provided in *Renfield's Diary*, by Roger Martin Tudor. The subtitle is *The Dracula Companion*. And as Tudor, who lives in Whitby, says in his foreword: "Renfield, the madman in Dr Seward's asylum, insectivore and idolizer of Dracula, has kept a journal of his incarceration. In it he has logged his thoughts and his visits from the vampire. His version of events is not quite the same as recorded in Dr Seward's diary. For afficionados of Dracula, this is the background story which explores the workings of the mind of the man to whom he promised eternal life and whose love he destroyed."

FYFI: https://www.goodreads.com/book/show/27569341

RENFIELD-4: stage adaptations of *Dracula* are increasingly being subjected to gender-bending (see FEMALE). In early 2020 Renfield became a woman. The *Dracula* adaptation, produced by the Classic Stage Company of New York, was the work of American playwright Kate Hamill, who specialises in putting a modern twist on the classics. And in this case she also had a starring role – playing the insect-gobbling mad (wo)man.

REPRESSION: academics, popular culture critics, just readers, have a massive range of reactions to the novel *Dracula*. But one thread runs through all thoughts – that of sexual repression. As *e-notes.com* points out: "Dracula was published during the Victorian era when sexual repression was at its height. This was also an age which saw a tremendous rise in prostitution and pornography. The novel shows this paradox and the consequences of sexual repression. Gentlewomen were supposed to be ladylike and were thought inferior to men. Lucy writes, 'My dear Mina, why are men so noble when we women are so little worthy of them?'"

And the website *Bartleby* – "your guide to better learning" – says: "... in Dracula, though we have a vampire myth novel filled with terror, horror, and evil, the story is a thinly veiled disguise of the repressed sexual mores of the Victorian era ... throughout the novel we see that vampirism most equates with sexuality. Without overdoing a Freudian analysis of the story, there are enough sexual references to satisfy the least Victorian in nature among us. However, the Victorian repression theme plays a role in the sexuality of the novel because though good women and men were able to control their sexual appetites in Victorian society, we see them unable to resist giving into their desires in Dracula."

FYFI: https://www.enotes.com/homework-help/how-does-dracual-portray-sexual-repression-53871; https://www.bartleby.com/essay/Analysis-Of-Dracula-By-Bram-Stoker-F3SRN2VYSEFP; for more on this theme, see SEX.

RICE: most people assume that Anne Rice, author of the phenomenally successful *Vampire Chronicles*, owes much to *Dracula*. Not so. At least not very much. Her first exposure to *Dracula* was as a nine-year-old when she went to see a re-release of the 1936-made *Dracula's Daughter*, that was showing at a cinema near her childhood home in New Orleans. She told the *Wall Street Journal*: "It was a turning point for me. I was captivated. I fell totally in love with Countess Marya Zaleska, Dracula's daughter, and left the cinema with the notion that vampires were glamorous, doomed, artistic people. I was enchanted by the film, not creeped out."

So she took *Dracula* out of the library – and had a vastly different reaction. The first few scenes scared her so much, she told *Biography* in October 2013, she swiftly returned it. It was not until *Interview with a Vampire* – the first in the 11-book *Vampire Chronicles* series – was published that she finally got round to tackling *Dracula* again. A different story this time. "I loved it. Bram Stoker did a bang-up job. He had a great imagination – and, of course the fact that Dracula was transferred to black-and-white movies really kicked off the vampire of the 20th century."

FYFI: to see/hear the interview, https://www.biography.com/video/anne-rice-on-bram-stoker-58197571735

RIDES: dreaming of a drive in a fancy, open, horse-drawn carriage with Dracula as your driver? Then head to historic Fayettville, North Carolina, USA, for its legendary Halloween event. Since 2000, the Downtown Merchants' Organization has staged a trick-or-treat event, with all the shop owners handing out sweet-goodies to the in-costume kids. Then, in 2016, Dracula came roaring into town, offering his Perfectly Horrible Carriage Rides from 3:00pm to 8:00pm. His black wagon, pulled by two monstrous black horses – decorated to look skeletal with non-toxic paint – and festooned with cobwebs, giant spiders, and whitened bones scattered about on the wagon floor, was an instant, scary hit.

Dr Hank Parfitt – a founder of the downtown group who, along with his wife Diane, owns City Center Gallery and Books – says: "The Count may seem like a vicious, loathsome creature, but he does have a soft spot for children and he would never disappoint the many kids who clamor to ride with him every year." The merchants also host various other carriage rides. Apart from Dracula there are rides with Santa, the Easter Bunny and those designed to celebrate Valentine's Day and Mother's Day.

RINGO: for Ringo Starr's venture into the *Dracula*-world, see FILMS–4

ROBERTS: one of the latest stars to take up the Dracula mantle is Eric Roberts. The award-winning actor (and btw brother to Julia) plays the lead role in *Halloween Hell*. A low-budget movie, made in 2014, it was described as a: "biting, satirical horror movie where a reality show's contestants are trapped on set with a deadly devil doll from hell, and a psychotic host who thinks he is Dracula."

FYFI: to watch the trailer, https://www.youtube.com/watch?v=UJK8oCO7D4Q

ROBINSON: to ensure he got the unique dialect of Whitby right, Stoker consulted Francis Kindale Robinson's *A Glossary of Yorkshire Words and Phrases Collected in Whitby and the Neighbourhood* (sub-title: *With Examples of Their Colloquial Use, and Allusions to Local Customs and Traditions. By an Inhabitant*). It was published in 1875. Stoker used the book to help him write the dialogue for the old seaman, Mr Swales, whom Lucy and Mina meet in the graveyard. In 2018, Trieste Publishing, which specialises in reproducing classic titles, responded to the surge of academic interest in how *Dracula* was written and reproduced the book, with much of the original scanned to simulate the "real" thing.

FYFI: original copies can still be found. Search antiquarian book-sellers. Expect to pay around from £60 to £100. To buy the replica, https://triestepublishing.com/search/?q=A+Glossary+of+Yorkshire+Words+

ROSENBACH: the Rosenbach Museum and Library in Philadelphia, with its priceless collection of rare books, manuscripts and artefacts, draws visitors and researchers from around the world. One of its jewels is its Bram Stoker Collection. And its presence, in this treasure of literary bounty, is a marvellous indication of how Stoker is acknowledged as the author of one of the finest pieces of literary work ever. Others represented in the Rosenbach include such giants of the written word as: Geoffrey Chaucer, John Bunyan, James Boswell, Robert Burns, Walter Scott, William Wordsworth, Charles Lamb, Percy Bysshe Shelley, John Keats, Charles Dickens, Lewis Carroll, Oscar Wilde, Conan Doyle, James Joyce and Joseph Conrad.

FYFI: www.rosenbach.org

ROSENBACH–2: every October the museum stages a month-long Dracula Festival. As the blurb for the annual event says: "Each Halloween season the Rosenbach Museum and Library opens the crypts and plumbs the depths of its collections to present the annual Dracula Festival, a month-long series of events inspired by Stoker's classic novel and iconic figure."

The museum – tucked away in a back street in the heart of historic Philadelphia – also opens up its Stoker collection a few times a year for one of its Hands-on Tour. In 2019 it advertised the event thus: "Get up close and personal with Bram Stoker's handwritten notes – character and chapter outlines, chronologies, and more – for *Dracula* as Rosenbach staff explore what it takes to create an enduring monster."

Reservations, for the $15 tickets, are recommended. Because of the corona-virus, the 2020 event was cancelled but to compensate the museum staged a virtual series, on Sundays over 27 weeks, from May to November, exploring all aspects of the novel.

FYFI: www.rosenbach.org

ROSS: in 1996 Jonathan Ross hosted *In Search of Dracula* for the defunct London Weekend TV. He brought together a shining list of British thespians and Hollywood luminaries to recall and discuss their involvement with *Dracula* movies. Those that took part were: Christopher Lee (played Dracula in nine Hammer films); Francis Ford Coppola (director of *Bram Stoker's Dracula,* 1992); Gary Oldman, Sadie Frost and Richard E Grant (stars of aforementioned); Jack Palance (TV movie, *Dracula*, 1973), Stephanie Beacham (Jessica van Helsing in *Dracula A.D.,* 1972); Grace Jones (Queen Katrina in *Vamp,* 1986) and the late and brilliant film-maker Ken Russell.

FYFI: until recently the show could be seen on You Tube but inexplicably it's disappeared. To discover why Russell was on the show see next entry.

RUSSELL: in 1978 Ken Russell – he of *Women in Love*, *Tommy* and *The Elephant Man* fame – wrote a *Dracula* film script. Sadly, it was never made. But in 2012, five months after his death, the script was published as a book – *Ken Russell's Dracula*.

FYFI: www.goodreads.com/book/show/21251025

RUSSIAN: it's believed the first film adaptation of *Dracula* was made by a team of Russian film-makers. Made in 1920 – and simply titled *Drakula* – it predated the lost Hungarian film, *Dracula's Death* (see FIRST–2) by a year. But, sadly, no evidence survives of its existence. There is a YouTube item that claims to be a trailer but it's been roundly discounted as "fake".

RUTHVEN: the first fictional vampire, in English literature, was Lord Ruthven – the main character in John Polidori's *Vampyre* (see VAMPYRE). Every March, the Lord Ruthen Award is presented for the best fiction on vampires and the best academic work on the study of the vampire figure. It's presented by The Lord Ruthven Assembly, an international group of scholars who specialise in vampires as portrayed in literature, film, and the other arts, founded in 1988.

FYFI: https://www.facebook.com/lordruthvenassembly

S

SABERHAGEN: the late Fred Saberhagen was an American writer famed for his science fiction and fantasy work but particularly for his *Dracula Series*, which was a collection of 10 books. The first was *The Dracula Tape* in 1975, in which Dracula told his story from his own point of view. Saberhagen was such an expert on interpreting the novel he was chosen to write the book about the film that claims to be closest to the original, ie, Francis Ford Coppola's *Bram Stoker's Dracula*.

FYFI: https://www.goodreads.com/author/show/10082

SALAD: nothing escapes Dracula! Not even a salad. For over 100 years The Dracula Salad was forgotten about. Then in July, 2020, it – like its namesake – sprung back into life, thanks to the vicar of Cruden Bay, the Rev Sean Swindells. In one of his regular on-line postings, he wrote to maintain contact with parishioners while the church was closed because of the corona-virus pandemic, he revealed all. Turns out that the salad was the culinary creation of someone very, very close to the creation of Dracula. In 1912, Florence, the wife of Bram Stoker – with whom she shared many happy holidays in Cruden Bay (see CRUDEN BAY) – contributed the salad to a pamphlet of recipes published to raise funds for an extension to the historic parish church. Not that The Dracula Salad is much of a recipe – just an imaginative juxtaposition of sliced tomatoes and deep purple sliced plums. The colour contrast is vampire perfection. And when dressed in a vinegar and olive oil vinaigrette, will tempt everyone, especially those dying to taste anything with a link to Dracula.

FYFI: to see a photo of the recipe and more, https://news.stv.tv/feature/authors-wife-donated-dracula-salad

SALKIN: David M Salkin is an American author with an enviable track record for churning out gripping thrillers. In 2012 he turned to a Dracula-like character as the anti-hero in *Forever Hunger*. New York police are looking for a mass killer who has been undead for over 200 years. Their prey is a Prussian soldier who was rendered a monster with an insatiable appetite for blood after being attacked by Napoleon's victorious army during the 1806 Battle of Jena. As one enthused reviewer wrote on Amazon: "Even if you're not into vampires this is still a very good read. A fascinating take on the life of a reluctant vampire! Fast paced, steamy and sexy! I love the twisted end." And in the end, *Forever Hunger* became the number 3 Best Selling Horror, for 2012, on Amazon.

FYFI: https://www.goodreads.com/book/show/13829451

SAMUELSON: James Samuelson was a Liverpool barrister who made his name by writing books about the history of the Balkans. His best known volume is *Roumania: Past and Present*. Published in 1882 it was central to the research Bram Stoker did when compiling information about "Roumania" (in those days the country was invariably spelt with an "ou") for his novel *Dracula*.

In the foreword to the book Samuelson observed: "There is no country in Europe which at the present time possesses greater interest for Englishmen than does the Kingdom of Roumania, and there is none with whose present state and past history, nay, with whose very geographical position, they are less familiar." The book has several passages about Vlad the Impaler, including one that describes how he killed his enemies by skewering them to the ground with a sharpened pole, leaving them to writhe in agony until "relieved by death". There's also a reference to Vlad also being called "Dracul", which Samuelson said translated to "devil".

FYFI: https://www.goodreads.com/book/show/35311867

SANGUINARIUS: is the condition attached to a human who feeds on blood. The name comes from "sanguis" the Latin for "blood". And because of the age we live in, there is a website catering for the wants and needs of such. There's also a book – well, a dictionary – titled *Vampspeak*. Its aim is to help those dubbed as "real vampires" communicate with each other.

FYFI: http://www.sanguinarius.org/dictionary-of-vampspeak.shtml

SCHLAGE: in 1987 the American company Schlage Security Systems, that specialises in high-security lock systems, produced a TV commercial that opens with a Veronica Lake-like (the 1940s Hollywood siren) woman in bed. A bat flies up to the French window and turns into Dracula. With lust all over his face, he opens the door – only to reel back in horror at the sound of a piecing alarm bell. As the message "Schlage Security System – starting from under $200", flashes up on the screen a voice-over coos: "It won't cost you an arm and a neck".

FYFI: to see it, https://www.youtube.com/watch?v=WfWQqJXnqXE

SCOTLAND: had a major part to play in the creation and writing of *Dracula*. Bram Stoker wrote most of it while on holiday there. See entries: BUFFALO, CRUDEN BAY, GLASGOW, KILMARNOCK ARM, and SLAINS CASTLE.

SCREAMING: in one way and another there's a lot of screaming in *Dracula*. So, no surprise that something of a hit song in 1964 was *Dracula's Daughter* by "Screaming Lord Sutch". Remember him? Heard of him? If you're under 70, probably not. But (and hence his "stage" name) what a scream he was. The flamboyant rock 'n' roller – real name David Edward Sutch – formed the Official Monster Raving Loony Party and stood in 40 parliamentary elections before dying, aged 58, in 1999. The song is a jaunty number with darkly funny lyrics, which should be on everyone's Halloween play-list. The refrain goes:

> *Lips are blue, eyes are red,*
> *A laugh like gurgling water.*
> *But I can't resist that passionate kiss,*
> *I'm in love with Dracula's Daughter.*

In 2005 *The Sharks* – sadly, a no-longer-around American new wave band – did a re-make of SLS's hit.

FYFI: listen to the original, www.youtube.com/watch?v=nfItXLQnOro &and the re- make: www.youtube.com/watch?v=4-DCvtBh_y8

SECRETARIES: when *Dracula* was published, and for generations later, secretaries around the world were delighted with it. Nothing to do with the high-horror or literary talent of the book but because of the way it championed their, often under acknowledged, skill and hard work. If it hadn't been for Mina's shorthand, typing and filing, the anti-hero would never have been tracked down. Of course, these days it has to be explained to many of a "certain age" exactly what shorthand is. Though of course everyone now "types".

FYFI: for an introduction to shorthand and an explanation of how the different systems work, www.omniglot.com/writing/shorthand.htm

SESAM 1: even *Sesame Street* has got in on the Dracula act! The American children's TV series has a character called Count von Count – who helps teach kids how to count. A permanent Muppet since 1972, he is a friendly vampire, who does not worry about going out during the day and has a slew of bat pets – which he constantly counts.

SESAME-2: in the 2020 US Census Count von Count was used in a public service announcement to ensure that youngsters – who for 40 years have been "dramatically" un-counted – were accounted for. In a fun exchange with Elmo, Rosita and her mum Rosa, he tells them: "Everyone in your home counts – especially little kids and babies."

SEVEN: it took Stoker seven years to research and write *Dracula*.

SEX: the sexual connotations of the book have been discussed, debated and dissected, ad infinitum. The basic theme of most analysis centres on how the book is full of symbolic references to the sexual repressions of the Victorian era and how the author writes passages that underline his own, possible – never disclosed – homosexuality.

FYFI: to explore the sexual repression of the book, http://www.inquiriesjournal.com/articles/1678/bram-stokers-dracula-a-reflection-and-rebuke-of-victorian-society; https://phdessay.com/sexuality-in-bram-stokers-dracula;&and https://www.erudit.org/en/journals/ron/2006-n44-ron1433/014002ar

SHAKE: yes, there is an ice-cream shake dedicated to the creator of *Dracula*. Sprinkles, in Whitby – owned and operated by Chris Hadley (his family has one of the best "chippies" in town) – has a "Bramble Stoker" on its extensive menu. Along with milk and ice-cream, it includes – for the needed dark look – brambles, blueberries and a good splash of grape juice. It's topped off with white chocolate chunks.

SHAKESPEARE: underlying the scholarly aptitude of the man who created a monster, is the way there is a Bram Stoker Collection housed in the Shakespeare Centre Library and Archive in Stratford-upon-Avon. The 69-box collection covers the 30 years Stoker was associated with Sir Henry Irving (see IRVING), the Victorian theatrical icon.

The Collection is enormously diverse – with all manner of mementoes, letters, business actions and travel details, that mount up to a fascinating insight into Stoker's lifr.

FYFI: to access the collection online, www.shakespeare.org.uk and search "Bram Stoker".

SHERLOCK: it was only a matter of time before the two great fictional characters of the Victorian era – Sherlock Holmes and Dracula – were brought together. In 1978, *Sherlock Holmes vs Dracula*, by American Western and detective writer Loren D Estleman, was published. The story pretty much follows the novel, with Holmes and Dr Watson getting involved as parallel forces. In 1981, it was adapted as a play for BBC Radio 4, starring the famed Timothy West as Watson and the late John Moffatt (best known as the voice of Hercule Poirot in 25 BBC radio productions, from the 1980s through the 2000s, of Agatha Christie's renowned Belgian detective) as Holmes. It's been aired numerous times since.

FYFI: to buy a copy, https://www.goodreads.com/book/show/1963165 to listen to the play, https://www.youtube.com/watch?v=0TX4rvB6mIs&t=304s

SHERLOCK-2: legendary British film director Gerry O'Hara was the one to merge Dracula and Sherlock into one story. One would have thought, because of his background, it would have been in a movie. But no, surprisingly, he also did it in a novel. In *Sherlock Holmes and the Affair in Transylvania*, published 2011, he has the great Baker Street detective and his side-kick Dr Watson venturing forth to Castle Dracula in a bid to solve the disappearance of Watson's nephew-in-law.

FYFI: https://www.goodreads.com/book/show/12660683

SHOPPING: there's tons of shopping to be done when it comes to Dracula. Be it books, films, jewellery, memorabilia, etc. But there is a new phrase in the lexicon. It's, "Vampire Shopping". These are shoppers, who in the depth of night, be it from: an inability to sleep; just got home from a late shift at work; the only time they have any peace and quiet at home; or just sheer loneliness, open up their computers and go mad, buying stuff they don't want, or need or can't afford. It's estimated that in-the-wee-small-hours-of-the-morning shoppers spend more than 20% of that of daytime online customers.

SIGHISOARA: the historic walled city in Transylvania, Romani, (see BANNED), is the 1431 birthplace of Vlad Tepes (Vlad the Impaler) who inspired Stoker to create the fictional Dracula. According to the Romanian Tourism Authority, the town, founded in the 12th century: "stands as one of the most beautiful and best-preserved medieval towns in Europe." Designated as a World Heritage Site by UNESCO, the tourism board claims: "it rivals the historic streets of Old Prague or Vienna for atmospheric magic."

SIMPSONS: even the fabled animated sitcom is not immune from the *Dracula* obsession. Mr Burns – Homer's boss and the oldest man in Springfield – turns into a vampire now and then, usually around Halloween. These episodes are among the most revered in the history of the TV show, which has been running worldwide since 1989. They are known colloquially as *Bart Simpson's Dracula*.

FYFI: www.simpsons.fandom.com/wiki/Count_Burns

SLAINS CASTLE: there's every reason to believe that this beautifully eerie Scottish castle – or what's left of it – was the inspiration for Dracula's castle. Especially as it matched Bran Castle in Transylvania in many ways, with its gaunt spires and towering turrett. Bran Castle also lays claim to influencing Bram Stoker when he wrote about Dracula's lair. Set high on a cliff-top that drops down into Cruden Bay (see CRUDEN BAY), 26 miles north of Aberdeen, Stoker looked upon Slains Castle and clambered around it on his many holidays there. In the book he describes it thus: "A vast ruined castle, from whose tall black windows came no ray of light and whose broken battlements showed a jagged line against the moonlit sky."

Sadly the castle is now closed off to the public. In 2004 a consortium of investors drew up plans to convert it into holiday accommodation – and threw up barriers to keep people away. Although plans were drawn up twice and presented to the local authority for planning permission, which was duly granted despite local opposition, nothing happened. In August 2017, the planning permission expired which delighted the protestors who wryly claimed that commercial development would "drive a stake through the heart of the castle". But it left the remote, beautiful region with a historic landmark that was crumbling away.

SLAINS CASTLE-2: but things are looking up for the neglected, deserted castle. In April 2018 the Castle was – after a long fight – awarded B-listed building status by Historic Environment Scotland. To qualify, it had to be judged of regional importance and/or, be a major example of a particular period, style or building type. Slains Castle more than fulfills both these requirements. In the petition to win the valued B-status, Neil Baxter, secretary of the Royal Incorporation of Architects in Scotland, said: "There are a number of ruined castles on cliff tops in Scotland, however, Slains Castle has a unique and internationally important literary relevance and therefore has special merit and should have special consideration in terms of care and preservation." The decision to give Slains Castle that recognition meant that it would be protected from development or demolition – two outcomes that had been feared by many,

Particularly Joe Allan, a retired civil servant of East Kilbride, South Lanarkshire. For years he led the bid to save Slains Castle, including lobbying HES and Scotland's First Minister, Nicola Sturgeon. On hearing that his battle had been won he said: "This is excellent news." But his fight was not over. The developers appealed the decision. Finally the long battle to save Slain's Castle from being turned into holiday flats was won. In October, 2018, the Scottish Government handed down the decision that the Castle should stay as is – under the protection of its conservation status.

FYFI: https://www.pressandjournal.co.uk/fp/news/north-east/1592499/new-slains-castle-to-keep-its-listed-status;& and https://www.historicenvironment.scot/about-us/news/new-slains-castle-awarded-listed-status

SNEEZE: these days the thinking on how to sneeze and cough has changed. Since 2009, US health experts have pushed for us all to sneeze like a vampire. That is: don't do it into your hand – but strike a Dracula pose and sneeze and cough into your sleeve. It's dubbed "The Dracula Sneeze"

because the idea is to hold your arm up over your face in a position similar to The Count holding up his cape. It's a move first recommended by the US Centers for Disease Control and Prevention, then followed up by scores of other healt bodies, schools and colleges, in the bid to fight the spread of germs.

So, no surprise that in 2020 the message was re-issued in powerful terms, in the hope of getting everyone to practice the "Dracula Sneeze" – as coronavirus swept the country and the world. Pediatrician Doug Later of Provo Utah, USA, used it succinctly when, in an article he wrote for his local paper the *Daily Herald*, giving tips with how to cope with the virus, he said: "Feel a sneeze or a cough coming on? Grab a tissue or use the inside of your elbow – this is commonly known as the 'Dracula Sneeze'."

FYFI: to see a typical poster, http://campushealthmedia.arizona.edu/images/large/Large_FLU_VampireCough_Poster.jpg

SNEEZE–2: in 2009 the American Dialect Society – founded in 1889, eight years before *Dracula* was published – declared "The Dracula Sneeze" the most creative phrase of the year.

SNOOKER: a legendary player who dominated the game for years was known globally by the nickname: "Dracula". One look at Welshman Ray Reardon – he reigned as the world champion and world's number one player from the mid-70s to the mid-80s – and it's easy to see how he got lumbered with it. All down to his dark-haired prominent widow's peak and sharp-toothed grin.

FYFI: for a photo of the snooker-playing Dracula go to, www.bigredbook.info/images/rayreardon.jpg

SNOWBOARDING: there are dozens of official acrobatic moves when it comes to the "tricks" that snow-boarding judges mark. And "Bloody Dracula" is one of them. To pull it off, the snow-boarder has to grab the tail of the board with both hands; the rear hand grabs the board as it would do during a regular tail-grab but the front hand blindly reaches for the board behind the rider's back. It got its name because the probability of failing and ending up with a bloodied mouth and/or, face is high. The amazing, stomach-churning manoeuvre brought wild applause from snowboarding fans at the 2014 Winter Olympics in Sochi, Russia, and then again in the 2018 games in PyeongChang, South Korea, particularly when American Kyle Mack pulled off a "Bloody Dracula" in 100% style and won silver in the Big Air event.

FYFI: https://fansided.com/2018/02/10/olympics-2018-what-is-snowboarding-bloody-dracula-trick; and https://ftw.usatoday.com/2018/02/watch-kyle-mack-land-a-gnarly-bloody-dracula-to-win-big-air-silver

SOCIALISM: like Dracula it keeps coming back – or tries to. That was the opinion expressed by leading American libertarian economist Richard M Ebeling, in a July 2018 article for the *American Institute for Economic Research*. He wrote:."… like Dracula rising once more from the grave, socialism has been making a comeback among academics, a growing number of other intellectuals, and college students. It is reflected in the Democratic Party primary win of Alexandria Ocasio-Cortez over an established

Democratic incumbent in a New York City congressional district. She's hailed as a member of the Democratic Socialists of America (DSA)."

In the 2018 mid-term election, Ocasio-Cortez was elected to the US Congress – where she continually creates headlines for her controversial socialist views and activities. She was up for re-election in the 2020 election. And of course, in the 2020 "race for the White House" the one-time-front-runner, Senator Bernie Sanders didn't deny the "socialist" label.

FYFI: www.aier.org/article/socialism-like-dracula-rises-again-from-the-grave

SOCIETY: The Dracula Society was founded in 1973 – mainly to organise trips to Transylvania, which back then was rarely visited, particularly in relation to the book. Since then it's evolved into a group that celebrates the whole genre, sparked by *Dracula*. Explaining the Society's mission its website says: "Since it is named after one of the most evocative titles in the whole genre, one of the most enduring and influential of Gothic novels, the Dracula Society naturally devotes a good deal of its attention to *Dracula*, the novel, and its author, Bram Stoker. However, the Society's field of interest embraces the entire Gothic literary genre, and incorporates, too, all stage and screen adaptations, and the sources of their inspiration in myth and folklore."

The Society makes two annual awards. One is the "Hamilton Deane Award" – in remembrance of the Irish actor, playwright and producer, who in 1924 was the first to bring *Dracula* to the stage (see DEANE). It's presented for the best dramatic performance or involvement in the staging or presentation in the Gothic, horror, supernatural genres. It's open to writers, actors, producers, and anyone in any of the performing arts such as stage, television, radio or film. The other award is "The Children of the Night Award", which is given for the year's best book in the Gothic literature category.

FYFI: to join the society – fee £19 a year for UK residents, £25 for non-resident go to, http://thedraculasociety.org.u

SON: Bram Stoker had one child – a son, Irving Noel Thornley Stoker. He was always known as Noel. His first name was to recognise the influence on his father's life of Sir Henry Irving (see IRVING). His third name was a Stoker family name. Noel was a boarder at Winchester College when *Dracula* was published. He died in 1961, aged 81, at his home on the Isle of Wight.

SON-2: the third *Dracula* movie, from Universal Pictures in 1943, was *Son of Dracula*. It was the first film showing Dracula's transformation into a bat on screen. It starred Lon Chaney as Count Alucard – and, in hindsight, is now considered a true "classic".

FYFI: to watch it for free, https://archive.org/details/UniversalStudiosMonsters1943SonOfDracula

SPACE: when outer-space was invaded by Dracula, in 2004, the result could have, should have been, top-notch entertainment. But no, it was, according to all the TV critics who bothered to watch *Dracula 3000: Infinite Darkness*, overwhelmingly awful.

Mitchell Hattaway of *DVD Verdict* said, "Dracula 3000 is a shining example of complete film-making ineptitude. You can look all you want and you won't find even the slightest hint of intelligence on any level ... it sucks."

According to the movie site *Rotten Tomatoes*, The storline, which showed promise but didn't deliver, goes: "The undead discover a new home in the far reaches of space in this blend of science fiction, action, and horror. In the year 3000 ... the crew of a commercial space freighter happens upon the wreckage of the *Demeter* (the name of the ship in the novel), a massive spaceship that has been missing for nearly a century. Aware that there's a substantial bounty being offered for the return of the ship's cargo, the freighter's crew begin exploring the *Demeter* to see what remains, and they discover that the ship's hold includes a large cache of black coffins. However, the real surprise lurks inside the coffins. A gang of vampires, taking advantage of the darkness of deep space, have taken refuge in the *Demeter*'s payload, and they soon begin attacking those who have discovered them. Can the freighter's crew keep the menace at bay until the ship's orbit takes them into the path of the sun?"

FYFI: if you really want to judge for yourself how bad it is, https://letterboxd.com/film/dracula-3000

SPANISH: for Spanish or Hispanic fans of *Dracula* there is the famed Madrileñs (ie, someone from Madrid) entertainer Andres Pajares, paying vocal homage in the song he wrote and recorded in 1968, *Dracula – YYye*.

FYFI: to listen, to buy, go to, www.discogs.com/Andres-Pajares-Dracula-Yeye/release/12147797

STAMP: the wonderfully talented British actor Terence Stamp (think of *Billy Budd*, *The Collector*, *Superman*, and *Star Wars*) played Dracula in a barely recognised 1978 stage production at The Shaftesbury Theatre, in London's West End. In a BBC interview he explained the attraction of playing Dracula. "I always think of evil and the Devil as being terribly groovy – not unattractive at all. They can be really interesting and really seductive."

FYFI: to see the poster, http://1.bp.blogspot.com/-B4dFXWQewMQ/U9r-pbyFymI/AAAAAAAAg38/il3AFhr7Ylw/s1600/689144_view_02.jpg

STAMPS: the Royal Mail's first commemorative stam, honouring Dracul, was issued in 1997 – with The Count being pictured as partially bald with long, snowy white hair and a flowing moustache to match. The 26p stamp was followed 11 years later by one for 48, that featured the poster for the 1958 *Dracula* movie, starring both Peter Cushing and Christopher Lee. Other countries to have put Dracula on their stamps are: Romania, Eire, Canada, USA and Chad.

FYFI: to buy them, https://www.freestampcatalogue.com/search?q=Dracula or go to eBay; to see them, http://www.artonstamps.org/Countries/Romania/About/dracula.htm

STAMPS-2: in 1996, the United Nations issued stamps that put the spotlight on plants that were "endangered". Issued by the UN in Vienna, they came in a set of four, all with the value of seven schillings (the Austrian currency before the Euro), which was about 60p. One of the four stamps was a painting of *Dracula Bella*, one of the many types of Dracula

Orchids (see ORCHIDS). Endemic to Colombia, *Dracula Bella* was discovered in 1878 by an expedition team from the Botanical Garden in Hamburg. It's on the endangered list because of the destruction of its habitat (see FOREST) – a threat shared by many types of Dracula Orchid, most of which originate from South America.

FYFI: https://www.stampworld.com/stamps/UN-Vienna/Postage-stamps/g0209

STAYED: when, on holiday, in Whitby, Bram Stoker – along with his wife and son – stayed at Number 6, Royal Crescent. He took "rooms" in the fine Georgian terraced ("row" for American readers) house set on the West Cliff, which is now adorned with a "blue plaque" which records a VIP once occupied the property. They enjoyed panoramic views out to sea. You can too. The house is now divided into two holiday rentals, Bram's Lair and Bram's View

FYFI: to rent, https://www.yorkshireholidaycottages.co.uk/yorkshire-coast/whitby-cottages/brams-lair and https://www.cottages.com/cottages/brams-view-28336?

STOKER: so much to say about Bram Stoker, the author of *Dracula*. Several fine biographies are out there (see BIOGRAPHIES), but basically: he was Irish; born in Dublin on November 8th, 1847; the third of seven children. He was sick for most of his childhood with an undefined but debilitating condition that rendered him mostly bedridden until he was seven years old and started school. To keep him amused, his mother regaled him with a deluge of Irish folklore tales, laced with mystery, horror and things that go-bang-in-the-night, which provided him with an endless interest in the weird and the ghoulish.

Despite being sick as a child, he became a fine athlete at Trinity College, Dublin, where he graduated with a degree in Pure Mathematics. He joined the Irish Civil Service but was never happy there. At university he'd acquired a love and interest in the theatre. On a part-time basis, he became the unpaid theatre critic for the long gone, *Dublin Evening Mail*. The paper was owned by Joseph Sheridan Le Fanu, who – as a pioneer author of fantasy and ghoulish novels – became a great influence on Stoker, particularly through his famed work, *Carmilla* (see CARMILLA).

In December 1876, Stoker reviewed a production of *Hamlet*, starring Sir Henry Irving (see IRVING). The famed thespian was so taken by the review he invited Stoker to dinner at his Dublin hotel. They became friends and in 1878, Stoker and his wife moved to London where he became Irving's personal assistant and manager of The Lyceum Theatre, in London's West End, which Irving owned. Throughout his 27 years at Irving's side, Stoker churned out many novels, including *Dracula*. Later he wrote the definitive biography of his boss, whom he clearly adored – though the affection was, never really returned.

STYRIA: the first manuscript of *Dracula* – dated March 8th, 1890 – placed the Count's castle in Styria. Stoker changed it to Transylvania six days later. Styria also links *Carmilla* (see CARMILLA) with *Dracula*. The story about the lesbian vampire – published 25 years ahead of *Dracula* – is set in Styria, which was part of the Austro-Hungarian Empire and is now an Austrian state.

SUCKING: something that Dracula's world certainly revolves around. *Bram Stoker's Dracula: Sucking Through* *the Century, 1898–1997*, published to mark the novel's centenary, is a series of scholarly essays compiled by Dr Carol Margaret Davison, Professor and Head of the Department of English the University of Windsor, Canada.

In the preface, the British Gothic fiction writer Patrick McGrath writes: "The essays, by some of the world's leading scholars, analyze Stoke"s original novel and celebrate its legacy in popular culture. The continuing presence of Dracula and vampire fiction and films provides proof that Dracula is 'alive and sucking'. Dracula is a Gothic mandala, a vast design in which multiple reflections of the elements of the genre are configured in elegant sets of symmetries.

"It is also a sort of lens, bringing focus and compression to diverse Gothic motifs, including not only vampirism but madness, the night, spoiled innocence, disorder in nature, sacrilege, cannibalism, necrophilia, psychic projection, the succubus, the incubus, the ruin, and the tomb. Gathering up and unifying all that came before it, and casting its great shadow over all that came and continues to come after, its influence on twentieth-century Gothic fiction and film is unique and irresistible""

FYFI: the book is out of print but used copies can be found for as little as £2.28, while "new" copies run from £63 to £150; check, https://www.goodreads.com/book/show/8776

SURF: The Count has taken to riding the waves. A hugely popular T-shirt for surfers shows a Dracula caricature, in beach-boy gear, clutching a sur-board emblazoned "R.I.P." It's exclusive to the global funky apparel and accessory company, Threadless, Chicago.

FYFI: http://www.threadless.com/designs/surf-dracula

SUTCLIFFE: the photograph that caught Bram Stoker's eye in the *Whitby Gazette* – of the beached Russian cargo ship *Dmitry* (see DMITRY) was taken by Frank Meadow Sutcliffe. Copies of the photo are available from the Sutcliffe Gallery in Whitby – which showcases the pioneer work of the lauded Victorian photographer. It's a must buy for *Dracula* enthusiasts.

FYFI: www.sutcliffe-gallery.co.uk/_photo_3182347.html

SWALES: is a legendary family name in Whitby, the historic Yorkshire harbour town, that Bram Stoker used as the setting to get The Count into Britain. In the book, a pivotal character, in the early chapters set in Whitby, is an old man, called Mr Swales. In Chapter 6 he meets and starts talking – in his broad, hard-to-understand, Yorkshire dialect – to Mina and Lucy as they sit on a bench in the cliff-top cemetery of St Mary's Church overlooking the harbour. He tells them tales of how the ruined Abbey (see ABBEY, behind the church, is home to goblins and ghouls. Then, after they've digested that scary news, he tells them it's all rubbish.

One day, when the three of them are again chatting in the graveyard, in the distance they see a ship drifting towards Whitby, which looks as though there is no one at the helm. Mr Swales says it's Russian and they're likely to hear more about it. The next day, after the drifting boat has been swept by a raging storm into the harbour, Mr Swales is found dead. His neck has been broken and a look of horror is etched on his lifeless face.

In Whitby, the Swales family of today tell the story, handed down over the generations, that when Bram Stoker was on holiday in Whitby he chatted to their ancestor John Swales, as they shared a bench on Cliff Street, close to where Stoker, his wife and young son, were staying. Stoker, taken by John's character and speech – he was in his late 60s – incorporated him into the novel. And the churchyard bench where the fictious Mr Swales met and chatted to Mina and Lucy is close by the real Swales family grave, alongside St Mary's Church.

SWEETS: since the 1960s, "Dracula Teeth" have been a favourite sweet (candy for American readers) for British kids – young and old. They are strawberry-flavoured, with the gum-like part red and the fangs white. There are two versions, plain and fizzy. They are widely available in independent sweet shops – many of which specialise in retro products – and sales soar around Halloween. Made by Hancock's of Loughborough, Leicestershire, the UK's biggest sweet and confectionery cash-and-carry, they sell around the world – even to Romania. When asked what had inspired Hancock's to make "Dracula's Teeth", Customer Liaison Officer, Claire Oguz, had fun. "As Dracula cannot see his own reflection, we wanted to make a version of his teeth so he can see what they actually look like for himself," she quipped.

FYFI: you can buy from Hancock's (https://www.hancocks.co.uk) but they only do bulk ordering so, if your local sweet shop does not stock them, go to, https://www.keepitsweet.co.uk/all-sweets/dracula-teeth or https://www.heavenlysweets.co.uk/products/dracula-teeth

SYPHILIS: it's generally believed that Bram Stoker actually died – despite a series of strokes – from untreated syphilis. His death certificate states his cause of death as "locomoaor atayia". In the repressed Victorian era in which Stoker lived, that was code for "syphilis". Stoker died in April 1912, aged 64. It was his great-nephew, the late famed writer and broadcaster, Daniel Farson (see FARSON), who revealed publicly that the death certificate recorded the euphemis, for the sexually transmitted disease, as the cause of death.

T

TAP: don't get too excited – or scared – but a "Vampire Tap" is now very much part of our world. Don't worry, it's not something you turn on and trigger a flow of blood. It's a device used to connect a computer into a network. The device clamps onto and bites the cable (hence the name) allowing the outer and inner conductors to be attached.

TAXI: the historic town of Yeovil, Somerset, has no connection with *Dracula*. Well, it didn't until Romanian Marius Virgil Botiu turned up and made it his home. Now he's the proud owner of Dracula Cabs. And what fun he has, trading on the name. The jokes and cracks about his business are non-stop. Such as, when someone might take issue with a fare, they will declare (usually in jest) "I should have known – after all you're a bloodsucker." But Marius takes it all in good part. But then he has to because his website for Dracula Cabs takes the mickey out of the name. For instance it opens with "Welcome humans …". And as he tells potential passengers: "No need for garlic but if it makes you feel better you can bring some with you … just in case."

And as for Marius's life in Yeovil, where he's lived since 2016, he says: "This is the first place for me in the UK. I like it here – the people are tasty. I will stick around …"

FYFI: https://draculacabs.co.uk

TEA: the drinking of tea is not usually associated with The Count. But the grounds of the Turkish Tokat Castle (see TURKEY), where Wallachian Prince Vlad III the Impaler (on whom Dracula was based) was imprisoned for 12 years, circa 1462, now boasts a teahouse. It opened in May 2017, two years after archeologists excavated tunnels and caves where Vlad was believed to have been held.

TEA-2: in humorous verse, former civil servant turned author-come-illustrator, Graham Corcoran, of Lichfield, Staffordshire, tells the tale about Dracula and his love of dropping in on folk for tea. *When Dracula Came to Tea* (2007) is the lead poem of a volume of his fun poetry of the same name. It is 24 verses long, some of which, after Dracula – "call me Drac" – has knocked on the door and been admitted by his nervous hosts, go:

> *I was up until dawn chasing virgins, he sighed,*
> *And they're all a lot younger than me.*
> *The succulent, juicy ones don't hang about.*
> *I could murder a nice cup of tea!' ...*

After chomping on beetroot and cress sandwiches and attacking the cake tray, he reveals:

> *I'm getting too old for romping all night,*
> *then sleeping it off through the day.*
> *I'd love to go out in the sunshine, like you.*
> *This sponge is superb by the way.*

FYFI: to buy a copy contact, http://www.lichfieldpress.moonfruit.com/#/booklist/4521232127

TECHNOLOGY: Dracula is alive and well in the world that was unimaginable when the novel was written. A French company that specialises in renewable energies is called Dracula Technologies. Its logo is a cartoon-like bat and its slogan is: "Even vampires can see in the light". Its website describes their work as: "Dracula Technologies uses the source of renewable energy and integrates electronics in many mobile products of everyday life. Their aim is to put energy and light in new products without altering their primary function, making these devices energetically autonomous."

FYFI: to find out in depth what the company really does, https://dracula-technologies.com/

TELEGRAMS: the text and twitter messages of yesterday! For readers brought up in the internet age it will be of interest to know that this form of "instant" communication, used by the characters in *Dracula*, was – back in the day – a pivotal part of life. The first one was sent in 1845 – marking the start of a global phenomena. And although they stopped, in 1982, being the staple of how, within hours, to send breaking, good or bad news, along with messages of congratulations and best wishes, they are still with us. Even if only in the capacity of a novel method of communication.

In Britain you can get a telegram delivered and handed over to a recipient by a "personal messenger". Costs a pretty penny though. For delivery before 9:00 am you'll fork out £29.95. For personal delivery without the time deadline, a mere £19.95. But if you've forgotten to get that vital greetings card in the post, a "first class" telegram will come to your rescue for £4.95. Up the price to £7.95 and return to the "golden age of telegrams" with your message sent on a replica, historic looking design.

FYFI: http://www.telegramsonline.co.uk/index1.asp; and in the US, https://sendtelegram.com

THIRTEEN: the mere mention of Dracula along with the number 13 and so many people – youngsters and grown ups alike – have the same instant reaction: "Room 13" they yell. Followed by either, depending on their age: "I was so frightened but so loved it" or "My kids' favourite read". They are of course talking about the children's book *Room 13*. Written by Yorkshire author Robert Swindells, and with its roots firmly in the *Dracula* story, it's a perennial top-ten choice for ages five to 11.

Inspired by a real week-long trip to Whitby (see WHITBY) by pupils from the now closed Mandale Middle School in Bradford, where Swindells used to teach, it's a tale based in a creepy boarding house where "Room 13" only exists at night.

FYFI: https://www.goodreads.com/book/show/1366989

TOURS: package deals to Dracula-land are big business. Lots of options to chose from. Just search "Dracula Tours" online and take your pick.

TRAIN: plying the Yorkshire coastal rails between Scarborough and Hull – with stops in Filey, Bridlington and Beverley – is a very special train. It bears the name *Bram Stoker – Dracula Creator*. The rather ordinary, bog-standard diesel received its prestigious literary moniker in a ceremony at – for obvious reasons – Whitby station in November 2014.

TRANSLATIONS: *Dracula* has been translated into 52 languages. The first was in 1901, four years after publication, into Icelandic (see ICELAND). It was only one of two foreign-language editions during Bram Stoker's lifetime. The second one was in 1908, into German.

TRANSLATIONS-2: the novel *Dracula* was not translated into Romanian until 1990. That should read "... not translated and readily available until ..." There are claims that copies in Romanian were around in 1923. But the evidence is basically non-existent. And once the Communist regime took hold in 1948, any copies – in any language – were banned. Copies that were held in libraries – along with any publications from capitalist countries – were locked up in "special collections". As liberalisation crept back into Romanian society, it's believed that a translation was sanctioned in 1970. But copies were never released. Finally, November 1990 saw the shackles undone and the novel, in translation, went on sale.

FYFI: to see a rundown of the history of the novel go to, https://kutztownenglish.files.wordpress.com/2015/09/jds_v11_2009_light.pdf

TRANSYLVANIA: is a region in central Romania bound on the east and the south by the majestic Carpathian mountains. Its history – like so many places in that part of the world – is complicated. It was part of the Roman Empire from 106 AD to 271 AD; from the 9th to the 11th century it was ruled by Bulgaria; then the Hungarians moved in; then the Ottomans had a go; followed by the Habsburg Empire and finally the Austro-Hungarian Empire. After the latter's collapse, in the wake of World War I, Transylvania became part of Romania. Every December 1st, the unification is celebrated with a national holiday, "Great Union Day".

TRANSYLVANIA-2: amazingly, Bram Stoker never visited Romania, let alone its region so intertwined with *Dracula*. His in-depth descriptions of the scenery and lifestyles of the people who called Transylvania home were all gleaned from various books he found mainly in the London Library (see LIBRARY) as well as the Whitby Library.

TRANSYLVANIA-3: there is another Transylvania! And it's been around for as long as the one most of us are more familiar with. It's an American county, with a population of 33,000, in the state of North Carolina. The county seat is Brevard. The region acquired its name – from the Latin for "trans" which means "across" and "silva" which translates to "the forest" – after the wooded land was taken from the Cherokee tribe and founded as a "colony" in 1775.

The town sports a biweekly newspaper, *The Transylvania Times*, which was founded in 1887, ten years before *Dracula* was published. Neither the town nor the paper is unaware of its more famous region. It recognises Romania and Dracula in various ways. The editor, John Lanier, dresses up as Dracula for the town's Halloween festival and leads the opening parade, either in a horse-drawn carriage or hearse; Dacre Stoker, Bram Stoker's great-grand-nephew, visited to promote his book *Dracul* (see DACRE); and there have been several exchange visits between Brevard city officials and their opposite numbers in Oradea, Romania, with which it is twinned.

TRANSYLVANIA-4: and then there is the university. It's not in Brevard (see above) but 309 miles away in Lexington, Kentucky. Transylvania University – a top liberal arts college with 1,000 students – was founded in 1780 and named (like the county, above) because of the forest by which it was originally surrounded. Colloquially it's known as "Transy".

The university's motto is: *In Lumine illo Tradimus Lumen*, or "In that Light, We Pass on the Light". With contorted thought that can relate to the light-hating Dracula. The same goes for the University's heraldic seal. It's made up of symbols of a torch, a hand, a book and a globe, which represent truth, faithfulness, learning and service to the world. But all could refer to Dracula – in that the "torch" is so he can see in the dark; his "hand" is not one that you want placed on you; the "book" because *Dracula* the novel is known around the "globe".

But the University goes out of its way to embrace the inevitable vampire and Dracula jokes. Its mascot is even a bat! And when the students decided, in 2016, to chose a bat (a bid to make the mascot a vampire was defeated) the Rafinesque's big-eared bat made the cut. Chosen because it's named after the legendary but eccentric Turkish botanist, Constantine Rafinesque, who taught at the university in 1819 and who is buried there.

And it does not shy away from celebrating Halloween. It's a riotous occasion with "Raf Week" taking over student life. It's non-stop fun and games dedicated to the aforementioned botanist and his bat, with lots of Dracula and vampire costumes.

But the joke can go too far. In 1988, Hallmark produced "Transylvania University" T-shirts emblazoned with the claim "Dracula's alma mater". The University complained and Hallmark immediately withdrew the T-shirts, admitting it didn't realise it was a real university.

FYFI: https://www.transy.edu

TRANSYLVANIA-5: in the funky environs of Key Largo, Florida, there is Transylvania Avenue. There are also other Transylvania Avenues in: Jacksonville, Florida; Chesapeake, Virginia; Raleigh, North Carolina; Berkeley Springs, West Virginia; and Prospect, Kentucky.

TRAVEL: a much-awaited book will pinpoint all the locations and settings mentioned in the novel. It promises to be a gem of a read for all those anxious to visit Whitby, Romania, Scotland, Ireland and London – with Dracula on their minds. *Dracula by Bram Stoker – The Travel Guide* is being compiled by Dacre Stoker, great-grand-nephew of Bram Stoker (see DACRE), and *Dracula* scholar, Hans de Roos. The blurb promises: "The book will lead you to the places where Bram Stoker lived and to the locations mentioned in *Dracula*. It will present many new insights with a wealth of exclusive route descriptions, photos and maps."

FYFI: to check on its progress, http://dractravel.com

TRUMP: in February, 2020, when the US Senate failed to find President Donald Trump guilty of impeachment, Joe Blundo, a columnist for the *Columbus Dispatch*, penned a mocking condemnation. He wrote: "The US Senate voted today to acquit President Dracula, ending an impeachment trial that saw him accused of biting the necks of women and drinking their blood on midnight forays. The outcome was expected, as Senate Republicans lined up to support their leader. Republican Senator Lindsey Graham of South Carolina had even taken to sleeping in a coffin to signal his solidarity with the president. Presidential lawyer Alan Dershowitz argued during the Senate trial that if a president genuinely believes it is in the public interest for him to sip the blood of unsuspecting citizens, then his actions are not a crime. The verdict is expected to further erode Dracula's support among women. Online site amazon.com reported record sales of garlic necklaces and wooden stakes."

TSD: sounds like a nasty disease! But no, it stands for "Transylvania Society of Dracula". Founded in 1991, its headquarters are in Bucharest, Romania. There are chapters in North America, Italy, Germany, Russia and Japan – but, strangely, there isn't one in the UK. There's an annual symposium; an official travel agent; a quarterly newsletter and an annual journal.

All the chapters – which charge around $30 a year for membership – introduce themselves online with the same statement. It reads: "TSD is an international, non-profit organization dedicated to the study of both Count Dracula of fiction and Vlad Tepes, the Dracula of history. The TSD in Romania hosts an annual Symposium and World Dracula Congresses. Its official travel agency – Company of Mysterious Journeys – offers Dracula tours in Romania. The head office of the TSD is in Bucharest, Romania. TSD members come from all walks of life: scholars, writers, artists, film buffs, tourism officials, students, computer programmers, home-makers, librarians, etc., all united by a common interest in the myth and the history of Dracula."

FYFI: https://en.wikipedia.org/wiki/Transylvanian_Society_of_Dracula

TURKEY: in September 2014, Tokat Castle in northern Turkey was put on the *Dracula* fan map. Archeologists doing restoration work on the castle – that dates back to the 5th century – uncovered dungeons, caves and tunnels. The discovery hit the headlines because it's where Vlad the Impaler (the inspiration for *Dracula*) was held prisoner for 12 years by the Ottoman Turks. Because of the discovery, plans to turn the castle into an international tourist were accelerated. "The castle is completely surrounded by secret tunnels. It is very mysterious," said archaeologist Ibrahim Çetin. "It is hard to estimate in which room Dracula was kept, but he was around here."

FYFI: https://www.ancient-origins.net/tokat-castle

TV: the terrific news is that the 2020 *Dracula* TV series (see LATEST) – the first small screen adaptation of the novel since 2013 – was, and still, is a smash hit. A sequel is on the cards.

TV-2: meanwhile before the above, the latest (as of publication) TV sort-of Dracula offering was *The Passage*, which premiered, on Fox, on both sides of the Atlantic, in January, 2019. The blurb reads: "When a botched U.S. government experiment turns a group of death row inmates into highly infectious vampires, an orphan girl might be the only person able to stop the ensuing crisis." Based on the best-selling vampire trilogy, by award-winning author Justin Cronin, the plot is faithful to the novels.

FYFI: https://www.cbr.com/the-passage-vampire-scarier-than-dracula

TV-3: there have been several TV series adapted from the novel. In 1968, Thames TV made one starring the legendary British actor Denholm Elliott. It was followed by a 1973 version starring Hollywood Walk of Fame star Jack Palance (see PALANCE). Then there was the 2013 10-parter, from America's NBC, with the wonderful Irish star Jonathan Rhys Meyers in the lead role (see ELECTRICITY).

U

UNCLE: as in *The Man From U.N.C.L.E.* – the top-rated 1960s American TV series that ran for four seasons with 105 episodes. Basically the plot was the man from U.N.C.L.E. (United Network Command for Law and Enforcement) against agents from THRUSH (Technological Hierarchy for the Removal of Undesirables and the Subjugation of Humanity). In season 2 (1966), *The Bat Cave Affair* drew heavily on *Dracula*. Count Zark, a THRUSH agent, operates out of Transylvania and has developed a worldwide menace involving bats. He plans to use radioactive bats to jam the world's radar systems. The U.N.C.L.E guys, one of them played by the great David McCallum (see McCALLUM) who's gained renewed fame as Ducky in the American drama series *NCIS*, must stop him before it is too late.

Also, in 1966, one of the 24 novels based on the TV series was extremely influenced by *Dracula*. In *The Vampire Affair*, by the late American author David McDaniel, an U.N.C.L.E. agent is killed in mysterious circumstances – in a remote part of Transylvania. The man's footprints in the snow lead to the base of the tree where he's been killed. But from here on there are no further tracks to follow. No clues at all as to what doom has overtaken him. There are only two small holes in the neck, and a complete absence of blood. The U.N.C.L.E. team didn't believe in vampires –

but as they investigate their fellow-agent's death they're forced again and again to wonder if perhaps the old terrors of the region have more reality than the world would like to think.

FYFI: to buy the episode go to YouTube, http://www.tv.com/shows/the-man-from-uncle/the-bat-cave-affair-70425; for the book, https://www.goodreads.com/book/show/2682980

UNDEAD: that was the original name of the novel, *Dracula*. Bram Stoker switched the title at the very last moment – just before the manuscript went to the printer.

UNDEAD-2: there are two novels referencing "Undead". Both titles are, for all intents and purposes, identical. A colon marks the difference. The first, published in 1997 then re-issued in 2009, was *Dracula the Un-Dead* by British writer Freda Warrington (see WARRINGTON). The other – *Dracula: the Un-Dead* – is by Dacre Stoker (see DACRE) Bram Stoker's great-grand-nephew.

UN-MADE: the film script for *The Unquenchable Thirst of Dracula* – in which Dracula ends up in India – was written for the famed British Hammer horror-film studio in the 1960s. But it was never made, despite the fact it was written by the late British screenwriter Anthony Hinds, the son of Hammer founder William Hinds. Now, decades later, it's risen from the grave – well, the coffin lid is partially lifted. The long-forgotten script first saw the light of day again in October 2015 when there was a reading at The Mayhem Film Festival – which specialises in cult cinema – staged at the Broadway Cinema in Nottingham.

Then, for Halloween, 2017, it was broadcast as a radio play on BBC Radio 4. It was directed by all-round thespian Mark Gatiss – he of the massively popular TV shows *Dr Who*, *Sherlock* and the 2020 *Dracula* writing fame – who said of the project: "What better way to celebrate Halloween than with a lost Hammer movie? Anthony Hind's thrillingly titled The Unquenchable Thirst of Dracula is a wonderful, rich and atmospheric script and way ahead of its time, set in the 30s, a sort of 'Heat and Dust and Fangs'! It was nearly made in the early 70s on location in India and I was thrilled to assemble a fantastic cast headed by Nikesh Patel, Michael Sheen, Meera Syal and Anna Madeley to bring this forgotten gem to gory radio life."

Welsh actor Sheen, a leading star of stage and screen, who played Dracula, commented: "The prospect of a long-lost Dracula script offering itself to me like a succulent pale neck was just too tempting. I devoured it in one sitting and cannot promise I won't strike again." The big hope is that one day soon Hammer will help him sink his teeth again into the juicy script by finally making good on its long ago commitment and make the film! But Gatiss did not wait for that call. The *Dracula* genre had really got under his skin ... see LATEST.

FYFI: one evening, turn off the lights and listen to the play in the dark, via Internet Archive – go to, https://archive.org/details/TheUnquenchableThirstOfDracula; buy the book https://www.goodreads.com/book/show/40717632

ULTRAVIOLET: the TV mini-series of that name, aired in 1998 and was hailed as a hit. But it only survived one season on BBC Channel 4. A boxed set, of the six episodes, was made available in 2013. The plot follows a covert government squad tasked with neutralising the vampire threat in London and beyond. The bloodsuckers have been around for centuries but prefer to keep their existence secret so as not to send the general public – their food supply – into a panic. Tracking them down is tricky, though, not least because they're invisible to cameras. But under ultraviolet light, their telltale neck bites become visible. The series was also notable for the way it was, for most people, their first introduction to the award-winning actor Idris Elba.

FYFI: binge on the series, via Netflix, https://www.netflix.com/Title/80225020

UNIVERSAL: when it comes to *Dracula* films, this is the company to conjure with. Under both its names – Universal and Universal Classic Monsters – it has made seven movies since 1931 based on the novel. And it has, of March 2020, another one in the pipeline. With the working title of *Dracula*, it will be set in modern times and promises to bring full-on global recognition to the Hollywood trio of director Karyn Kusam, her scriptwriter husband Phil Hay and his writing partner, Matt Manfredi. Their previous movies were *The Invitation* and *Destroyer*.

Kusam has promised that her take on the iconic novel, while a faithful adaptation, will provide "a fresh look", mainly through the way she plans to feature the voices of all the characters, just as the book does. She said: "I think something that gets overlooked in other adaptations of Dracula is the multiple voices ... the book is filled with different points of view. Also, Dracula is not going to be the same kind of romantic hero that we've seen in the past ... in past interpretations of Dracula."

UNIVERSAL–2: one of the lead roles – opposite Nicole Kidman – in *Destroyer* (see above) was played by Sebastian Sam. He wasted no time in letting Karyn Kusam know he'd love to be Dracula. When the production was announced he emailed her, pointing out: "You know I'm from Romania, right?" She replied: "Yes, yes, but it's very early ..."

URINE: cows urine will keep Dracula at bay. That is the "unpeelievable" opinion of the Indian state of Gujarat. In October 2016, an advisory board stated that sprinkling cow urine around where you live "can protect from evil forces like Dracula and Satan." As a result, a flourishing business has sprung up of selling something from a cow – other than milk – bottled or in a carton.

FYFI: https://timesofindia.indiatimes.com/city/ahmedabad/Sprinkle-cow-urine-to-combat-Dracula/articleshow/54968431.cms

UPHOLSTERY: in the novel, Dracula's castle had – according to Jonathan Harker's observation in Chapter 2 – soft-furnishings of the finest materials. As he said: "... the curtains and upholstery of the chairs and sofas and the hangings of my bed are of the costliest and most beautiful fabrics, and must have been of fabulous value ..." And the same can be said of theatrical productions of *Dracula*. For instance in the 2013–2014 NBC TV drama series (see ELECTRICITY), no expense was spared in decorating Dracula's digs in London. A major feature was the sumptuous Chinese hand-painted silk wallpapers.

V

VALENTINE: a romantic gift for a *Dracula* fan can be found via the novel. There are two venerable quotes which have been used in artwork to express the ways of the heart and love. One appears in Chapter 5, in a letter from Lucy to Mina when she writes: "I am longing to be with you and by the sea, where we can talk together freely and build our castles in the air." The other is: "There are darknesses in life and there are lights, and you are one of the lights." That comes from Chapter 14 when Van Helsing is talking to Mina.

FYFI: to find them as art pieces, check-out Etsy, Bookishly and Red Bubble; https://www.etsy.com/listing/204517632/bram-stokers-dracula-quote-typed-on; and https://www.bookishly.co.uk/products/dracula-one-of-the-lights-best-friend-watercolour-quote-print?_pos=1&_sid=4d158f813&_ss=r; also for every imaginable thing, emblazoned with the quotes, from T-shirt to clocks, https://www.redbubble.com/shop/bram+stoker+dracula

VAMPIRE: if you really want to know and understand vampires – real vampires, not the fictitious Dracula sort – there are many books to consult. In all there are at least a dozen books cataloguing the world of vampires. Probably the earliest is *Vampires and Vampirism* by Montague Summers, first published in 1929 and reissued in 2005. But several, more recent ones, are paramount when it comes to excellence in explaining what goes on in the real world.

Phenomenon Vampire: A Casebook was published in 1998 and is still a best seller. Compiled by the late Alan Dundes, the eminent American folklorist, who had a high-profile career in the department of anthropology at the University of California, Berkeley, through 11 leading scholars, it explores the true nature of the vampire from its birth in graveyard folklore to the modern day psychiatric patient with a penchant for drinking blood. As the blurb for the book says: "It takes the legend out of the realm of literature and film."

Another expert tome is *Vampires, Burial and Death: Folklore and Reality* by Paul Barber. Published in 1988, it was updated in 2010. Reviewing it, *Booklist* – part of the American Library Association – said: "In this engrossing book, Paul Barber surveys centuries of folklore about vampires and offers the first scientific explanation for the origins of the vampire legends. From the tale of a sixteenth-century shoemaker from Breslau whose ghost terrorized everyone in the city, to the testimony of a doctor who presided over the exhumation and dissection of a graveyard full of Serbian vampires, his book is fascinating reading."

The latest, published in October 2018, is *The Vampire: A New History* by Nick Groom. *The New York Times* hailed it as: "An authoritative take on the history of the vampire."

FYFI: to find them and many more, put "Vampire Encyclopedia" into The Book Depository (free shipping worldwide).

VAMPIRISM: in the world of abnormal psychology, "vampirism" is sadly alive and too well. It's classed as paraphilia – a condition in which sexual arousal and gratification depend on fantasising and engaging in manic sexual behaviour, which is at the least offensive, at the worst illegal. Vampirism can of course be the monstrous calling card of criminal psychopaths. But not all vampires are breaking the law.

FYFI: for a deeper-bite, https://drmarkgriffiths.wordpress.com/2012/03/22/the-bite-of-passion-vampirism-as-a-sexual-paraphilia; and http://merticus.com/vampirenews/vampirism

VAMPYRE: the novel, *The Vampyre*, by John Polidori, preceded *Dracula* by 78 years. And while there is no record of Bram Stoker having referred to it in his research he surely did. Polidori, a doctor, was only 23 years old when he penned his short horror tale while on holiday in Switzerland. In June 1816, he accompanied his famed patient Lord Byron to Lake Geneva. There they met up with poet Percy Bysshe Shelley and his soon-to-be wife, 18-year-old Mary Wollstonecraft. The weather was atrocious, cold and wet – so bad it was universally dubbed "the year without a summer" – and the two pairs locked themselves into their adjoining lakeside villas with a literary challenge.

The aim was to produce fantastical tales, jammed with horror and outlandish conceptions. To provoke and unleash unimaginable thoughts, they consumed copious amounts of laudanum – an opium-laced medication that is now a "controlled substance" but in those days was freely available. The result, within a week, was Mary's *Frankenstein* and Polidori's *The Vampyre*. The anti-hero of *The Vampyre* is Lord Ruthven, a British nobleman.

Decades later, the *Dracula* story showed very similar traits: a suave aristocrat having his bloodsucking, deathly way with high-society's beautiful women. Over the years, there have been film and stage adaptations of *The Vampyre*. And it's scheduled to hit the silver screen again in 2021, in a feature film written and directed by independent British film-maker Rowan M Ashe.

FYFI: http://thevampyremovie.com

VAN HELSING: in the novel, Abraham Van Helsing (named by Stoker, whose first real name was Abraham, after himself) is the Dutch vampire hunter. A film and a TV series carry his surname as their titles – though they are not linked in any other way. The TV series *Van Helsing* (see FEMALE) produced by the *SYFY* cable channel, has been around since 2014 and is now in its 4th season.

The 2004 film *Van Helsing* starred two Australians – Hugh Jackman as Van Helsing and Richard Roxburgh as Dracula. It was made, by Universal, in homage to its Universal Horror Monster movies of the 1930s and 1940s. The plot revolves around the famed monster hunter being sent to Transylvania to stop Dracula, who now and then turns himself into a werewolf to expand his sinister lifestyle. But despite earning $300 million worldwide, it was deemed a disaster, after being universally panned by the critics. The only reviewer with a kind word was the legendary Roger Egbert who concluded it was: "silly, spectacular and fun". The film was intended to start a series of Van Helsing adventure movies, along with a TV series spin-off. However, because of the way the film flopped, all such plans were dropped.

FYFI: for info about the SYFY TV production, https://www.syfy.com/vanhelsing; to rent or buy the movie, https://itunes.apple.com/us/movie/van-helsing/id292731622?ign-mpt=uo%3D5

VARNEY: was an early fictional vampire. Fifty years before *Dracula* appeared, *Varney the Vampire* – aka *The Feast of Blood* – was a serialised, 1845 to 1847, *Penny Dreadful* publication. Co-authored by British writers James Malcolm Rymer and Thomas Peckett Prest (the duo who created the fictional *Sweeney Todd*), it's notable because it contains the first, very specific, reference to the lustful manner in which sharp-toothed vampires operate. As in this quote from one of the 232 chapters published over three years as a weekly pamphlet: "With a plunge he seizes her neck in his fang-like teeth."

FYFI: to learn more about the *Dracula* forerunner, and read the whole transcript, https://vampires.fandom.com/wiki/Varney_the_Vampire and http://www.gutenberg.org/ebooks/14833

VENEZUELA: the troubled South American country has a state governor nicknamed "Dracula". He is Rafael Lacava, who rules the region of Carabobo with an iron fist. He's earned the name because of the way he patrols the state's capital city of Valencia – the third largest in Venezeula – late into the night, in his beat-up batmobile-like vehicle, which is plastered with images of gold bats. He's also fond of locking up people he thinks are breaking the law into the large wire cage attached to the vehicle which he fondly calls his "Dracula car".

FYFI: to see him in action, https://www.youtube.com/watch?v=xR9HO564Q-4

VIENNA: is the setting for a 2014 novel that Bram Stoker appears in, as a character. In *A Matter of Breeding*, by J Sydney Jones, the author of *Dracula* is in Vienna, circa 1900, to give a talk about the book to the Concordia Club (the real name of the city's press club). He asks for protection as he fears he is being stalked by a "fan" out to do him harm.

FYFI: www.goodreads.com/book/show/19084532

VINEYARD: nothing, no product, no business, no genre is spared the *Dracula* influence. So, of course, there is a vineyard that produces three red varieties with the *Dracula* moniker: sangria, pinot noir and merlot – along with a sparkling rose. Despite its name, Vampire Vineyards is in the Napa Valley, California. In the States a place that produces wine is usually called a "winery", rather than the European "vineyard". The genesis of the vineyard was a starlight night, in 1985, over the Nevada desert. Owner

Michael Machat, then a New York-based music/trademark lawyer, was driving along a deserted road when the Milky Way in the sky inexplicably conjured up (to him) the image of red wine and vampires. The strange seed was sown. The vision stayed with him. In 1995, along with his English wife (hence the use of "vineyard") rock 'n' roll singer Lisa Dominque, he started producing wine in Transylvania. Then in 2005 they started production in California.

FYFI: https://www.vampire.com

VINEYARD – 2: Lisa Dominique Machat is co-owner of the Vampire Vineyards (see above). She's taken the love she and her husband have for the genre a step further – by writing about things that bite-in-the-night. Her book, *A Walk in the Sun,* got a rave review from Kirkus, which specialises in self-published books. Its verdict: "Reminiscent of the earliest vampire novels, such as Bram Stoker's *Dracula*."

VINYL: Dust Bug Records specialises in reproducing classic LPs for the ever-increasing, retro vinyl market. In 2014 – in co-operation with Hammer films – it released *Dracula*, narrated by Christopher Lee, who played The Count in nine Hammer movies. With only a limited edition of 500 and priced at £25, it quickly sold out but "used" copies can be found, from way below the original price, up to £49. And a few "unused" are still out there for £160.

FYFI: to (hopefully) buy "unused", http://dustbugrecords.com/index.php?route=product/product&product_id=52&search=Dracula; for "used",
https://www.discogs.com/sell/list?master_id=392456&ev=mb

VLAD: Bram Stoker never set foot in Transylvania – but gleaned all his knowledge via reading. One of the books he consulted – *An Account of the Principalities of Wallachia and Moldavia*, (see WILKINSON) which he found in the Whitby Library – introduced him to Vlad Tepes (or Vlad the Impaler) on whom he based Dracula.

In 2011, the Transylvania Society of Dracula (see TSD) made a documentary called *Dracula: The Vampire and The Voivode*. In Eastern Europe a "voivode" is a warlord or military leader – which is exactly what Vlad Tepes was. The film explores Vlad's background and how Bram Stoker used him as a format for Dracula. Romania takes center stage in the 84-minute film and, through the expertise of pioneer Dracula expert and founder of the TSD, the late Nicolae Paduraru, viewers follow in both Vlad Tepes' and Count Dracula's footsteps. The film also explains why Stoker never left any of his own footprints in Transylvania but instead left an indelible impression of the Romanian region on the Western mind.

Shot in Transylvania, Whitby, London and Dublin, the documentary tells the story behind Bram Stoker and the novel. It features interviews with leading international Dracula experts. Over the years there has been much confusion between Vlad Tepes (The Voivode) and Count Dracula (The Vampire). This film separates fact from fiction and looks at both characters in depth. Script consultant Elizabeth Miller (see MILLER) describes Vlad's reign of terror and debunks any association between *Dracula* and the iconic Castle Bran. Dennis McIntyre, of The Bram Stoker Society (see SOCIETY), takes us to key locations in the author's home town of Dublin and Tina Rath, also of the Society, visits Stoker's and Dracula's haunts in the capital city. In Whitby, Harry Collett – who led wonderful Dracula Walks in Whitby for years – gives a vivid account of Dracula's association with the Yorkshire seaside town where The Count arrived in England on a stormy night aboard the *Demeter* (see DEMETER).

FYFI: for a trailer and where to buy the DVD go to, https://movietube.online/movie/dracula-the-vampire-and-the-voivode-2011

WADDELL: Northern Irish writer Martin Waddell is a prolific author of children's books. And to many he is best known for his eight-book series of *Little Dracula* – which features a green-skinned child vampire whose dad is Dracula. He lives in fear of the villainous Garlic Man. In 2004, in recognition of his huge body of work, Waddell was given the highest of honours: The Hans Christian Andersen Award. Bestowed by the IBBY – the Swiss-based International Board on Books for Young People – it's considered the Nobel Prize for children's writers. Born in Belfast, Waddell lives in Newcastle, County Down.

FYFI: to buy all eight books go to AbeBooks, https://www.abebooks.co.uk/servlet/SearchResults?sts=t&cm_sp=SearchF-_-home-_-Results&an=Martin+Waddell&tn=Little+Dracula&kn=&isbn=

WALK: lots of *Dracula* things to do and explore if you go to Whitby. But one thing is a must. It's the "In Search of Dracula" guided walk. For a mere £5, "Dr Crank" will lead you on a 75-minute tour of all the spots featured in the book, along with all the places Bram Stoker frequented. As Dr Crank says: "Find out more about the legend of Dracula, and how the environs and setting of Whitby inspired Bram Stoker."

FYFI: http://www.whitbywalks.com

WALT WHITMAN: the iconic American poet (1819–1892) was admired by Bram Stoker. In his own words he "fell in love" with Whitman after reading his legendary collection *Leaves of Grass*. The two met on three occasions – forging a mutual admiration society through their face-to-face conversations and also their letters. Handwritten notes between Stoker and Whitman are among the vast amount of memorabilia in The Bram Stoker Collection, stored at the Shakespeare Library in Stratford-upon-Avon (see SHAKESPEARE). The first letter Stoker wrote was dated February 18th, 1872. But he hung onto it for four years before plucking up courage to post it.

It was thanks to Sir Henry Irving, the famed British Shakespearian actor (Stoker was his long-time manager), performing in the States that the two eventually met. Their first meeting was in Philadelphia, where Sir Henry was appearing. Over the next few years, Stoker and Whitman met twice more. Each occasion was made possible because of Sir Henry touring across "the pond". The second and third meetings were in Camden, New Jersey, which is just across the river from Philadelphia. Whitman had always hoped to visit Stoker in Ireland but ailing health – he was 28 years older than Stoker – never allowed him to make the journey.

Leaves of Grass, a poetry compilation, was initially published in 1855, with a dozen other poems. It was roundly condemned as obscene and pornographic because of its overt sexuality and Whitman's concentration on the delights of sensual pleasure, which in those days was an absolute literary "no-no". The last edition in 1892, just before Whitman's death, contained 400 poems. The controversy finally died down and *Leaves of Grass* is now considered one of the finest examples of the written word. In 1998 it garnered renewed interest for its sexual content when it was revealed that President Bill Clinton had given a copy to his sex-scandal intern Monica Lewinsky.

FYFI: to see the letters between Stoker and Whitman go to, https://lettersofnote.com/2013/11/11/you-are-a-true-man; and for a comprehensive and academic take on the relationship between the two literary giants go to, https://ir.uiowa.edu/wwqr/vol3/iss3/5/

WALT WHITMAN-2: here is an extract from the first letter Bram Stoker wrote to Walt Whitman in 1872.

> *I have read your poems with my door locked late at night and I have read them on the seashore where I could look all round me and see no more sign of human life than the ships out at sea: and here I often found myself waking up from a reverie with the book open before me. I love all poetry, and high generous thoughts make the tears rush to my eyes, but sometimes a word or a phrase of yours takes me away from the world around me and places me in an ideal land surrounded by realities more than any poem I ever read.*

WAMPYR: it would never have worked – so happily the original name for The Count was changed. At first Bram Stoker called him "Count Wampyr". But even if people had learnt to pronounce it properly – the "W" as a "V" – it would never have had resonated or had the ring of "Dracula".

WARHOL: there is little in popular culture untouched by the Dracula DNA. In 1974, Andy Warhol – the charismatic Pop Art genius who died in 1987 – immersed himself in The Count via an Italian film called *Blood for Dracula*. Warhol was billed as the producer. It will come as a surprise to many (though not diehard Warhol fans) that he wasn't just an artist and sculptor. He made upwards of 500 movies – some as short as 35 minutes, others as long as eight hours. But his venture into Dracula land was one that had some big-screen success. Though the film was made in English, its official title was in Italian, *Dracula cerca sangue di vergine – e mori di sete!* which translates as *Dracula is Searching for Virgins' Blood – and He's Dying of Thirst!* But for commercial reasons it was shortened to *Blood for Dracula*. Then for its US release it got yet another new title with a bigger commercial grab: *Andy Warhol's Dracula*.

FYFI: to see a trailer go to, https://www.youtube.com/watch?v=-mxhJzSKV08

WARHOL-2: in March 2015, the soundtrack for the above movie – by Italian composer Claudio Gizza – was re-released as a 1,000 limited-edition vinyl LP. The actual disc was blood red in colour. Titled *Andy Warhol's Blood*, there are 31 tracks with names like *Dracula's Theme*, *Fuel and Death of Dracula*, *Old Age of Dracula* and *More Blood*.

FYFI: it was available on both sides of the Atlantic, and new and used copies are out there. Go to outlets specialising in independent labels and rare recordings and check eBay. Expect to fork out up to £122 for a sealed, brand-new copy of the limited edition; or, https://www.last.fm/music/Claudio+Gizzi/Andy+Warhol%27s+Blood+for+Dracula+%2F+Andy+Warhol%27s+Flesh+For+Frankenstein

WARHOL-3: if you've got more than a few bob to spare, look for a Dracula image by Warhol. Some of a limited edition of 200 signed screenprints of his take on our man – drawn in pink and black – come on the market now and then. At the time of going to press Dane Fine Art, of Philadelphia, had one coming up for auction with an estimate selling price of $63,500 to $88,00. Before that, one was sold in October 2018 by Christie's in New York, for $27,500. But the record amount, to date, goes to the one that went (again sold by Christie's) for a mind-boggling £513,300.00, in London in 2007. But that one was signed differently: in ink, not pencil and Warhol included the date, 1981, the year he made the image.

FYFI: to see a picture of the half-million-pound-plus image, https://www.artsy.net/artwork/andy-warhol-dracula-from-myths-1

WARHOL-4: Studio 54 is the long gone, though never forgotten, Manhattan hedonistic night-spot of the 1970s. Known for its drug-fueled wild parties, it was haunted by the headline names of the times – including Warhol. British Gothic novelist, Kim Newman – famed for his *Anno Dracula* series (see QUEEN) – invoked both the maniac artist and the nightclub in his 1998 book *Andy Warhol's Dracula*. Its anti-hero is Johnny Pop, a Romanian vampire who, while cruising the streets of New York, comes up with the plan to ingratiate himself among Studio 54's power-personality regulars and sell vampire blood as a drug, particularly to Warhol – whom he knew painted pictures of soup cans and made whacky movies and so could be nothing else but a natural vampire.

FYFI: the out-of-print novel – now considered "collectable" – can be bought for as little as £10 or, for a hardback copy signed by the author as much as £174. Check for sellers on AbeBooks, eBay and Amazon.

WARREN: British actor Marc Warren played the title role in the 2006 TV movie *Dracula*. The movie was shown on the BBC and on PBS (Public Broadcasting Service) in the States. He was generally considered too "cute" and "boyish" for the part. However, there was no sign of such characteristics when, six years later, he played the thug husband of Kalinda in the long-running US TV drama *The Good Wife*.

FYFI: to watch the movie, https://www.youtube.com/watch?v=NGMWgk18M3Q

WARRINGTON: best-selling British author Freda Warrington, famed for her fantasy novels, was commissioned by Penguin Books to write a sequel to *Dracula*, to mark the centenary of its 1897 publication. The result was *Dracula The Undead*, which went onto win The Dracula Society's Best Gothic Novel Award. The synopsis reads: "It is seven years since a stake was driven through the heart of the infamous Dracula. Seven years which have not eradicated the terrible memories for Jonathan and Mina Harker, who now have a young son. To lay their memories to rest they return to Transylvania, but can find no trace of the horrific events. But, beneath the earth, Dracula's soul lies in limbo, waiting for the Lifeblood that will revive him."

FYFI: www.fredawarrington.com

WEAR: show-off your fandom of *Dracula* round your neck, on your hands, in your hands via StoriArts. The Portland, Oregon, company specialises in producing scarves, fingerless writing gloves and totes – all dedicated to classic novels and inscribed with famous passages. The passage printed on the *Dracula* offerings is from Chapter 2, when Jonathan Harker arrives at Dracula's Castle. It includes one of the best known lines from the book: "Listen to them, the children of the night. What music they make." On its website, StoriArts explains it exists to "spread the love of great literature, bringing tangible reminders of your favorite books, poems, and stories. We believe a good book can change the world." Part of every purchase goes to LitWorld, a non-profit dedicated to fighting illiteracy in 28 countries.

FYFI: https://storiarts.com

WHITBY: the historic seaport, surrounded by extensive moorland, is 47 miles from York, 255 miles north-east of London. Almost uniquely, for an east coastal town, it faces due north. So, in the long summer light, the sun rises and sets over the sea. Twin piers, flanked by soaring cliffs, guard the entrance to the harbour, which is also fed by the River Esk.

Towering over the town is what's left of the 7th-century Abbey (see ABBEY), where legend says the famed Abbess Saint Hilda turned the snakes that over-ran the Abbey and infested the town to stone, a legend triggered by the ammonites that crowd Whitby's Jurassic east-side cliffs and shale beach.

Whitby has many fames to claim but three characters (two real, one fictitious) stand out. First, Captain James Cook – who "discovered" Australia and New Zealand – and who as a teenager lived in Whitby. His first exploration (1768) of the South Seas was as captain of *HMS Endeavour*, which started life as a Whitby-built collier (a bulk coal carrier) and was then converted into a barque (a vessel of three or more masts). Cook sailed the seas without the benefit of a crow's nest as a lofty lookout point. That was not invented until 1807. And it was Captain William Scoresby, who sailed out of Whitby as a whaler and Arctic explorer, who came up with the idea.

Then, of course, there is Dracula, who turned-up in Whitby as a ship's dog. Chapters 6, 7 and 8, in *Dracula* serve, to this day, as a great guide to the town – which is one of Britain's top seaside holiday spots.

Bram Stoker's words conjure up the magic of the place. For instance, in Chapter 7, describing the storm that sweeps the cargo ship that Dracula is on into the harbour, a *Dailygraph* correspondent reports: "White-crested waves beat madly on the level sands and rushed up the shelving cliffs; others broke over the piers and with their spume swept the lanthorns of the lighthouses which rise from the end of either pier of Whitby Harbour."

And in her journal, on the day she arrives, Mina records her initial thoughts about Whitby thus: "This is a lovely place. The little river, the Esk, runs through a deep valley, which broadens out as it comes near the harbour. A great viaduct runs across, with high piers, through which the view seems somehow further away than it really is. The valley is beautifully green and it is so steep that when you are on the high land on either side you look right across it, unless you are near enough to see down. The houses of the old town are all red-roofed and seem piled up one over the other. Right over the town is the ruin of Whitby Abbey ... it is a most noble ruin, of immense size and full of beautiful and romantic bits ... this is to my mind the nicest spot in Whitby, for it lies right over the town and has a full view of the harbour and all up the bay to where the headland called Kettleness stretches out into the sea."

FYFI: for a good guide to Whitby's *Dracula* links go to, https://www.youtube.com/watch?v=1ynMiPr7kUU; and for information about the town just put "Whitby" into any search engine for dozens of sites – but a couple of good ones, to find out what's going on, where to stay, with lots of information, are, https://www.visitwhitby.com and https://www.thewhitbyguide.co.uk

WILDE: so how on earth does Oscar Wilde – as well known for being jailed for his homosexuality as his plays and novels – get an entry? What possible connection can he have to *Dracula*? There's no direct link but still an important one. Wilde (who in these days would now be considered bisexual) was in love with Bram Stoker's wife, Florence. They courted for two years but in the end she turned down his marriage proposal – and on December 4th, 1878, she married his close friend, Bram Stoker. She was 20 years old, he was 31. Shortly after her marriage a heart-broken Wilde wrote to her saying that their two years of courtship had been "the sweetest of all the years of my youth". He also told her that he was leaving Ireland and would never return. A vow he kept.

WILDWOOD: a seaside town in New Jersey, USA, which was once home to one of the most popular Dracula attractions. In 1977, the Nickel family, who'd owned the Midway Pier since 1944 and operated several funfair rides, built a replica of the alleged Dracula Castle in Transylvania. With its boat ride through the Castle it became an enormous hit and drew crowds from around the States and the world. But the playful horror of the Castle turned to real horror in January 2002. A couple of teenagers broke into the Castle, which was closed for the winter, and set fire to it. It was left a total, burnt-out ruin. As for the arsonists, aged 15 and 16: they were each given three years probation, 90 days of community service and fined $2,500.

FYFI: the Castle has kept its devotees. There is an "in memoriam" Facebook page, https://www.facebook.com/Castle-Dracula-Wildwood-NJ-795990590508946; and for a video of the "horror" boat ride through the Castle, along with a newscast of the fire, http://www.bobsblitz.com/2018/08/wildwood-nj-boardwalk-draculas-castle.html

WILKINSON: one of the books Bram Stoker consulted to glean information about Transylvania and its culture was *An Account of the Principalities of Wallachia and Moldavia: With Various Political Observations Relating to Them.* It was written by William Wilkinson who was British Consul to the principalities of Wallachia and Moldavia, based in Bucharest from 1813 to 1816. His book was published in 1820. The region became Romania in 1886.

FYFI: go to AbeBooks, the global site specialising in antiquarian and used books, https://www.abebooks.

co.uk/book-search/title/account-principalities-wallachia-moldavia

WORLD: mark the calendar! May 26th is "World Dracula Day". Why? Because that is the day, in 1897, that *Dracula* was published.

X: *Dracula X* and *Dracula X Chronicles* are video games and part of the massively popular *Castlevania* series – in which Dracula is the number one protagonist Japanese-produced – by Konami, a leader in the industry – the series was launched in 1986 and dozens of new games later is still going as strong as ever. All of the releases have received very high critical acclaim. Well advanced plans to turn *Castlevania* into a movie, first mooted in 2005, finally came to a halt in 2012 over script rights. But the British movie-maker Paul W S Anderson – known for his skill in converting video games into films – said he would make it if the rights' issue could be resolved. But in 2017 Netflix beat him to the punch when it premiered a four-episode season, followed in 2018 with an eight-episode season, then in March 2020 a third season with 10 episodes.

FYFI: https://castlevania.fandom.com/wiki/Castlevania:_Dracula_X; and https://castlevania.fandom.com/wiki/Castlevania:_The_Dracula_X_Chronicles

YARN: the story of *Dracula* is not the only yarn that carries his name. Artist Marie Redding, who has a shop on School Lane in Leominster, Herefordshire, sells wool and silk hand-spun yarn in 26 intriguing colour combinations, all inspired by images and quotations from the novel. Marie, who also sells to customers all over the world on Etsy, says: "I'm a big fan of the book *Dracula*, of Bram Stoker and the whole vampire culture that has grownup as a result. As an artist I wanted to bring the book to life through the evocative medium of colour – so the 26 Dracula colourways tell the story via key moments or phrases in consecutive order from the book. For instance, Marie's number five yarn is inspired by 'Listen to them, the children of the night – what sweet music they make ...' The colour is an alluring mix of grey, mauve and light bronze."

FYFI: https://www.etsy.com/shop/MarieReddingArts/items

YEAR: it's fascinating to note that while there are dates, there's no mention of any specific years in the novel. Stoker probably did this quite intentionally, for several reasons: to allow early readers to imagine it was happening in their time and to dissuade anyone from trying to check whether the story was indeed true – a belief that Stoker undeniably attempted to convey.

YELLOW: the colour of the front and back, cloth-bound, covers of the original editions of *Dracula*. A dull yellow with the title and author's name spelt out in, naturally, blood-red ink. There was special meaning behind the choice of yellow. In the era of the novel's publication, 1897, it indicated that the contents could be considered degenerative and decadent. Yellow was synonymous with the more adventurous and transgressive elements of Victorian society. It was the colour used for the jackets of disreputable French novels. And from the mid-1890s, the term "yellow press" was in common use for newspapers that catered to the "sensational". As the British Library, describing the first edition, says: "By giving *Dracula* a yellow cover, the publishers were deliberately aligning the novel with an experimental, and for many, a rather disreputable form of literature."

YORKSHIRE: Whitby is not the only Yorkshire connection with Bram Stoker. After the publication of *Dracula* he became good friends with J S R Phillips, the, then, editor of the *Yorkshire Post*, with whom he often stayed at his home in Headingley, Leeds. In recognition of their friendship, Stoker gave Phillips his desk (see DESK) – the one at which he wrote *Dracula*.

YOUNG: the BBC had tremendous success with *Young Dracula*. The first series was shown in 2006 and the fifth – and final – series ended in March 2014. The horror-comic drama, aimed at six-to-twelve-year-olds, was centred round a vampire family that leaves Transylvania to live in

Wales. The hugely popular and critically acclaimed series was based on the book *Young Dracula and Young Monsters* (published 2006) by British author Michael Lawrence.

FYFI: to see all TV episodes, https://www.youtube.com/results?search_query=young+dracula; to buy the out-of-print book, go to AbeBooks, https://www.abebooks.com/servlet/SearchResults?sts=t&cm_sp=SearchF-_-home-_-Results&kn=&an=&tn=Young+Dracula

YOUNG-2: could our man Dracula have been really onto something with his predilection for sucking the blood from young maidens to keep himself alive and horrifically well? In 2014, a Californian company called Ambrosia set up business to see whether transfusions of young blood could help the middle-aged-plus stave off life-threatening conditions and diseases.

It charges those over 35 years old $8,000 to have two litres of the blood of 16-to-25-year-olds racing through their veins. Earlier tests, using young and old mice, threw up some positive results. And while Ambrosia's mind-bending business has been generally mocked – and condemned by America's Federal Drug Administration as "unproven" – it now claims to treat patients in all 50 of the American States.

FYFI: https://www.ambrosiaplasma.com

YOUNG-3: but the work of Ambrosia – which in Ancient Greek means longevity or immortality – does have some support from top-notch medical minds. Leading the "it has promise" charge is one of the world's leading geneticists, the UK's Professor Dame Linda Partridge, head of the Institute of Healthy Ageing at University College London. In the September 2018 issue of the prestigious journal *Nature,* she published analysis of data about the research. She said it showed the tendency that when older mice were given the blood of young ones they did not develop age-related diseases, like cancer, dementia and heart disease, and that the "bloody" scientific bid to enhance the health of the elderly deserved closer study.

FYFI: https://www.dailymail.co.uk/health/article-6144799/Top-scientists-claim- transfusions-young-blood-END-sickness-old-age.html

ZIEMBA: Paul Ziemba is the American composer who gave birth to *Dracula, the Opera*. The four-act performance opens with Jonathan Harker leaving for Transylvania, parting with his fearful fiancée Mina, who gives Jonathan a small crucifix. The final scene has Dracula, as he lays dying, calling out to Mina for just one last embrace. As she tenderly cradles him in his last moments, he lifts his curse on her. After Dracula dies, all the cast burst into a brief singing tribute – *May You At Last Find Peace* – to mark Dracula's regained honour through death.

The songs and arias that punctuate the opera could only be motivated by the *Dracula* story. They include: *Beloved Mina*, *Blood Is Life*, *Demons and Monsters*, *Whitby Waltz*, *We'll End His Evil Reign* and *Your Soul Shall Now Be Free*. The opera premiered in Lancaster, New York, in 2001. Ziemba has plans to fine-tune *Dracula, the Opera* and market it internationally.

And his *Dracula* opera is not the only way he's been inspired by the Prince of Darkness to produce music. For several years the Riviera Theatre in Buffalo, New York – where Ziemba lives – showed the famed silent movie *Nosferatu* (see NOSFERATU) every Halloween. It was accompanied by a Gothic musical score by him, that was played on a classic Mighty Wurlitzer organ. In the words of Ziemba, Dracula is portrayed as a "tragic nobleman" who is plagued with "guilt" about his obsession and "longs to be reunited with his long lost love".

FYFI: originally the opera was titled *Dracula, Prince of Night*. To hear an extract, https://www.youtube.com/watch?v=m_bzBW5EtJs

ZOOS: there are several zoos that feature "Dracula deer". Their proper name is "Chinese water deer" and the bucks are instantly recognisable by the fact they do not have antlers but sport unique, long tusks, ie, elongated canines. Hence the vampirish moniker. In Britain DD can be seen only in Bedfordshire. Not for any specific geographic reason but just by coincidence. They are on show at the famous Whipsnade Zoo, near Dunstable. They also roam – along with nine other deer species – in the 3,000 acre Deer Park of Woburn Abbey, one of the country's finest stately homes, which is just 14 miles north of Whipsnade. In the USA, the Chattanooga Zoo, Tennessee, is home to a herd of them.

FYFI: https://allthatsinteresting.com/chinese-water-deer-vampire-deer

ZOOPHAGOUS: means feeding on animals. In the novel, Dr Seward diagnoses Renfield – who feasts on flies and spiders – as a "zoophagous maniac". In other words, a carnivorous madman.

ZORRO: the dashing Mexican-American outlaw is only 22 years younger than Dracula. But it took 74 years for them to challenge each other. Zorro – the 1919 creation of pulp writer Johnston McColley – has been portrayed in so many ways and genres, in books, movies, comics, computer games, toys. But in 1993, the short-lived (but legendary) *Topps Comics* brought them together. Their fiery clash is described thus: "Zorro squares off against the most dangerous enemy in his life: the lord of the vampires, Count Dracula! And there is a woman caught between these two powerful foes: Carmelita Rodriguez, who has faced tragedy and loss, only to be confronted by a spine-tingling battle of blood and sacrifice!"

FYFI: copies of *Dracula vs Zorro* can be bought from, https://www.mycomicshop.com/search?TID=127161

ABOUT THE AUTHOR

Maggie Hall is fascinated by the hold *Dracula* – the novel and the character in equal measure – has on society. Although she doubts that her interest would have reached such heights, that she was compelled to compile this book, if it were not for her lifetime love of Whitby – the historic Yorkshire harbour town where, in the book, Dracula arrived in Britain. Born and brought up in Cleckheaton, 70 miles inland, she spent every childhood holiday in Whitby, eventually buying a "bolt-hole" there – to which she escaped from her London life as a Fleet Street reporter for the *Daily Mirror* and still does from her long-time home in Washington, DC. After quitting the reporter's road, as a foreign correspondent throughout the Americas, she amused herself by researching and writing a book about Marmite – *The Mish-Mash Dictionary of Marmite: an anecdotal A–Z of 'Tar-in-a-Jar'*. It proved to be as equally a compelling and fascinating subject as Dracula. As one friend quipped: first the dark goo, then the dark count – what "dark" subject next Maggie?